Sally Hemings

AN AMERICAN SCANDAL

Also by Tina Andrews

Essays:

"The First Time I Got Paid For It...
Writers' Tales From The Hollywood Trenches"

Short Stories:

"Daddy and Miss Bankhead"

Screenplays:

"Why Do Fools Fall In Love?"
"Sally Hemings: An American Scandal"

Plays:

"The Mistress of Monticello"
"Frankie"

Sally Hemings

AN AMERICAN SCANDAL

The Struggle To Tell The Controversial True Story

TINA ANDREWS

THE MALIBU PRESS
New York • Malibu

The Malibu Press logo and colophon are registered trademarks
of The Malibu Press, Inc., Reno, Nevada. All rights reserved.

Grateful acknowledgement is made to the following for permission
to reprint previously published material:
Excerpts from The Los Angeles Times, copyright, May 24, 1977;
TV Guide, copyright, February 12, 2000; Wall Street Journal, copyright,
February 11, 2000; Philadelphia Inquirer, copyright, February 10, 2000;
Washington Post, copyright, February 12, 2000.
Excerpt from "Sound In Space" appearing in "Blues: For All The
Changes" reprinted by permission of Nikki Giovanni

Cataloging-in-Publication Data

Andrews, Tina
    Sally Hemings, an American Scandal : the struggle to
tell the controversial true story / Tina Andrews, — 1st ed.
    p. cm.
    Includes screenplay
    Includes bibliographical references.
    LCCN: 00-104155
    ISBN: 0-9701295-4-8

1. Television authorship—Biography. 2. Sally
Hemings An American Scandal (Television program)
3. Andrews, Tina. 4. Screenwriters—United States
—Biography. 5. Hemings, Sally. I. Title.

PN1992.4.A53A1 2000   812.6

FIRST EDITION

Printed in Korea

10 9 8 7 6 5 4 3 2 1

Dedicated to the memory of

SALLY HEMINGS

and

her children

and

their children

and

all the generations of

Hemings descendants

known, unknown,

accepted and unaccepted

moving into the light

WE HOLD THESE TRUTHS TO BE SELF-EVIDENT: THAT ALL MEN ARE CREATED EQUAL, THAT THEY ARE ENDOWED BY THEIR CREATOR WITH CERTAIN INALIENABLE RIGHTS, AMONG THESE ARE LIFE, LIBERTY AND THE PURSUIT OF HAPPINESS, THAT TO SECURE THESE RIGHTS GOVERNMENTS ARE INSTITUTED AMONG MEN. WE···SOLEMNLY PUBLISH AND DECLARE, THAT THESE COLONIES ARE AND OF RIGHT OUGHT TO BE FREE AND INDEPENDENT STATES···AND FOR THE SUPPORT OF THIS DECLARATION, WITH A FIRM RELIANCE ON THE PROTECTION OF DIVINE PROVIDENCE, WE MUTUALLY PLEDGE OUR LIVES, OUR FORTUNES AND OUR SACRED HONOUR.

An excerpt from the Declaration of Independence photographed from a wall at the Jefferson Memorial in Washington, D.C.

FOR

My husband,
Stephen Gaines

Who endures all the struggles with me

and

My mother, Eloyce Andrews
My brother, Donald Andrews

REMEMBERING

My father, George W. Andrews
My mentor, Alex Haley
and
Dr. Fawn M. Brodie

HONORING

All writers everywhere struggling for respect

Contents

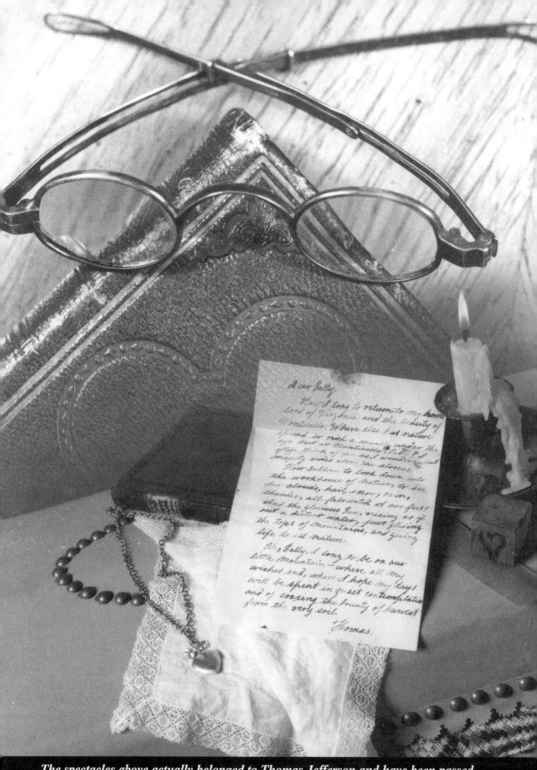

Dear Sally,

How I long to return to my home land of Virginia and the beauty of Monticello. Where else has nature spread so rich a mantle under the eye, but at Monticello? Stately? Of often think of you as I wonder what majesty rides above the storms.

How sublime to look down into the work-house of nature, to see her clouds, hail, snow, rain, thunder, all fabricated at our feet! And the glorious Sun, rising as if out a distant water, first gliding the tops of mountains, and giving life to all nature.

Oh, Sally, I long to be on our little Mountain, where all my wishes end, where I hope my days will be spent in quiet contemplation and of coaxing the bounty of harvest from the very soil.

Thomas.

**The spectacles above actually belonged to Thomas Jefferson and have been passed
down five generations to Mary Cassels Kearney, a Woodson descendant who let me
use this photo. Jefferson's spectacles sit on top of Mary's photo album of Woodson
descendants which appear later in this book. The letter at bottom, was from, our film**

Acknowledgements

First and foremost, I thank father/mother God for all the blessings, and my prayers are, and will always be, in gratitude and appreciation. Secondly, there would never have been a "Sally Hemings: An American Scandal" had it not been for Wendy Kram and her fierce tenacity, encouragement, development skills and talent. I am also deeply indebted to Craig Anderson of Craig Anderson Productions who put his reputation and much of his own money on the line to executive produce the miniseries and imbue the story with the dignity and class it so richly deserved. Additionally, I owe a great deal of gratitude to CBS and its executives Sunta Izzicupo, Joan Yee and, most especially, President/CEO of CBS Television Leslie Moonves, who shared my enthusiasm for the material, and green-lit the script.

Then, there are my special angels...

Writing is arduous business, so trust me, I could not have written the script, survived the production, or written this book without the assistance of Stephen Gaines and my dear friend Erik Aston, both of whom spent many sleepless nights researching and making endless phone calls to help me create as factual a historical drama as possible. I also extend my deepest thanks to photographer Jane Feldman, who introduced me to descendants; Reuben Cannon, Euzhan Palcy and Mario Van Peebles, who remained loyal friends throughout the production; Pamela Sharp of Sharp & Associates; professor Annette Gordon-Reed; longtime friend Stanley Bennett Clay; professor Thelma Wills Foote; Joseph J. Ellis; Rita McClenney of the Virginia Film Office; Jody Frisch; Hemings family researcher Beverly Gray; my editors at Malibu Press, Austin Foxxe and Leigh Kirkwell; photographers Cliff Lipson and Peggy Harrison; Ira Trattner; Gerard Chok, Arman Yerzinkyan & Lennart Christofferson; Reggie Resino & Screenplay Systems; the gang at Mail Boxes Etc. in Malibu; Tiffany Williams; Nick Davidson & Dave Ingland; Reverend David E. Chambers & the Church of the Good Shepherd and the George W. Andrews Memorial Foundation in Chicago for divine intervention; E. Lynn Harris, Tina McElroy Ansa and Iyanla Vanzant for sheer inspiration; and "Team Tina"—Todd Harris, Rob Carlson, Patti C. Felker, Charles King and Alan Kaufman, who make me see the possibilities when I cannot.

Most importantly, this work is dedicated to those numerous Hemings and Jefferson descendants who graciously shared their stories, photos and time with me. I want to particularly thank Madison Hemings descendants, Shannon Lanier, William F. Dalton, Shay Banks-Young, Priscilla Lanier, and Patti Jo Harding; Eston Hemings descendants, Julia, Marshall and Dorothy Jefferson Westerinen; Thomas Woodson descendants Michele Cooley-Quille, Byron & Trena Woodson, Robert Golden, Mary Kearney, and Connye Richardson; and Jefferson descendant, Lucian K. Truscott IV.

With your love, support and encouragement I was lifted on wings of grace.

Tina Andrews, January 2001

WHO WILL SPEAK FOR ME?
As I am the slave with no voice
No record of existence, my presence silenced
By centuries of denial, by betrayal
By the admonishments of the purists, and the puerile

Who will speak for me?
While my spirit roams without rest
Without peace, without a place
For the kindred to gather
To acknowledge my presence or know my name

Who will speak for me?
To hear my story when I have been expunged
From the history that enlightened America
Yet repressed the human drama which
Bore me, defined me, explained me, accepted me

Who will speak for me?
When the roots of racism negate my place
In the truth of the man
Who wrote on the equality of men
And the pursuit of happiness

Who will speak for me?
I pray their names to be Madison and Eston
And Sarah and Harriet and Thomas and Beverly
And the hundreds who came after me, with me
Through me

Who will speak for me?
They will speak for me, and to me
Without recriminations, or science, or documentation
Without denying who I am and who I was
Without DNA, which only confirmed the
Denial of Negro Ancestry
And the rejection of oral tradition

They will tell the tale of my struggle and my survival
Of my courage, my sacrifice, and of my being
For they are here, because I was there

And I was loved

Introduction

By:

THELMA WILLS FOOTE

Associate Professor of History and African American studies,
University of California-Irvine

An average of 20 million TV viewers watched "Sally Hemings: An American Scandal," a two-part, four-hour CBS mini-series written and Co-Executive Produced by accomplished dramatist Tina Andrews and aired in February 13 & 16, 2000. The mass audience garnered by Andrews' dramatization of the liaison between Thomas Jefferson, author of the Declaration of Independence, and Sally Hemings, his female slave, not only attests to the widespread public interest in that controversial relationship but also confirms the enormous popularity of TV dramatizations of the past. More influential than conventional documentaries, the historical drama made for TV audiences is fast becoming the principal means through which people learn about the past. What ramifications has this film genre had on the production of historical knowledge? In the following assessment of "Sally Hemings: An American Scandal" I hope to provide an answer to this question.

A meticulously researched film project, Andrews' TV mini-series draws on written source materials, as well as oral histories handed down to the surviving Jefferson-Hemings descendants, to render a richly detailed portrait of Thomas Jefferson, Sally Hemings, and their world. In this respect Andrews' film has much in common with docudrama. In its current usage 'docudrama' refers to a drama for television, motion picture, or theater that tells the story of historical events and personages, often of a controversial nature, through action and dialogue, usually involving emotions and conflicts. What distinguishes docudrama from conventional drama is the "documentary imperative" — or, the requirement that docudrama must be based on empirical evidence that verifies the truth or accuracy of the historical events and personages portrayed on stage or screen. The "documentary imperative" is imposed on the makers of docudrama not only by the historians who often preside over the critical reception of their work but, more fundamentally, by the ideal of empiricism bequeath to us by the Enlightenment. According to the protocols governing empiricist representations of the past, whether conveyed through the written word, film, or some other medium, only those events that can be verified by documentary evidence, usually derived from a contemporary eye-witness account, assume the status of historical truth.

Such a definition of historical truth not only privileges particular subjects as historical agents but also limits what can be known about the past. Although Andrews is fully acquainted with the extent documentary records, she moves beyond the limiting frame of docudrama and its 'documentary imperative' in order to bring to life on screen what cannot be known about the Jefferson-Hemings liaison through rigid adherence to the conventions that ordinarily govern the production of historical knowledge.

Andrews' film dramatization directly challenges the authority of written documentation to validate historical truth. In a remarkable scene Andrews stages a volatile confrontation between Jefferson and Hemings — but this is no ordinary lovers' quarrel. In this scene Hemings reads aloud to her lover the infamous passage from his *Notes on the State of Virginia* in which he asserts his aversion to Negroes and his belief in the moral and intellectual inferiority of the Negro race. Interestingly, it is this same text that defenders of Jefferson's reputation often cite as evidence that the Sage of Monticello found Negroes so repulsive that he could never have entered into a sexual liaison with Sally Hemings or any other member of the Negro race. With her outraged citation of the evidence documenting Jefferson's racism, Hemings confronts her lover with the contradictions of his own life. The author of a text attacking the Negro race is the same man who has taken for a lover a member of the race he maligns. Andrews might have also called attention to Jefferson's contradictions by writing a scene in which Hemings recites a passage from the Declaration of Independence. But, the brilliance of the scene she offers not only lies in its exposure of Jefferson's inconsistencies but also in its questioning the privileged status of documentary evidence as the sole means of authenticating complex historical truths.

By taking into serious account the oral tradition of the Jefferson-Hemings descendants and other subjugated knowledge Andrews retrieves the story of Sally Hemings, her centrality in the life of Thomas Jefferson, which the guardians of the Jeffersonian legacy have, until quite recently, disavowed, and importantly her central role in the lives of the slaves who inhabited Monticello. In many respects Andrews frees her female protagonist from the fetish structures that have entrapped female slaves in the Mammy/Jezebel stereotype. As the film drama unfolds the young Sally matures into a complex woman who is much more than the nurturing handmaid of a wealthy white girl and the mistress of a powerful white man. Instead, Hemings is portrayed as a multi-dimensional figure, as concubine, mother, aunt, sister, teacher, and conductor for the Underground Railroad. Sally Hemings' story thus becomes representative of the subjugated histories of female slaves, numbering in the millions, whom the protocols of conventional history have consigned to oblivion.

Prologue

"…Our deepest fear is not that we are inadequate.
Our deepest fear is that we are powerful beyond measure.
It is our light, not our darkness, that most frightens us…"

1994 Inaugural Speech, Nelson Mandela

BUT WAS IT LOVE?

"...History is but a lie agreed upon..."

Napoleon

People, upon hearing my take on the Sally Hemings and Thomas Jefferson relationship, always ask why an African American woman would write a love story between a slave master and a slave. How could any affection have been possible between the owner of chattel and his disenfranchised chattel? Especially when conventional wisdom dictates—in fact demands—that every instance of miscegenation must be born of rape. My response is always, "It depends on the situation and the two people involved."

Any dramatization of this story is bound to be controversial no matter how it is characterized because stories dealing with interracial relationships frighten us. We are still afraid of genuine emotion between white folks and black folks. Even in this day and age we are still uncomfortable with affection between the races. We frown when we see an African American man sitting in a restaurant holding the hand of a white woman. Visions of O.J. tear at our psyche. We shake our heads at the sight of a white guy with his arm around a pretty black sister. We swear there's an ulterior motive or some purely sexual component. We've all heard the lines:

"It can't be love. It has to be lust."

"You know what they say about those hot-blooded Black women."

"It won't last."

"It's a phase."

"She's only in it for the money."

"He's only in it for the sex."

These relationships are like an accident on the freeway. No matter your sensibilities, you have to look at it and make some mental commentary. And somehow, you always want these relationships to end. Preferably badly. That would make the point not to ever engage in such a practice again. It's the line from West Side Story, "Stick to your own kind." We refuse to believe that we, as human beings, can actually interact, care, need, disagree, share, worship with, be intimate and most important, love someone who does not look like us—whose background doesn't jibe with ours. It doesn't fit into our neat, understandable, acceptably packaged precepts. But it happens every day. And it happened more than we care to acknowledge during that abominable period in America's history when African Americans were held in bondage slavery.

Sally Hemings has been called many things by Federalist slanderers of Thomas Jefferson, historians and die-hard Jefferson traditionalists. It pained me to read how a slave who could not alter her circumstances has been categorized by history. James Thompson Callender, the most villainous scandalmonger and betrayer of Jefferson, variously referred to Sally in his *Richmond Recorder* attacks as: "the Negro wench and her mulatto litter," "an African Venus," "a slut as common as the pavement," and as being a "mahogany colored charmer." Scathing songs and poems were written about her. She has been referred to as "Dusky Sally," "slave whore," "wanton woman," "black Aspasia," "Black Sally," and "black seraglio." And although Jefferson, too, was attacked by Federalist propagandists as trying to increase the population of Virginia with "mulatto offspring" and experimenting with "racial inbreeding," he was never referred to by these same Caucasian writers as a rapist or sexual abuser. No matter how poorly the Virginia gentry may have thought of Mr. Jefferson's behavior regarding his liaisons with slave women, they always stopped short of accusing him of abuse toward a human being. That was because Negroes were not considered human beings and slaves less than that. Slaves were chattel. Objects to be bartered. Things with no souls to be bought and sold. As long as Sally Hemings was a slave, as long as she was a black woman, no matter how much "Caucasian blood" was accorded her by geneticists, genealogists, historians, and oral histories, she would never ever be considered a woman of worth by the majority culture. Not then. Not now. Even as I sat recently at a meeting of the descendants of Thomas Jefferson through his daughters Martha and Maria, and the descendants of Thomas Jefferson through Sally Hemings, I personally witnessed the degree to which Sally has been denied her rightful place in the history of Thomas Jefferson.

While researching documents and source references for the miniseries, I discovered that a number of our illustrious former presidents had mistresses, e.g., Andrew Jackson, Warren G. Harding, Franklin Roosevelt, George Washington, John F. Kennedy and William Jefferson Clinton. While Jimmy Carter may have acknowledged that he "lusted in his heart," Grover Cleveland actually admitted to having an illegitimate child. But none of them—other than Clinton—has suffered the scorn, indignation and ignominy from the puritanical right as did Thomas Jefferson in his relationship with Sally Hemings—a relationship though not adulterous—was interracial.

I read a passage in the appendix of Joseph J. Ellis' book, *"American Sphinx: The Character of Thomas Jefferson,"* which struck me as ironic. *"...Long before we learned about the sexual escapades of Presidents Kennedy or Clinton or, before them, Harding and Franklin Roosevelt, there was the story of Jefferson and Sally. Indeed the alleged liaison between Thomas Jefferson and Sally Hemings may be described as the longest running miniseries in American history..."*

I found this passage interesting for two reasons. One, Professor Ellis, a noted historian and Jefferson biographer, had once denounced the relationship as out of character for Mr. Jefferson. But upon disclosure of the DNA evidence, Mr. Ellis became one of the first to publicly change his position and has been very vocal in defense of how the relationship may have been probable. In fact Mr. Ellis, in a November 9, 1998 article for *U.S. News & World Report*, wrote, *"...Jefferson has always been Clinton's favorite Founding Father. Now, a sexually active, all-too-human Jefferson appears alongside his embattled protégé. It is as if Clinton had called one of the most respected character witnesses in all of U.S. history to testify that the primal urge has a most distinguished presidential pedigree..."*

And, two, I was the one who was finally writing and would produce that *"...longest running miniseries in American history."*

So many had tried to tell the story over the years. So many had been thwarted in their efforts. I was not aware of it until well after we were in production, but at one point in 1979 or 1980, CBS, under a different regime, had been serious about presenting a miniseries based on Barbara Chase-Riboud's fictional novel, "Sally Hemings." But a group of Jefferson historians, including Virginius Dabney and Dumas Malone among others, wrote letters of protest and made well-placed phone calls, and the project, for whatever reason, was ultimately shelved. Malone, who called the relationship "utterly impossible," told the *Washington Post* at the time, the miniseries "will be a mockery of history."

Other networks and movie studios also lost interest in the various scripts floating around Hollywood on the story when told advertiser support might be withdrawn. So the dreams of many good writers out there attempting to see their books, plays and screenplays of the Thomas Jefferson/Sally Hemings imbroglio on film went unrealized.

Had I known, when first engaging in this subject matter, that my own quest would consume 16 years from page to stage, I may not have pursued it.

First and foremost, I am a dramatist—a screenwriter who uses all available information on a subject to craft a script. I am not a historian or a Jefferson biographer and the opinions I express in this book are mine alone. I do not represent any production company or network. But I felt compelled to write this book for several reasons. Though there were many who felt the miniseries should have had its primary emphasis on Jefferson and his political or scientific career, I was more interested in Sally Hemings' perspective, the disregarded perspective, the slave perspective, which meant the project would be primarily dealing with Jefferson's *domestic* life at Monticello.

Frankly, it is the illumination of the private Jefferson which makes people uneasy. We place our icons on very lofty pedestals indeed. We canonize them, glorify them and forget that they, like the rest of us mortals, have weaknesses, vulnerabilities and frailties—none of which makes them any less magnanimous, just human and, therefore, relatable. There is not one among us who would want the sexual aspects of our being to be explored and exploited for public consumption, but we have to acknowledge we have them. So to assume that Mr. Jefferson was incapable of engaging in sexual activity is foolish presumption. His genius as an architect of the perfect republic and his primal urges were not mutually exclusive. They worked in tandem.

Second, even though the events upon which my screenplay is based are true, some may have felt the miniseries contained substantial historical inaccuracies. As a result, I realized many people are unfamiliar with the facts or are unaware of how much actual data was utilized in the miniseries. So, I want to share my research and source references to establish that there is an abundance of historical data or "dots to connect."I also want to show how I connected those dots in a structured and emotional way to create a compelling *drama* designed to hold an audience's attention for four hours.

Third, I want to share my personal odyssey of "finding, processing and producing the story"—which was exhaustive and taxing—so that people will understand what writers go through. Many times we must wrestle demons and traverse our own dark tunnels to emerge from the other side changed and more evolved as a result of the experience. This is what happened to me along this journey.

People are neither benign nor agnostic on the subject of Thomas Jefferson and Sally Hemings, and my take on the subject would deal with disquieting issues. Those of race, sex, blood, genes-and shame. I would also discover there was no "right" way to present such taboo subject matter without offending someone's sensibilities. Had I written it as 38 years of the rape of mother Africa, white Americans would have dismissed it as conjecture, racism and the continued demoralization of Virginia's "favorite son." Lovers of the third president simply cannot wrap their brains around the concept of his "alleged" miscegenation with a black woman, period, let alone his being sexually violent with her. And if I presented a love story, there would have been those to say "impossible" because it was morally reprehensible to even suggest that Jefferson could have a deep and abiding affection for a black woman, because, to them, white men cannot possibly love black women. It also had the potential of alienating African Americans for whom the subject of slavery has as an inviolable component numerous scenarios of the heinous abuse of black females. For most African Americans the "master/slave" relationship is inherently coercive and the question of miscegenation will always be the absolute and painful result of rape. Consequently, no rendition of the story other than abuse and sexual depravity will be tolerated. So where was the politically correct middle? I was damned if I did, and damned if I didn't.

Thus my dilemma.

In investigating the story, there is no question there were far more examples of sexual abuse against slave women by slave masters than the few isolated incidents of affection I discovered in the research. There was even evidence of this in my own family genealogy. But the Hemings/Jefferson liaison was leaning, for me, toward being one of those isolated incidents. Whenever I encountered bias it was always in keeping with the idea that the relationship had to be debauched *if* there was in fact a relationship at all. My attempt to understand and thus dramatize Thomas Jefferson was not an attempt to debase him, but rather to place him in some mortal context. It would be mythology to assume that because Mr. Jefferson was a white, wealthy, politically positioned aristocrat that he could not be sexually attracted to a woman of color. Whether he was besotted by Sally Hemings or simply took sexual pleasure in her was not as much the issue as the fact he indeed *did* sleep with her and had children with her no matter how their sexual arrangement is characterized. Conversely, can we deny Sally Hemings her right to a private life without representing her as a passive victim? Whether she was slave or free, she had her own private passions. Did she use Jefferson for personal gain? For the freedom of her children? For protection? Or did she in fact find in him a kindred spirit longing to simply love and be loved in return? So many of us place entirely too much politics behind the simplicity-of genuine affection.

So many questions burned at my soul as I embarked on this project and there will never be more important, more meaningful work to me than my work on "...American Scandal." In the end, I found that it was better to tell the story as I discovered it. By presenting the story as truthfully and with reverence to the deprecated Sally Hemings, I knew that the visual telling of this controversial story would resonate far beyond its airing for, ultimately, it is a story of America--and America's struggle with unfinished family business.

"...Daughters, who should have been the principal object of his domestic concern, had the mortification to see illegitimate mulatto sisters, and brothers, enjoying the same privileges of parental affection with themselves. Alas! Mr. Jefferson, did not your philosophy teach you the impropriety of such proceedings?... Why have you not married some worthy woman of your own complexion..."

Richmond Recorder, November 3, 1802

"...Information assures us that Mr. Jefferson's Sally and their children are real persons. And that the woman herself has a room to herself at Monticello in the character of seamstress to the family, if not as housekeeper... but her intimacy with her master is well known, and on that account she is treated by the rest of his house as one much above the level of his other servants. Her son, whom Calendar calls president Tom, we are assured, bears a strong likeness to Mr. Jefferson."

Richmond Recorder, December 8, 1802

This bell, according to Hemings family oral history, was given to Sally Hemings by Thomas Jefferson's wife, Martha Wayles Skelton Jefferson shortly before Mrs. Jefferson died. The bell is presently on display at Monticello but is owned by Howard University's Moorland-Spingarn Research Center.

Center: Madison Hemings descendant Shannon Lanier flanked by Sam Neill as Thomas Jefferson and Carmen Ejogo as Sally Hemings.

Act One

THE CONTROVERSY

"...science fiction is much better than science fact because
science fact tries to prove things like Thomas Jefferson wasn't
diddling Sally Hemings and everybody knows people didle
people all the time especially when they can't say no..."

Nikki Giovanni
"Sound in Space"

Interracial TV Romance Goes Pffft

Actors Charge Racism but Show's Producers Deny It

BY WILLIAM K. KNOEDELSEDER

If the course of true love never runs smooth, it bounces like a buckboard on daytime television.

The latest from NBC's Days of Our Lives is that the chaste, year-long engagement of David Banning and Valerie Grant, soapdom's only interracial couple, is kaput. According to the script, the reason for the rift is David's infidelity. But according to the actors portraying the color-crossed lovers, the reason is racism, real-life racism.

"They're breaking us up because the story line is unpopular," said Richard Guthrie, who plays David. "The studio has been getting a lot of hate mail from people threatening to stop watching the show."

"When they get enough of those letters, they respond," said Tina Andrews, the black actress who appears as Valerie. "One letter said, 'I hope you're not going to let that nigger marry that white boy.' Apparently they are not. I'm being canned."

Tuned in again on your program yesterday - and note that you are still making a cheap trashy ass of yourself - - - -

with that black and white love affair . . . .

helping those goddam Marxists-Communist-serving producers . . .

to bring about a change in social mores - as they work towards the disintegration of american society.

A review of the TRUE history of the convictions of the "Hollywood Ten" - ought to be good thinking exercises for you.

ANGRY FAN—Excerpt from letter sent to show; name of sender is withheld.

Chapter One

"IN THE BEGINNING, THERE WAS THE WORD"

FADE IN:

My interest in the Sally Hemings story began, curiously enough, with my demise on "Days of our Lives." Prior to 1983, I had been a young working actress with a degree of recognition who was also a playwright. Two of my plays—"The Very Best of Friends" and "Frankie's Song" had been presented in Los Angeles. The latter was based on the life of '50's rock & roll star Frankie Lymon, and eventually became the screenplay, "Frankie," which ultimately became the Warner Bros. film, "Why Do Fools Fall In Love?" I had worked hard and my resume brimmed with quality projects of which I was proud. I had played Ermengarde in "Hello, Dolly" both on Broadway and in a touring company with Pearl Bailey and Cab Calloway. I had appeared in Alex Haley's "Roots" with LeVar Burton and Louis Gossett, Jr.; secured lead roles in movies for television such as "The Atlanta Child Murders," "Born Innocent" and "Billy: Portrait of a Street Kid"; and co-starred in the films "Hit" with Billy Dee Williams, "Conrack" starring Jon Voight, and "Carny" opposite Jodie Foster. I had even guest starred on "The Brady Bunch" with Davy Jones from The Monkees. Sure, those projects were few and far between, but I was making a living and supporting myself as an actress while I toiled as a writer.

Tina Andrews as "Valerie Grant" and Richard Guthrie as "David Banning" on " Days of our Lives" in the late 70's. One kiss ended it all.

Then I landed what I thought was the perfect steady job: a soap opera. It would be a weekly paycheck and a huge audience base. "Days of our Lives" gave me the security I needed to continue writing my plays, screenplays and novels leisurely, and to buy my first house. I had found a way to render myself debt-free while doing what I enjoyed doing most—plying my trade in my chosen profession while hopefully influencing and/or educating a mass audience. I also loved my character on the show. "Valerie Grant" was a working professional—a nurse who was studying to be a doctor.

Over the course of two years of storytelling, Valerie got her medical degree and made her family proud. She was educated and ambitious, not poverty-stricken as so many African American characters were on network television—and she was moral. She came from a good home—complete with a hard working father—and went to church every Sunday, where her mother sang in the choir.

In fact, the show boasted the first black family in daytime history. We became so popular that the powers-that-be decided to make our story more mainstream by introducing my character to the son of the lead white female character on the show. There was such wonderful chemistry between Valerie and David Banning, played by actor Richard Guthrie, that the writers slowly developed an interracial relationship between the two.

Thus began my first taste of controversy regarding televised interracial relationships. My fan mail, which earlier in the storytelling was 100% positive, shifted. When it dawned on the Bible belt that David was finding himself serious about Valerie, 40% of my mail became downright hostile. Fans pointed fingers to the tune of "Stay in your place." Naturally, I was upset. Here I was introducing America to a black character they hadn't often seen. I was coming into their homes on a daily basis. I was educating otherwise uninformed people that not all black folks were alike. And, in point of fact, my character, had she been evaluated in a purely colorblind, status-oriented, highbrow society, would have been considered "too good" for his. He had only graduated high school, didn't have a job, and had developed amnesia after an accident. That's right, amnesia. Understand, the writers had to give themselves an out. After all, what self-respecting white guy is going to actually fall in love with a black woman AND be in control of all his faculties? If something went wrong, like protests, advertiser pullout or falling ratings, they could always give David back his senses and he could go scurrying back home to his "real" life and forget he'd ever had a relationship with Valerie. He could always claim he wasn't responsible. *He wasn't in his right mind.*

But I took it in stride because I knew our success on the show had the potential to lead to the casting of other African Americans on other soaps as regulars. I understood we had a higher purpose and no matter how much stress was involved on a day-to-day basis, we were being held to a higher standard for a reason. Now that I look back on it, I realize my character had many of the qualities Sidney Poitier's character had in "Guess Who's Coming To Dinner," and I often chuckle about it. It seems that in order to present America with the notion of true love between the races, the black character must be overly educated with Ivy League degrees to outmatch Einstein, be chaste as the driven snow, beyond reproach morally, and, most importantly, must speak proper "King's" English, completely devoid of ethnic slang. In my experience as "...That Black Diva they got on 'Days...'" there could be no Aretha blasting in the background, or snapping your fingers, rolling the head signifying, "You go, girl." *Au contraire.* Hearing me recite my lines with closed eyes was like hearing JULIE Andrews, not TINA Andrews.

But none of it meant a thing to those die-hards out there who would just not accept such a relationship simply because of my skin color. And those folks are the ones who holler and write the most. And write they did. A year later, when the producers finally had the courage to script in the couple's first kiss, America went ballistic. We received a note from the network brass saying in effect, "There should be no evidence of open mouth kissing." The "Valerie/David kiss" episode aired on a Friday. Monday morning 2,000 letters had flooded the network in protest. At the same time our soap rose to number two, just behind "General Hospital" and their Luke and Laura story. David asked Valerie to marry him—and I began to see the handwriting on the wall. Protesters continued to be vocal. Suddenly nervous about potential loss of viewers or being tried in the court of public opinion for appearing racist, the soap tried to appease all by introducing a black doctor, played by the divine Michael Warren, into the mix. When that didn't work, they copped out altogether. David's mind returned (See? I told you), he had a fling with a white character on the show, she got pregnant, and on the day we were to be married, Valerie got word she was to receive a grant to study in Stockholm…that's Stockholm in Sweden. She left David at the altar…

…And I lost my job. Not the actor who played David, but the show's primary black character. Additionally, in eliminating my role, there was no need for the other black characters. So all four of us joined the ranks of the unemployed. So much for progress. So much for social change. So much for a successful amalgamation between the races leading to better understanding. The "R" word that dare not speak its name had won.

Now, if you're wondering *why make an issue of this?* It's simple. The entertainment industry is under constant scrutiny for undue influence. An act of terrorism in reality, which mirrors a similar event in a film, is blamed on the film and its filmmakers. It's life imitating art. A violent scene played out on a television series, which is then repeated in a classroom, will subsequently evoke negative commentary about the media taking responsibility for its part in the perpetuation of violence in society.

But of equal importance to me are the images of minorities shown the public. If we aren't careful about the characterizations we program to the viewing audience when we only present ghettoized, ignorant, racist portrayals of minorities, the world will become only familiar and comfortable with one myopic, closed-minded, stereotyped impression. Blacks, Hispanics, Asians and Native Americans cannot and should not all be painted with one brush stroke dipped in one color, nor do we all think as one massive monolith.

So there I was without steady work. Six months go by, then a year, then three. Work was so sparse that I quickly went through my unemployment, my unemployment extensions, then my savings. Soon, my friends were loaning me cash. I felt worthless. There I had been high in the Hollywood Hills in a house overlooking the Hollywood Sign. But by '84, I was in a rented apartment overlooking the Hollywood Freeway.

I was also upset by the lack of good roles for African American actresses and had a tendency to call my dear, sweet father to bemoan the issue. My father was a supportive, hard-working, dignified man who had come through the depression, fought in World War II and dealt with abject racism on a daily basis yet made a decent living and kept his values. He invested in stock, bought land, built his own home which my mother still lives in today, and put food on the table. Daddy imbued my brother Donald and me with a sense of morality and spiritual integrity and the lesson that "hard work always pays off." He more than provided for Donald and me, and we were expected to make something out of our lives. "After all," he said, "whatever you become, you become on the backs of your ancestors. People who could not and did not have the opportunities you have. People who went through extraordinary odds to survive and hand you the ability to sit out there in Hollywood under a palm tree acting ethereal."

"Ethereal, daddy?"

"Sugar, (my nickname) what else is it, when your entire day consists of whether or not you'll have an audition, or whether or not you'll get a residual check, or whether or not you'll get a call back for some commercial praying they'll use a black girl?"

"But daddy, that's how it is. If you're an actress you get your jobs by auditioning for whatever comes along."

"But when they don't, your answer is to go to the movies and critique films for not having enough black characters, or complaining that every black female character is a policewoman, a hooker, or the first to die. Sugar, you know how to write. You could be part of the solution instead of complaining about the problem. You could be writing empowering roles for black women. When will you take yourself seriously as a writer? That's why you left for New York—to write. Remember?"

He was right. I had been writing plays, essays and articles for the school newspaper all through high school even though my public claim to fame was as an actress. And since the longevity of an acting career can be similar to that of an athlete's, I'd always imagined when my ten-year dramatic career slowed I'd concentrate on writing. I just hadn't counted on a slowing career after only five years in Hollywood.

"Daddy, that's not really why I called. I could really use some money. Could you send something by Friday? Before they staple a three day pay-or-quit notice to the door?"

"Again? This is the fourth time this year? Where is all your money?"

"Gone, dad. I've been out of work three years. I've run through my savings."

There was a long silence followed by a sigh. "And for this, I sent you to NYU? This is sad, Tina, really sad. I'm so disappointed in you."

"I am so disappointed in you." Words which stab through the heart of any self-respecting daddy's girl. Just the tone in his voice haunted me for days afterwards. Disappointing daddy was tantamount to a pox. Especially since I'm supposed to be the one in the family with such promise. I was supposed to be a winner. The golden girl. The overachiever daddy urged to explore all options, have a career, and do all the things I dreamed of so I wouldn't live a life of regret before I got married. The one he was so proud of. The one who was supposed to be a "credit to the race." By this point in my career, Judy, my best girlfriend from Chicago, had her Master's degree and her teaching certificate. She had earned great respect, made terrific money and had a husband with a doctorate degree. But me? I had found myself the "Former star of 'Days of our Lives.'" "The Girl Who Played Valerie Grant." Talk about your let downs.

But daddy couldn't stay upset with me for long and generally, by the appointed date, he'd send the necessary funds. He was still the daddy of a daddy's girl holding out hope for his daughter. He didn't want me in the streets. God forbid I should become a hooker instead of *play* one on TV. How could he or mom face the folks at church?

But, unfortunately, along with daddy's check came an anticipated albeit unnerving ritual. I would have to suffer through a never-ending conversation with mother which always amounted to, *"Get a REAL job! Stop trying to push into areas they don't want you in. Teach! Plenty of people want to be actors. Teach, or you can always get a good job at the post office. After all, daddy's second job at the post office is how he put you in school and sends you bail-out cash all the time."*

I was screaming inside my head. It hurt for me to be encouraged so far away from my dream—especially with the oldest adage in the world stuck in my brain: "Those that can—do. Those that can't—teach." But mom wasn't content to leave it there. This particular time she added: *"...Either that or come back home to Chicago. Your father and I will finance a little dancing and acting school. Your Uncle Lionel can build it, do all the carpentry work, and you could have a big grand opening. Think about it. A lot of kids would be thrilled to be taught by the girl who played Valerie Grant."*

That was it. Written on my epitaph: "Here lies Tina Andrews, her sole accomplishment in life was being the girl who played 'Valerie Grant.'" Just the mental image of "GRAND OPENING: The Tina Andrews School of Performing Arts–Drama, Dance, Voice. All ages welcome. Brought to you by the girl who played Valerie Grant," made me pursue my writing with a vengeance.

It was the last time I accepted a dime from my parents or anyone else for that matter. Whether symbolic or metaphoric, it was important for me to visualize my higher self, and that self was capable of success. I vowed to become more pro-active in my future as a screenwriter.

I took daddy's advice and began writing seriously. I enrolled in a screenwriter's course in the UCLA Extension Program that met twice weekly in the evenings. I also took my mother's advice and got a real job. Well, ok, so I signed up with a temporary job agency. I had a modicum of secretarial abilities and possessed what was known as "Front Office Appearance," so I worked fairly regularly as a receptionist for Kelly Girls. On days I had auditions I scheduled them during my lunch hour or I didn't accept work that day. The good news was bills were paid, and best of all, most of the jobs I went on had computers. So if my job was answering phones, I would work on my plays between calls.

Occasionally I would call daddy to chat and keep him abreast of what I was working on. God bless him, but whether I asked him or not, he always offered up his opinion on what I should be doing. On one such occasion, after having read my script on Frankie Lymon, he suggested I combine my ability to write biographical material with my interest in history. Some of my best conversations with daddy were about historical events. We debated the Kennedy assassination, compared feelings about the civil rights movement, the Vietnam War and Watergate. We'd argue the merits of birth control or women's rights. But this day, daddy had some specific thoughts on what he wanted to see on stage and on the screen. "We don't get to see our stories told very often," he said, "And I like the kind of movies where you get a personal story within the historical or political story. To me that makes it more interesting than just stating the facts. Take 'Roots.' That one was told from the right perspective. We were really drawn into the lives of all those people even though it was set during slavery. And look how well it did. America was stopped in her tracks for eight nights straight."

"Yeah, imagine writing something like that," I responded.

"But you could write a story like that. There are so many good ones in our experience. Like, why doesn't someone write something about Frederick Douglas? Or Dr. Charles Drew? Or Sojourner Truth? Or the slave Thomas Jefferson was involved with…?"

He rambled off several others, but I was still back at *"…the slave Thomas Jefferson was involved with…"*

"Daddy, wait a minute. What *slave* was Thomas Jefferson involved with?"

"You don't know? Jefferson was involved with one of his slaves named Sally Henning (sic). She was his mistress a long time, had quite a few children with him. It was in Ebony magazine years ago. Plus, don't you remember when I used to go visit my cousin in downstate Illinois? She lived across the way from a real light-skinned woman who claimed she was descended from Jefferson and the slave."

I was stunned. It was the first time I had heard of the relationship. Not that I was shocked by the idea of miscegenation during slavery because I knew that at one point the number of mulattos in the State of Virginia alone outnumbered the number of whites. But I was unaware that Jefferson had a slave lover or that he was a slaveholder. Not the man who wrote "All men are created equal…" A slaveholder? Bedding one of his slaves as well? This was too compelling not to explore. Here I had been thrown off the air for depicting a contemporary interracial relationship, yet one of the Founding Fathers, whose power of the pen is well documented, whose image is perched on Mount Rushmore and the flip side of the nickel, had actually engaged in one centuries earlier. The title came to me immediately…"The Mistress of Monticello." My research began at the Santa Monica library that very evening.

My quest for the Sally Hemings story first took me to the bible of the Sally Hemings saga. Dr. Fawn M. Brodie, professor of history at the University of California at Los Angeles, had written a biography in 1974 titled "Thomas Jefferson An Intimate History," which contains the most comprehensive gathering of evidence and information on Sally Hemings available. In 1972 Brodie had written an article for *American Heritage* called "The Great Jefferson Taboo," and in 1976, in response to her Jefferson biography, she wrote another article for *American Heritage* called "Jefferson's Unknown Grandchildren." Professor Brodie's research placed Sally at every important event in the life of Thomas Jefferson, and her scholarly suppositions became the basis for my theory of affection between Jefferson and Hemings. But Ms. Brodie also came under attack by the historical community for assuming there was more to the relationship between Ms. Hemings and Mr. Jefferson other than one of master and slave/servant.

In reading the chronology of events I, too, saw a pattern emerge which suggested some degree of care between the two beyond 17th- and 18th-century conventions. I only had to read between the lines to see a simple human drama which possibly played out between a grieving widower and the young woman who closely resembled his dead wife—who was in his ownership. Many years later, when working on the four hour, made-for-television version of the story, I utilized the works of Annette Gordon-Reed and her excellent book, "Thomas Jefferson and Sally Hemings: An American Controversy," Judith Price Justus' "Down From The Mountain," and Samuel Sloan's "The Slave Children of Thomas Jefferson." I also incorporated the oral histories of 33 Hemings/Jefferson descendants, which filled in many emotional blanks. After that, I connected the dots with my own dramatist's imagination, utilizing anecdotes from my own family history which we have documented on both sides dating back to slave masters in Mississippi and Alabama.

The more I researched the story of Sally Hemings and Thomas Jefferson, I came across other stories of ownership and possession in which the boundaries of "acceptable" behavior were blurred between slave owners and slaves. I began to uncover that, like most human beings, the process of raging endorphins, which stimulate chemical components in the brain to attract men and women to one another, knows no discrimination. Who we find ourselves sexually attracted to has nothing to do with who we are racially. Two people lock eyes from across a room…and nature inevitably takes its course. Now this, of course, makes a good argument for sex. What it doesn't make a case for is love. Love is a far more abstract and complicated thing. And in the case of Thomas Jefferson internal conflict and irreconcible character flaws tortured him all his life. He was not a man willing to express his emotions in an overt, physical way. Jefferson left his more ardent feelings to the interpreters of the future. His political sentiments, however, we have in abundance. Jefferson biographies and biographers overflow like Victoria Falls.

That became my first obstacle in discerning who Thomas Jefferson, the man, really was. My biggest question was how could he have written '...*Endowed by their creator with certain inalienable rights, among these life, liberty and the pursuit of happiness...*' then deny liberty, happiness and those very same "inalienable rights" to the 235 men, women and children of color on his plantation. On top of this, he was simultaneously involved with the object of this very denial for 38 years.

Then, in the course of my research, I read his incendiary, "Notes On The State Of Virginia," which he published in English in 1787, four months before Sally Hemings came into his life in Paris, thus beginning their "long term" relationship. The book sent me into a rage from which I would never recover. After reading that tome, I realized my dramatic Sally Hemings had to also read that book somewhere in the screenplay and speak out. She had to become the voice for all of the slaves and freed blacks in America then and now. She had to express outrage at Jefferson and his racist, divisive views about Blacks and their contribution (or lack of according to him) to American culture. She had to become the voice of the silenced. And that presented my second dilemma.

Who was Sally Hemings? After all, if she was the woman who obviously dominated the private life and passions of Thomas Jefferson and kept the American icon and genius for peace interested in her until his death in 1826, then she had to have been an intriguing woman. Thomas Jefferson never remarried and never dated again after beginning his liaison with Sally in Paris. He would keep her close no matter the political consequences. He named their children after friends of his. He was at the brink of losing his second term as President based on the discovery of his relationship with her, and still he did not sell her. Why? What did she mean to him? How much did she mean to him? Where did she come from? Who was her family? How did she cope? What kind of mother was she? What happened to her after Jefferson's death? I had to do more research. I had to go where my story had taken place.

In August of 1984, I took a train cross-country to visit Monticello for the first time. It was sweltering in Charlottesville and I was wearing a black suit that made me feel as though I was on fire. Yet, as I made my way from the parking facility where I left my rented Pinto and saw the magnificent red brick mansion sitting there just beyond the book shop, I suddenly felt cool tears on my face. I was actually at the site where the bulk of my story would take place. I was at Monticello. Not a set, or a mock-up, or a painting. The real thing. My breath grew short and I stopped walking. I just stared at it.

Nothing prepares you for Thomas Jefferson's home in the Blue Ridge Mountains of Albemarle County, Virginia. Monticello, which in Italian means "little mountain," is an amazing feat of architecture that consumed forty years of Jefferson's life in its construction. As you gaze at the majestic structure boasting Greek and Italian inspired stone columns, intricately detailed cornices, underground passageways and tunnels, and an impressive white-trimmed octagonal dome, you cannot help but be transported back in time. You find yourself in a time when our Constitution and American laws and dictates were being formulated. A time when reasonable men gathered to discuss and put before mankind those resolutions and precepts which would ultimately become, "We the People…" The men who were the creators and architects of our American justice system, our American government. A government *of* the people, *by* the people, and *for* the people.

Yet, as I thought about the people who came to Monticello and sat at the great Jefferson dining table—intellectuals like Volney, Adams, Lafayette, Madison, Tom Paine and countless others, I couldn't help thinking about the people who served and satiated them. The people who brought their food and wine, made their beds, cleaned up after their horses, washed their clothes, emptied their chamber pots and performed a host of other menial labors. Soon a flood of emotion swept over me. These were also "We the People." But these "people" did not own homes with gardens replete with foliage they could place in crystal vases to decorate classically designed rooms filled with European antiques. No. These "people" had been expunged from our government's system of justice. These "people" were denied and ignored in the creative tapestry of America. Why? Because these "people" were not considered people at all. They were Jefferson's slaves. They were chattel property which, 200 years ago, I could have so easily been.

As I looked down at the bricks which created an inviting path up to the Grand East portico of the house, with its glass front doors and stone columns inspired by the architecture of Palladio, I thought about Monticello's slaves who two centuries earlier painstakingly mixed and made the mortar, poured and formed the bricks, and laid them in the ground. I looked at the mansion again. How many dozens of slaves had cut trees, carried lumber, made nails, laid bricks, forged the iron, and troweled plaster to help Jefferson create this magnificent masterpiece? Then I thought about Sally Hemings—Jefferson's most prized chattel, and I wondered about her place on this plantation. I wondered how she must have felt, how she may have used her position as a Hemings, a favored slave family, and as the master of Monticello's celebrated "concubine" to not only change the condition of slaves there a modicum, but to also ensure the freedom and safety of her children.

As I entered the house with a group of others led by a tour guide, I found myself impressed with the entrance room with its detailed friezes and cannonball clock, etc. But I also thought about Sally Hemings, whose job it was to polish and dust the statues, books, busts, maps, mastodon jaws and other oddities which were housed throughout. As I learned more about the day-to-day life of Jefferson at Monticello, I was surprised that I didn't learn more about the slave community there—except for bits and pieces. When we were shown into Jefferson's famous bedroom/study I looked up at the three porthole-type windows high above the wall over the alcove bed. I had seen a photo in a 1974 article called "Treasures of America" in *Reader's Digest* magazine, which featured Jefferson's bedroom and a set of stairs leading up to this area. Observers had made comment that the stairs led to a room where Sally Hemings purportedly lived. I asked about this room and Sally Hemings, and a hush fell over the group. Our tour guide stammered then insisted the room was a closet where Jefferson kept his winter clothes and that stairs were added after Monticello came under the ownership of the Levy family who held it for 90 years.

As for Sally Hemings, the response was much more rote. We were informed Sally was a member of a slave family whom Jefferson cherished, of whom several had contributed greatly to Jefferson's lifestyle and well-being. Among them were Sally's brothers, John Hemings, whose carpentry and furniture designs are still in evidence at the home today, and James Hemings, who was Jefferson's most trusted valet and chef. Both had ultimately been freed by Jefferson. But nothing specific or special was accorded Sally by our guide except that Ms. Brodie's research and Ms. Riboud's novel had grossly exaggerated her importance in Jefferson's life.

By the time I left Monticello that day I had a real sense of the layout of the mansion and grounds, and after seeing the ruins of Mulberry Row where the slave artisans and craftsmen lived and worked, and the tiny 10-by-10 foot foundations of slave cabins accorded special slaves, I was convinced of how to tell the story. It would be Sally's story and all sequences would be told from her slave's point-of-view.

Upon my return to Los Angeles, I drew a chart which became my chronology of events in Sally's life utilizing the voluminous amount of material I had collected from Jefferson biographies or magazine articles. Daniel Griffin, a friend who worked at the main branch of the Los Angeles library downtown, found most of the information relating to the story and made copies available for me. I then drew a diagram which consisted of "dots" of truth—and connected them from there. Surprisingly, the information revealed not only the known history of Sally and Tom, but the history of the Hemings family and their contribution to both Monticello and the life of our third President. In reading the actual texts and "between the lines," I saw a story emerge.

The author at Monticello, 1984.

"...We hold these truths to be self evident..."

Thomas Jefferson

The Hemings and Jefferson Family Tree

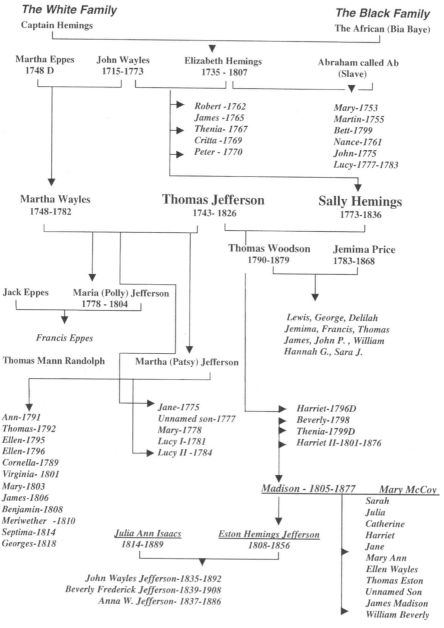

The White Family

Captain Hemings

The Black Family

The African (Bia Baye)

Martha Eppes 1748 D	John Wayles 1715-1773	Elizabeth Hemings 1735 - 1807	Abraham called Ab (Slave)

Robert -1762
James -1765
Thenia- 1767
Critta -1769
Peter - 1770

Mary-1753
Martin-1755
Bett-1799
Nance-1761
John-1775
Lucy-1777-1783

Martha Wayles 1748-1782

Thomas Jefferson 1743- 1826

Sally Hemings 1773-1836

Thomas Woodson 1790-1879

Jemima Price 1783-1868

Jack Eppes

Maria (Polly) Jefferson 1778 - 1804

Lewis, George, Delilah
Jemima, Francis, Thomas
James, John P. , William
Hannah G., Sara J.

Francis Eppes

Thomas Mann Randolph

Martha (Patsy) Jefferson

Ann-1791
Thomas-1792
Ellen-1795
Ellen-1796
Cornella-1789
Virginia- 1801
Mary-1803
James-1806
Benjamin-1808
Meriwether -1810
Septima-1814
Georges-1818

Jane-1775
Unnamed son-1777
Mary-1778
Lucy I-1781
Lucy II -1784

Harriet-1796D
Beverly-1798
Thenia-1799D
Harriet II-1801-1876

Madison - 1805-1877

Mary McCoy

Julia Ann Isaacs 1814-1889

Eston Hemings Jefferson 1808-1856

Sarah
Julia
Catherine
Harriet
Jane
Mary Ann
Ellen Wayles
Thomas Eston
Unnamed Son
James Madison
William Beverly

John Wayles Jefferson-1835-1892
Beverly Frederick Jefferson-1839-1908
Anna W. Jefferson- 1837-1886

'D' indicates date of death

Chapter Two

SALLY AND TOM – THE RESEARCH

*"The weary statesman for repose hath fled
From halls of council to his negro's shed
Where blest he woos some black Aspasia's grace
And dreams of freedom in his slave's embrace!"*

Thomas Moore

According to Hemings family oral history and the memoirs of Sally Hemings' second-to- last son, Madison, Sally's grandmother was a full-blooded African owned by John Wayles, a plantation owner and slave trader. Wayles, who would become Thomas Jefferson's father-in-law, was an acquaintance of an English sea captain named Hemings, whose whaling vessel regularly sailed between England and Williamsburg, Virginia. It is unknown what the African woman's name was or the specific area of Africa she may have been stolen from. Some suspect she may have been from the Bia Baye tribe. But until further research is done, we cannot say for sure.

We can assume from everything we know about the Trans-Atlantic slave trade, that this woman was probably snatched from all she knew and understood. She was dragged kicking and screaming into the bowels of a slave ship where she was tightly packed "spoon style" next to other stolen Negro bodies. She was forced to live in her own waste, humiliation and wretchedness. Her body was poked, prodded, examined and otherwise degraded by slave traders. She was stripped of her dignity, her language, her religion, her culture— her complete humanity—to be made chattel. A thing to be bought and sold for the sole purpose of laboring under whites in America.

According to James A. Bear Jr., a former curator at Monticello,

> *JUST ARRIVED from* AFRICA, *the ship* PRINCE *of* WALES ,*Capt* JAMES BIVINS,
> With about FOUR HUNDRED fine healthy
> ## S L A V E S,
> The S A L E of which will begin at BERMUDA HUNDRED, on *Thursday,* the 8th of *October,* and continuing until all are sold.
>   JOHN WAYLES.
>   RICHARD RANDOLPH.

A recreation of ad in the Virginia Gazette, October 15, 1772, announcing the sale of four hundred slaves by John Wayles, Jefferson's father-in-law. Wayles owned the African woman who gave birth to Betty Hemings and the Hemings clan.

the African woman was originally owned by Colonel Francis Eppes IV and was deeded to John Wayles in consideration of Wayles' marriage to Martha Eppes. She would become free labor and a sexual bartering tool for Wayles who eventually, according to one decendent, gave her as a bedmate to Captain Hemings when he would come into the port of Williamsburg. As alluded to in Madison Heming's memoirs, Captain Hemings impregnated the African woman sometime during one of those stays. Months later, when he returned to Williamsburg, he learned of and ultimately acknowledged he had fathered the honey-colored daughter of the African. Wayles named the child Elizabeth (Betty) Hemings, thus beginning the Hemings clan and what would later become one of the most indomitable slave matriarchies in Virginia. Captain Hemings attempted to purchase the woman from John Wayles, offering him a large sum of money to take both mother and child back with him to England. But Wayles, after seeing the light-skinned, biracial baby, found himself curious as to its outcome and did not want to part with either. He refused to sell. The captain vowed to return for mother and daughter, stealing them if necessary. But a slave in the Wayles household forewarned John Wayles of Hemings' arrival and Wayles had the African and baby Elizabeth removed to the main house under his protection. Captain Hemings was thus thwarted in his attempt to steal mother and daughter and he sailed away from Williamsburg, never to contact Wayles again.

ELIZABETH (BETTY) HEMINGS (1735 – 1807)

In 1847, Isaac Jefferson, a former slave at Monticello, described Betty Hemings to a reporter as a "bright mulatto woman" in his reminiscences. The beautiful, fair-skinned daughter of Captain Hemings and the African woman grew up in the household of John Wayles at The Forest, a few miles west of Williamsburg, Virginia, in Charles City

Diahann Carroll as "Betty Hemings"

County. Betty was industrious and hard working. She became the personal maid to Wayles' daughter, Martha. She had several children with a slave named Abraham, among them, Martin, born 1755, Mary, born 1753, Bett, born 1759, and Nance, born 1761. Then much later, after the death of John Wayles, she had two children with John Neilson, a white carpenter at Monticello—John, born 1775, and Lucy, born 1777. But it is the six children she bore John Wayles which have come into controversy.

John Wayles had three wives. His first wife, Martha Eppes, died shortly after the birth of her daughter, Martha Wayles, the future wife of Thomas Jefferson. His second wife, a Miss Cocke, bore Wayles four daughters, three of which would survive to adulthood. Upon Miss Cocke's death, Wayles married Elizabeth Lomax, but Lomax, too, died in less than a year. After the death of his third wife, John

Wayles sought sexual refuge in Betty Hemings, taking her as his concubine in 1761. There is no evidence to support whether Betty Hemings and John Wayles had consensual sexual relations or if it was another example of coercion and assault—as was usually the case, but Betty bore Wayles six children nonetheless: Robert, born 1762; James, born 1765, Thenia, born 1767; Critta, born 1769; Peter, born 1770, and Sally Hemings, born 1773. While all six children had their mother's last name of Hemings, Isaac Jefferson is quoted as saying, *"Folks said that these Hemingses was old Mr. Wayles' children."* Madison Hemings also confirmed this in his own memoirs later in 1873. All of these children were said to be light-skinned enough to pass for white. According to Isaac Jefferson, Betty differentiated between her "browner" children with Abraham and her "lighter" children with Wayles and Neilson. How this differentiation manifested we do not know.

After John Wayles' death in 1773, Betty, her children and a total of 135 slaves became the property of his daughter, Martha Wayles Skelton (now a widow). They were given special privileges when they came under the ownership of Thomas Jefferson upon his marriage to Martha. Thomas Jefferson may have known and understood his father-in-law's interest and preoccupation with Betty Hemings, having had as a mentor George Wythe, Jefferson's law teacher and a signer of the Declaration of Independence. Wythe also had a preoccupation with his slave, Lydia Broadnax. Lydia bore Wythe a child, Michael Brown, who was to inherit Wythe's property upon his death. Betty Hemings thus became the "Matriarch of Monticello" and ultimately the Hemings family would hold most of the important positions on the plantation, particularly those domestic positions in the house. They had better clothing and were left to their own devices for the most part, which distinguished them from many of the field hands and other slaves on the little mountain. Several of Betty Hemings' sons could travel freely about and Jefferson only sold a Hemings when they requested so as in the cases of Thenia and Robert.

There was always a great affection for the Hemings family. Jefferson would keep Betty apprised of her son James' well-being while they were in Paris. As an example, in a letter to a gardener at Monticello, Jefferson indirectly informed Betty that, *"James is well. He has forgot how to speak English, and has not learnt to speak French..."* Later, Betty would send back her "compliments" to her son, and in another such communication sent through this same gardener, she informed Jefferson that her own daughter Lucy had died. Historian Dumas Malone believed that Betty was accorded special considerations from Jefferson because Jefferson's wife Martha treated Betty and her family with such consideration. Accordingly, Betty was at the pinnacle of the slave hierarchy at Monticello. Betty died in 1807 at age 72. She'd had 14 children. Of these, 11 survived.

JAMES HEMINGS   (1765 – 1801)

James Hemings, Sally's second oldest brother, according to historian Virginuis Dabney was "exceptionally intelligent" and served as house servant, messenger and driver to Jefferson while he was governor of Virginia. James and his brother Robert were allowed to freely travel in and around Virginia without "passes" or "permission slips" from the Master of Monticello and at one point James served as a guide for an Englishman traveling in Richmond. When Jefferson accepted the position of ambassador to France, he insisted

This indenture made at Monticello in the county of Albemarle & commonwealth of Virginia on the fifth day of February one thousand seven hundred and ninety six witnesseth that I Thomas Jefferson of Monticello aforesaid do emancipate manumit & make free James Hemings, son of Betty Hemings, which said James is now of the age of thirty years so that in future he shall be free and of free condition, & discharged of all duties & claims of servitude whatsoever, & shall have all the rights and privileges of a freedman. In witness whereof I have hereto set my hand & seal on the day & year above written and have made these presents double of the same date, tenor & indenture one whereof is lodged in the court of Albemarle aforesaid to be recorded, & the other is delivered by me to the said James Hemings to be produced when & where it may be necessary.

Signed, sealed & delivered
in presence of

John Carr

Francis Anderson

Th Jefferson

Above: *Deed of manumission which freed James Hemings dated December, 1796 and signed by Thomas Jefferson.*
At right: *Mario Van Peebles as "James Hemings"*

James accompany him as his valet. James left for France in 1784. After arriving in Paris, Jefferson trusted James to go ahead of Martha and him to make hotel reservations for them. He also began a culinary apprenticeship under the chef for the Prince de Conde and became a pastry chef. Ultimately James became "chef de cuisine" for Jefferson at the Hotel de Langeac, Jefferson's Paris residence, and invented new culinary dishes which were a mixture of French and southern cuisine. He was soon in demand to cook for other aristocracy in and around Paris.

It has been noted by Fawn Brodie that James also had a volatile personality. In a letter to Thomas Jefferson dated January 9, 1789, Monsieur Perrault, the same tutor utilized for Martha and Maria Jefferson, and hired by James for himself and sister Sally, complained of, *"mauvais traitemens de gimme"* and *"Sotisses les plus durs…"* an indication that James was hot tempered. We also know that according to Madison Hemings' memoirs, James had refused to return with Jefferson to America when Jefferson was recalled unless Jefferson promised to free him in writing. But Jefferson didn't agree in writing until September 15, 1793 adding a clause that if James taught *"such a person as I shall place under him for the purpose to be a good cook,"* James would be freed. Why James didn't elect to remain in France where he was already a free man despite his color, and use his culinary skills in a country which would have appreciated his abilities, is unknown. What is known is that upon their return from France, Jefferson continued to pay James wages thus making him a slave paid a salary.

Still, in spite of his high rank in the slave hierarchy, James wanted his freedom, as any slave would want, and began drinking. Per his agreement with Jefferson in 1793, he taught his younger brother Peter how to cook French-style, then petitioned Jefferson for his freedom. James' deed of manumission was signed in December of 1796 and James was freed. Jefferson gave him $30 for his expenses to Philadelphia. After a time in Philadelphia, James went to Paris and talked of a trip to Spain but could find no peace. He returned to the United States where he worked odd jobs here and there, but unfortunately life as a free black man proved as arduous as slavery. He gave his life over to alcohol. Jefferson discovered his whereabouts through a friend who had been one of James' employers. Jefferson asked James to return to Monticello and offered him a salary, but James refused. In 1801, at age 36, James Hemings committed suicide.

SARAH "SALLY" HEMINGS (1773 – 1835)

With as much infamy as Sally Hemings has come to garner in recent years, there is not an overabundance of historical specifics about her. Fawn Brodie refers to it as "a record of extraordinary concealment." However, there was enough information in my research to construct an image, personality and the circumstances which led her to intertwine with Thomas Jefferson on their road to controversy.

There are two physical descriptions of Sally

Hemings. One by Isaac Jefferson, a former Monticello slave, who in his 1847 reminiscences described her as *"...Mighty near white,"* and *"very handsome, with long straight hair down her back."* The other was from Thomas Jefferson Randolph, Jefferson's grandson who is quoted in a letter dated June 1, 1868 from Henry S. Randall to James Parton, and who described Sally as *"light colored and decidedly good looking."* Fawn Brodie broached the idea that because Sally was Jefferson's wife's half-sister, she may have favored Mrs. Jefferson.

We also know that nine-year old Sally and her mother Betty were present in the room when Mrs. Jefferson, on her deathbed, elicited a promise from Thomas Jefferson that he never remarry. Jefferson made that promise and in fact did not marry again. Mrs. Jefferson gave Sally Hemings a small bell as a gift. The bell is now kept at Monticello.

THE STORY

In 1784, two years after the death of his wife, a still bereft Thomas Jefferson accepted the position of ambassador to France. He left for Paris on a sailing vessel called the Ceres and took his oldest daughter, Martha, nicknamed "Patsy" to avoid confusion between she and his wife named Martha, and his trusted servant/slave James Hemings, Sally's older brother. At the point Jefferson left for France, he had two other daughters residing with his sister-in-law, Elizabeth Eppes. They were Maria, nicknamed "Polly," and Lucy Jefferson. Sometime in 1786, young Lucy Jefferson contracted yellow fever and died. When word reached Jefferson in Paris, he was once again bereft. Of the six children he'd had with wife Martha, only two were still alive. Panicked at the possibility of losing more family, Jefferson sent for Polly to join him in Paris.

Jefferson requested that young Polly be accompanied by an older slave/servant. According to Fawn Brodie, the slave Jefferson suggested was named Isabel. All we know about Isabel is that she was nine months pregnant, ready to give birth at any moment and could not make the trip to Europe. Instead of sending another older, capable slave, the decision was made to send 14-year-old Sally Hemings. We do not know who made the decision to send Sally, but some speculation suggests it was Sally's mother, Betty Hemings. It is well known that the Hemings family held all the important household positions at Monticello, and that Betty Hemings was matriarch of the Hemings family and therefore in charge. Another account suggests that Elizabeth or Francis Eppes sent Sally over. In any event, Sally accompanied Jefferson's nine-year-old daughter on the five-week voyage to Paris.

On June 26, 1787, Abigail and John Adams met the ship at the port of London. Abigail expressed concern that an older slave had not attended Polly, but an adolescent girl. She then wrote Jefferson to say that Sally was "a girl about 15 or 16...the Sister of the Servant you have with you," and that Sally was "quite a child." Abigail also indicated that "...Captain Ramsey is of opinion (Sally) will be of so little Service that he had better carry her back with him. But of this you will be the judge. She seems fond of the child and appears good naturd (sic)." Indeed, Sally and Polly were friends, and this friendly relationship I included in both the play and screenplay. Sally and Polly stayed in London with the Adamses approximately two weeks before Jefferson's valet Adrien Petit arrived to take the two girls across the English Channel to the city of lights.

Prior to Sally's arrival, Ambassador Jefferson was involved in one of the great love affairs of his stay. It has been rumored that his relationship with the married Lady Maria Cosway was platonic. But like his relationship with Sally Hemings, it depends on the researcher or the attitude of the biographer as to whether there was actually a physical involvement. Whatever the characterization, on October 12, 1786, Jefferson wrote Lady Cosway one of most endearing love letters in American history, which has come down to us as "My Head and my Heart." I found this letter revealing in many ways. First, Jefferson's emotional conflicts were so clearly articulated here. He knew it was wrong to be romantically interested in a married woman, yet his heart would soar whenever he was in her presence. Guilt was consuming him, and he had to share the source of that guilt with Maria, thus expressing his deep feelings for her. Secondly, Jefferson had a habit of being attracted to unavailable women, and later, in seeing the error of his ways, would break off the relationship.

Upon Sally's arrival at the Hotel de Langeac in Paris, she was treated with what Fawn Brodie calls "special consideration." On November 6, 1787, Jefferson paid a Dr. Sutton 240 francs to have Sally inoculated against small pox, fearful of catching the dread disease himself or infecting the entire household. To inoculate a slave against disease is something most slave owners would never consider. In fact, the average slave master would have rid himself of a sickly slave in favor of a healthy one. So the first sign that Sally Hemings, upon touching French soil and the ultimate liberation France guaranteed, was being elevated to a condition above that of ordinary slave, was evident. Equally interesting is the fact Jefferson began to pay Sally wages. Initially it was 24 francs a month and was eventually increased to 36 francs, just as he had paid James Hemings. Wages are an indication one is an employee — not a slave in unpaid servitude. However, it must be noted that Jefferson was not an equal opportunity employer as he paid his French servants 50 to 60 francs a month. Also of interest was Jefferson having Sally Hemings tutored in French with the same instructor, Monsieur Parrault, who was also tutoring his daughters Polly and Martha…and James Hemings.

Sally was also trained as a "Ladies Maid." This gave her access to French aristocracy and the opportunity to observe and "mimic" people of privilege which none of the French servants working for Jefferson in Paris had. More than likely she attended Jefferson's daughters, Martha and Maria, and when they attended parties, balls and/or gatherings amongst the elite, Sally would have accompanied them as their ladies maid. Sally may have also had some special place amongst the domestic staff at the Hotel de Langeac as she was referred to as "Mademoiselle Sally" by Jefferson's butler, Adrien Petit. Later, when Jefferson was Secretary of State, Petit closed a letter to Jefferson by saying, "say hello to Gimme (James) and Sally."

Sometime in 1788, a relationship developed between Jefferson and Sally Hemings. Jefferson abruptly broke off his relationship with Lady Maria Cosway and according to his account books had begun spending an unusually large amount of money on Sally's clothing compared to the other staff. These expenditures rivaled those of his daughters. In April of 1789 alone, he noted expenditures of 96 francs for "clothes for Sally" on April 6; 72 francs on April 16; and 23 francs on April 26 for "making clothes for servts." On May 25, there is another item which notes "pd making clothes for Sally 25# 2." To give you an idea of what kind of money we're talking about, a pair of gloves in those days cost 2 francs, so an expenditure of 216 francs in one month would be considered excessive. There is also an observation on page 239 of Fawn Brodie's book where she cited in Jefferson's account books that *"...Jefferson in September 1788 went to his old haunts—St. Germain and Marly, and that he went back to the 'Desert' in May 1789. Was it Sally Hemings who accompanied him?"* Brodie goes on to rationalize: *"We know that he bought a "watch" for Patsy on January 5, 1789, costing 554 francs, and on June 30 a "ring for Patsy" costing 48 francs. Was it for Sally Hemings, on September 30, 1788, that he paid 40 francs for "a locket"?*

I wondered how Martha "Patsy" Jefferson might have felt with all the attention being paid to Sally Hemings by her father. Dr. Brodie comments on this as well, stating: *"One wonders if it ever occurred to him (Jefferson) that Patsy, upon coming home from school on Sunday, would look upon the spectacle of her maid newly dressed in stylish Parisian clothes with absolute incomprehension..."* *"...But there is the coincidence that it was in early April that Jefferson spent almost two hundred francs on "clothes for Sally," and that on April 18 Jefferson was appalled to get a note from Patsy formally requesting his permission to let her become a nun..."*

I utilized "the locket" idea in the play and the screenplay as well as Martha Jefferson's bitter jealousies over the women in her father's life. This gave the Martha/Sally relationship a universal and human understanding, and grounded it in the reality of two women fighting over the affections of one man—a time-honored conflict.

As for Sally's age at the time of the sexual liaison (15 or 16) and the charge Jefferson was a pedophile, one must remember that prior to the 20th century, women married shortly after puberty. A woman who found herself unmarried at age 18 was a candidate for spinsterhood. In fact, Jefferson's daughters Martha and Polly married at ages 17 and 16 respectively.

Equally curious is the question as to whether Sally and Jefferson had an epistolary relationship comprised of letters exchanged to each other. No letter between them has surfaced thus far, but more interesting to note is that the entire letter index for the year 1788, the year it is believed a physical relationship began between Sally and Jefferson, has mysteriously disappeared. According to Fawn Brodie, it is the only volume in the 43 year written history of Thomas Jefferson—a fanatic letter writer and keeper (thanks to his polygraph letter copier)—to vanish. According to historian Julian Boyd the letters once existed. Perhaps in an attempt to protect the image of Mr. Jefferson, they are now missing. Curiously, letters written by Jefferson to other members of the Hemings family exist, but anything remotely referencing Sally Hemings does not.

Sally Hemings became pregnant sometime in 1789. She must have known that both she and brother, James, were free by virtue of their presence on French soil. Thus any child born to Sally would have been born free as well. Madison Hemings' memoirs confirm that Sally did not want to return to America and elicited a promise from Jefferson that her child or any children she had would be freed by age 21. But what of Sally herself? Did she obtain a verbal agreement of freedom from Jefferson or that her movements in Virginia would be unrestricted as were her brothers Robert, Peter and James? We do not have any hard evidence. We do know that her brother James was given his promise of freedom if he returned. For two intelligent "free" persons of color to knowingly return to America and the American system of chattel slavery suggested some accommodation or arrangement was made to insure life in America would not be that of a bondaged servant.

We also can surmise that Sally's experiences in France must have been some of the most significant in her life. Edmund Bacon, one of Jefferson's overseers, said in his memoirs that Sally always talked about Paris and her time spent in Europe. Those 26 months must have been among the happiest and left an indelible impression on the young slave. As with her brother, James, she probably longed to return to Paris and recapture a time when race, color and ethnicity had less to do with a relationship than emotion. Still, something more than love, a sense of duty, or love of family would have induced Sally Hemings to return to America given the repercussions inherent to slavery. What that something was, I would later have to dramatize.

In January of 1790, Sally gave birth to a son. He was named Tom Hemings and was described as red-haired and fair-skinned. In March, Jefferson left Monticello to become America's first Secretary of State. Very little has been written about Tom's earlier years until 1802. Historian Winthrop Jordan noted that Thomas Jefferson was present at Monticello nine months before the births of each of Sally's children and that Sally did not have children when Jefferson was away in political office. Next, according to Brodie, Sally gave birth October 5, 1795 to a daughter, Harriet, and in 1796 to Edy. Jefferson was in retirement from January 16, 1794 to February 20, 1797. According to new information, biographer Annette Gordon-Reed notes Edy as not being Sally Hemings' actual daughter but a quasi "baby sitter" who had moved in to help with Harriet. But Harriet died in infancy. Sally next gave birth to a son, William Beverly, called "Beverly", on April 1, 1798 after Jefferson had been at Monticello from July 11, 1797 until December 4, 1797 when he returned to Philadelphia as Vice-President. A daughter, possibly named Thenia, after Sally's sister Thenia, was born to Sally in 1799. Jefferson was in residence at Monticello from March 8 through December 21, 1800. But this baby died soon after its birth. While Jefferson was serving his first term as President of the United States, Sally next gave birth to a second Harriet in May of 1801. Jefferson had been at Monticello from May 29, 1800 to November 24, 1800.

Sally would next have James Madison Hemings on January 19, 1805. Jefferson was at Monticello from April 4 through May 11, 1804. Madison wrote in his memoirs that he was named by Dolley Madison, the future First Lady of the United States. Madison was ultimately freed in Jefferson's will. Finally, Sally gave birth to Eston Hemings on May 21, 1808. Thomas Jefferson had been at Monticello from August 4 to October 1, 1807. Eston was also freed according to Jefferson's will in 1826.

Questions have been raised as to whether Sally Hemings ever followed Jefferson in his various posts or visited him in the White House (then called the Executive Mansion) as I presented in the miniseries. I got the idea from a notation in Aaron Burr's diary that he saw Sally Hemings in Philadelphia in March, 1797, attending Thomas Jefferson's inauguration as Vice-President. Also James Hemings was still serving as Jefferson's chef while Jefferson was Secretary of State in New York. As mentioned earlier, Adrien Petit ended a letter to Jefferson there stating "say hello to Gimme and Sally." So it became obvious, Sally Hemings may have traveled to Jefferson in every one of his positions in government, so why *not* the Executive Mansion?

Sally Hemings, Thomas Jefferson and their five living children would have gone on to conduct their relationship in relative obscurity had it not been for one ambitious, unscrupulous Scottish reporter for the *Richmond Recorder*. James Thompson Callender, once described by Jefferson as "a man of genius," had fled to America sometime in the 1790's to avoid a trial for sedition in England. Jefferson began purchasing political articles from him and when Callender was unemployed, sent him fifty dollars. But while Jefferson was Vice-President Callender found himself in jail for sedition again, this time against then President John Adams. When Jefferson became President he pardoned all convicted under the Aliens and Seditions Act including Callender, but the latter wanted more. He wanted to be Postmaster. Jefferson did not respond to Callender's correspondence, and Callender began questioning Jefferson's neighbors in April of 1801 and learned in detail about Sally Hemings. He then tried to blackmail Jefferson with threats of exposing "information" he had on Jefferson prompting Jefferson to assure Governor James Monroe that *"...He (Callender) knows nothing of me, which I am not willing to declare to the world myself..."* However, once Callender was certain Jefferson would not appoint him as Postmaster, he did reveal his information on Sally Hemings, and on September 1, 1802, the story appeared in the *Richmond Recorder* under the headline, "The President Again?" It set into motion the scandal which became the source of a deeply debated controversy. Among many charges, Callender wrote:

"It is well known that the man whom it delighteth the people to honor, keeps, and for many years past has kept, as his concubine, one of his own slaves. Her name is SALLY. The name of her eldest son is TOM. His features are said to bear a striking although sable resemblance to those of the president himself. The boy is ten or twelve years of age. His mother went to France in the same vessel with Mr. Jefferson and his two daughters. The delicacy of this arrangement must strike every portion of common sensibility..." *"...Some years ago, this story had once or twice been hinted at in Rind's Federalist. At that time, we believed the surmise to be an absolute calumny. One reason for thinking so was this: A vast body of people wished to debar Mr. Jefferson from the presidency. The establishment of this SINGLE FACT would have rendered his election impossible..."*

Later in the article Callender also wrote: *"We hear that our young MULLATO (sic) PRESIDENT begins to give himself a great number of airs of importance in Charlottesville, and the neighbourhood."*

This article and the information contained therein was dispatched to the world and Callender kept up his vituperative attacks for over a year. Other newspapers followed suit and the "Dusky Sally" stories almost cost Jefferson his presidency. Two events finally overshadowed the scandal, Jefferson's successful Louisiana Purchase in 1803 and the treaty with France; and the death in July 1803 of James Thompson Callender found drowned in three feet of water. Curiously, all throughout the scandal Jefferson never had Sally or his children with her removed from Monticello to another of his lodgings or farms, nor did he sell her as advised. Tom Hemings, however, left Monticello when the public attacks began and ran to a nearby plantation in Greenbriar County, Virginia belonging to one of Jefferson's cousins named Woodson. There he met Jemina Grant, a mulatto, married her and adopted the name Woodson. Thus, as Mr. and Mrs. Thomas C. Woodson, the two moved to Southern Ohio where they raised 11 children as mentioned. Sally and Jefferson went on to have two more children—Madison and Eston. Both were in fact conceived while Jefferson was still President.

Sally Hemings was not formally freed in Jefferson's will. In fact, she was listed on the slave inventory as "an old woman worth $50." Questions are raised as to why Jefferson did not include her on the list of five slaves he freed as all five were children or relatives of Sally's and had skills which would have prepared them for the free world. My assumption is one shared by the historians who believe there was a relationship between Sally and Tom. To name Sally Hemings in a public document such as his will could mean revisiting the scandal which had so plagued his presidency. It would forever tie Hemings to Jefferson in a way as to overshadow his accomplishments in public life, making what was essentially a private matter a public calumny all over again. Thus, the deed fell to Martha Jefferson who gave Sally "her time."

My question has always been, if Martha was not told specifically by Jefferson to attend to the informal freedom of Sally Hemings, why would she have done it given her quest to keep the image of her father pristine? Why not allow Sally to be sold and rid herself of the problem ever after? Was there some other reason Martha freed Sally? It was then I thought of James Hemings' manumission papers and the promise Jefferson made to James in Paris. He gave James his freedom five years after his return to America and James was not involved with Jefferson in any sexual capacity as was Sally. So, why wouldn't Jefferson have accorded Sally the same preference, given their relationship, and allowed Sally the freedom of choice? According to Madison Hemings' memoirs Jefferson did promise Sally that her unborn child and any children she'd have would have their freedom by age 21, and all of the children Sally had with Jefferson in fact became free. That is how I came up with the notion of a written promise given to Sally by Jefferson which she kept on her person and presented to Martha at the end of Jefferson's life. Granted, such a document hasn't come down to us in history as James' manumission papers have, but for Sally to have used such a written document and be desirous to stay in Virginia would mean Martha petitioning the Virginia legislature. This would also have rekindled the scandal—and Martha would have done anything to avoid this. Therefore freeing Sally quietly and surreptitiously was far more prudent and accomplished the same net result for Sally Hemings: freedom. Thus, Sally accomplished what no other slave at Monticello could: she secured her children's freedom, and her own as well.

Thomas Jefferson never admitted, acknowledged nor denied his involvement with Sally Hemings or the children he fathered with her. Some suspect it was because of his determination for privacy and that he felt it was no one's business. There is, however, one private letter dated July 1, 1805 which Jefferson wrote to Navy Secretary Robert Smith regarding a copy of a letter he wrote to Attorney General Levi Lincoln. In it Jefferson states, "*...You will perceive that I plead guilty to one of their charges, that when young and single I offered love to a handsome lady. I acknolege (sic) its incorrectness. It is the only one founded on truth among all their allegations against*

An ad in the Charlottesville Central Gazette dated January 3, 1827 announcing the sale of Thomas Jefferson's estate by his grandson Thomas Jefferson Randolph. The sale included 130 slaves at Monticello including many members of the Hemings family.

me."

In my attempt to deconstruct Jefferson in order to dramatize him, I came to the conclusion it was probably not prudent for Jefferson to admit to the relationship given the miscegenation laws in Virginia. As it was illegal for whites and blacks to have sex, Jefferson was committing a crime. A crime he, oddly enough, exacerbated when he drafted a bill in 1786 which stated: *"...a marriage between a person of free condition and a slave, or between a white person and a negro, or between a white person and a mulatto, shall be null..."* Thus when Mr. Jefferson wrote those words, he, in effect, drafted his own prescription for scandal.

As for Sally Hemings we can surmise from the fact she never had children for any other man at Monticello, that she did not have another lover or slave husband during her 38-year relationship with Thomas Jefferson. Also, according to several descendants, Sally walked up that steep hill for nine years after Jefferson's death to take care of Jefferson's grave at Monticello. As Sam Neill, our actor who portrayed Thomas Jefferson said recently, it was "hardly the act of an abused former slave. Had she been mistreated, intelligence dictates she would never have returned to Monticello again." I agreed. Additionally, any slave freed in Virginia was required to leave the State within one year. Thomas Jefferson had petitioned the Virginia Legislature to allow Madison and Eston to remain in Virginia if they chose. Both sons elected to remain in the State and took care of their mother in a small cabin four miles from Monticello when all three could have left the State and the memories of plantation life and slavery. It should also be noted, however, that when Sally Hemings died in 1835, both Madison and Eston sold the cabin and relocated to southern Ohio where many of their descendants still live today. So my guess is, it was their mother who insisted upon staying in Virginia in close proximity to Monticello.

Sally's other children, Beverly and Harriet, were allowed to "run away" and pass for white in 1822. Jefferson noted these departures in his farm book writing the word "run, '22" next to their names. Harriet was given $50 by Jefferson and placed on a stagecoach bound for Philadelphia. Both were thought to be lost to history except for brief mentions in Madison Hemings' 1873 memoirs. Madison wrote that Beverly married a white woman in Maryland and had a daughter who "was not known by white folks to have any colored blood coursing her veins." Harriet eventually moved to Washington and married a white man who, according to Madison Hemings, "...was in good standing..." and had children who were "never aware they had African ancestry." Madison and Harriet kept up a correspondence which lasted until sometime around the Civil War. Since the miniseries, new information has been forwarded to me by Dr. Thomas D. Best, a retired University of California professor and a purported descendant of Harriet Hemings. Dr. Best's research states that Harriet may have later migrated to Wisconsin where she changed her name to "Eliza Jefferson" (perhaps after her grandmother Elizabeth?). We also know that Sally's youngest son Eston also migrated to Wisconsin from Ohio in 1852 and changed his name to "E.H. Jefferson." At that point he, too, passed for white. Could brother and sister have reunited? Only new evidence or DNA will tell.

When Thomas Jefferson died in 1826, he was over $107,000 in debt. By 1830, Monticello and all of Jefferson's possessions had been sold to repay Jefferson's creditors. This included all of his remaining slaves including many Hemings family members. Sally had to know about the ad in the *Charlottesville Central Gazette dated January 3, 1827* announcing the sale of Jefferson's estate and his "130 Valuable Negroes" by grandson Thomas J. Randolph. She must have watched as her relatives and friends had their families separated, bid upon and sold to slave masters all over the South. She had to know that except for the few members of Monticello's slave community whose whereabouts she was aware of, life as she had known it on the little mountain had changed forever. By staying, she missed an opportunity to move on as a free woman. So either Sally felt too old to begin life anew elsewhere—or perhaps love is more binding than slavery, and when Jefferson died, so did a part of Sally. It just took her body nine more years to follow.

So many things about Sally Hemings we'll just never know. Equally enigmatic is the heart of Thomas Jefferson. But since I had to make a dramatic choice, my assessment became clear. These two people, Thomas Jefferson and Sally Hemings—a white man and a black woman—were both victims of the times in which they lived. They were forced to conduct their relationship in a cloistered, clandestine, sometimes tumultuous environment. But for what reason? Why would these two have continued together for 38 years, particularly under some politically untenable circumstances for Jefferson, unless there was some emotional attachment involved? Perhaps for the same reason we cannot choose the people we're related to, alas, human nature dictates we cannot repel the feelings we have for people we're captivated by either.

I give a gold watch to each of my grandchildren who shall not have already received one from me, to be purchased and delivered by my executors to my grandsons at the age of 21. and grand-daughters at that of sixteen.

I give to my good, affectionate, and faithful servant Burwell his freedom, and the sum of three hundred Dollars to buy necessaries to commence his trade of painter and glazier, or to use otherwise as he pleases. I give also to my good servants John Hemings and Joe Fossett their freedom at the end of one year after my death: and to each of them respectively all the tools of their respective shops or callings: and it is my will that a comfortable log-house be built for each of the three servants so emancipated on some part of my lands convenient to them with respect to the residence of their wives, and to Charlottesville and the University, where they will be mostly employed, and reasonably convenient also to the interests of the proprietor of the lands; of which houses I give the use of one, with a curtilage of an acre to each, during his life or personal occupation thereof.

I give also to John Hemings the service of his two apprentices, Madison and Eston Hemings, until their respective ages of twenty one years, at which period respectively, I give them their freedom. and I humbly and earnestly request of the legislature of Virginia a confirmation of the bequest of freedom to these servants, with permission to remain in this state where their families and connections are, as an additional instance of the favor, of which I have received so many other manifestations, in the course of my life, and for which I now give them my last, solemn, and dutiful thanks.

In testimony that this is a codicil to my will of yesterday's date, and that it is to be taken as part of it, I have written it all with my own hand, in ... me this 17th day of March one thousand ...

Th. Jefferson

Above*: Codicil to Thomas Jefferson's will dated March 17, 1826 freeing five slaves including Sally and Jefferson's sons, Madison and Eston Hemings.*

"...I give also to John Hemings the service of his two apprentices, Madison and Eston Hemings until their respective ages of twenty one years, at which period respectively, I give them their freedom..."

Jefferson also requests the Virginia legislature allow Madison and Eston to remain in the State of Virginia if they chose to.

Chapter Three

SCRIPTING SALLY'S STORY

"...An amalgamation between whites and blacks produces a degradation to which no one...can innocently consent..."

Thomas Jefferson

Oh the contradictions. Clearly Sally Hemings and Thomas Jefferson had an amalgamation which produced offspring. Did Mr. Jefferson think his own mixed children were a degradation to which he could not innocently consent? Or did they not even exist for him? And if they did, were they exempt from his assessment of biracial children? Such incongruities are indicative of the Jefferson paradox and are difficult to rationalize. Surely Jefferson must have witnessed that the biracial progeny of slaves and their masters fared better in a society which, like Jefferson, was conditioned to revile slaves socially, because they were generally more educated, more acceptable to whites therefore more likely to assimilate into white society, and were less threatening. Hardly a degradation. But then we must remember this is the same man who wrote, "All men are created equal" who was both a slave owner and opposed emancipation.

Sigmund Freud has been quoted as saying, *"Biographers frequently select the hero as the object of study because for personal reasons of their own emotional life, they have a special affection for him from the very outset. They then devote themselves to a work of idealization, which strives to enroll the great man among their infantile models... For the sake of this wish, they rub out the traces of his life's struggle with inner and outer resistances, and do not tolerate in him anything savoring of human weakness or imperfection... It is to be regretted that they do this, for they thereby sacrifice the truth to an illusion..."*

It's really too bad Freud had not lived during Jefferson's lifetime or vice versa, and that Mr. Jefferson could not submit himself to Dr. Freud's leather couch. As a dramatist, I could not resist imagining a session between the conflicted genius for peace and the psychoanalytic genius.

INT: DR. SIGMUND FREUDS'S OFFICE - DAY

JEFFERSON

Dr. Freud, thank you so very much for seeing me on such short notice. I shall only be in London a few days and it was imperative I see you.

FREUD
Dear Mr. Jefferson, I was only too pleased to accommodate
you. In fact, I rescheduled Mr. Beethoven for tomorrow.
He's depressed, you know. He is going deaf and having
difficulty writing anything other than masses and funeral
marches these days. Now, how can I help you?

JEFFERSON
I, too, have been depressed as I am prone to
experience a recurring nightmare. Ever the same.

He rubs his temples, in the throes of a migraine.

JEFFERSON
I am staring through my telescope at the site I
have chosen for my university, when suddenly
I am surrounded by slaves who resemble me.
Dozens of them—tall, auburn exact replicas. And
they are not slaves typical in manner, dress or
appearance, mind you sir, but well dressed,
well educated lads, all carrying bibles in one
hand and pitchforks in the other. They seem
disagreeable and after wrestling me to the ground,
shouting "Am I not a man?" some begin stabbing
me whilst others wave those bibles.
(a beat)
Then, as I beg for mercy, a beautiful mulatto
woman appears before me crying. Her tears fall
onto my person burning my flesh. I reach out for
her, but it is she who thrusts the last pitchfork into
my heart piercing it. Then I awaken...screaming.

FREUD
Interesting. How would you categorize your
relationship with your mother?

JEFFERSON
(thinks back)
She is dead, God rest her. But ours was a strained
pairing. I was always with one eye to the future.
She with one to the past. And she was British, you
know. Intractable, occasionally demanding.
(a beat)
Why should you inquire? How could it have bearing?

FREUD

You loved your mother, but could not tolerate
aspects of her, nor free yourself from the guilt of
resentment. You love your slaves, but they are still
slaves and you cannot free yourself from the guilt
of their resentment.

JEFFERSON

But what does it all mean? How does it correlate?

FREUD

Free your slaves—or forever torment your soul
to hell. For your conflicts have more to do with
complacence and avarice—than morality, good sir.

JEFFERSON

But what of the woman? Who is she?

FREUD

She, dear boy…is America. Mother of the world.

Indeed, Mr. Jefferson was a confused individual. Earlier in his life he had been
a fervent believer in slave emancipation. When he first wrote the Declaration of
Independence, he included a paragraph which denounced King George for *"waging
cruel war against human nature…"* and refusing to end the slave trade. But the Southern
constituents voted against the inclusion of the paragraph, thus it was deleted from the
final draft. Thereafter, Jefferson retreated from his once strong anti-slavery sentiments.
The problem is all while he was struggling with wavering attitudes regarding
emancipation, racial inferiority and slave liberation, he was having a relationship with
a black woman. He would refer to his slaves as his extended "family" as he did in 1776
when he made a census of the "Number of souls in my family" which counted in
addition to the white Jefferson's, some 83 slaves. Yet, while he may have vowed never
to sell slaves for profit, when he desired a case of imported French wine or a shipment
of Italian fabric, off went three or four "family" members to be quietly sold to private
buyers.

I used these aspects of Jefferson's inner conflicts along with Sally's outrage at
the racist sentiments he expressed in "Notes on the State of Virginia" which he wrote in
1781. Following are a few examples I excerpted from one chapter entitled, "Query XIV
LAWS." These references contain Jefferson's original spelling and grammar.

"…The first difference (between the races) *which strikes us is that of colour…"*
*"…Add to these, flowing hair, a more elegant symmetry of form, their own judgment in
favour of the whites, declared by their preference of them, as uniformly as is the
preference of the Oran-ootan for the women over those of his own species. The
circumstance of superior beauty is thought worthy attention in the propagation of our
horses, dogs, and other domestic animals; why not in that of man? Besides those of*

colour, figure, and hair, there are other physical distinctions proving a difference of race. They have less hair on the face and body. They secrete less by the kidnies, and more by the glands of the skin, which gives them a very strong and disagreeable odour. This greater degree of transpiration renders them more tolerant of heat and less of cold, than the whites..." "...They seem to require less sleep. A black, after hard labour through the day, will be induced by the slightest amusement to sit up till midnight, or later, though knowing he must be out with the first dawn of the morning. "...They are more ardent after their female: but love seems with them to be more an eager desire than a tender delicate mixture of sentiment and sensation. Their griefs are transient..."

"...Comparing them by their faculties of memory, reason, and imagination, it appears to me, that in memory they are equal to the whites; in reason much inferior..." "...and that in imagination they are dull, tasteless, and anomalous..."

"...The Indians... astonish you with strokes of the most sublime oratory; such as prove their reason and sentiment strong, their imagination glowing and elevated. But never yet could I find that a black had uttered a thought above the level of plain narration; never see even an elementary trait of painting or sculpture. In music they are more generally gifted than the whites with accurate ears for tune and time..." "...Misery is often the parent of the most affecting touches in poetry.-Among the blacks is misery enough, God knows, but no poetry..." "...Religion indeed has produced a Phyllis Whately; but it could not produce a poet..."

"...The improvement of the blacks in body and mind, in the first instance of their mixture with the whites, has been observed by every one, and proves that their inferiority is not the effect merely of their condition of life..."

"...But in this country the slaves multiply as fact as the free inhabitants. Their situation and manners place the commerce between the two sexes almost without restraint..." "...I advance it therefore as a suspicion only, that the blacks, whether originally a distinct race, or made distinct by time and circumstances, are inferior to the whites in the endowments both of body and mind..." "...This unfortunate difference of colour, and perhaps of faculty, is a powerful obstacle to the emancipation of these people..." "...The slave, when made free, might mix with, without staining the blood of his master. But with us a second is necessary, unknown to history. When freed, his to be removed beyond the reach of mixture..."

These observations led me to my final dilemma. How do I construct a historically accurate yet compelling script from 38 years of gaps, supposition, bits and pieces, and character contradictions? I sought the answer from an old writing teacher, who reminded me I was writing a drama—not a documentary, and that the dramatic imperatives present different challenges requiring different resolutions. With that in mind, I started writing.

Many times in the construction of my story, I found myself with no factual material with which to support either character arcs and motivations, or timelines for scenes. In dramatic structure every scene has two purposes: one, to advance the plot, or, two, to illuminate character. Sometimes the only facts I had were a chain of "events" in the activities of Thomas Jefferson in reference to Sally Hemings. These events or nuggets of factual information became the "dots" I had to connect in order to build a dramatically compelling narrative. On occasion, in order to fill in the many of the blanks in Sally's life, I had only to imagine what may have happened. Other times I used aspects of my paternal great-great grandmother, Addie Mae, and her granddaughter Annie, whose lives bore a striking resemblance to Sally Hemings' and were handed down to me through my own family oral history.

Addie Mae Washington had been a light skinned black nurse maid to the sickly wife of a white man in Birmingham, Alabama during Reconstruction. It is said that she was the result of a rape between her mother and her mother's white slave owner. Addie, it is rumored, also taught her medical "obeah arts" to other Negroes in her area. When the man's wife died, he grieved for a year, but would not let Addie Mae move on to other employment, asking her to instead continue to help take care of he and his two children. Addie Mae stayed on and sometime in 1874, the man's affections for Addie Mae grew into love and the two began a relationship which lasted nine more years until his death. During that time, Addie became pregnant with a son, who it is said was so light that he left Birmingham and passed into white society. My family has no more history on him other than that.

Due to the anti-miscegenation laws and the nature and attitudes in segregated Birmingham during the days of Jim-Crow, the white man and Addie Mae could not marry. Though they conducted their relationship surreptitiously, it was well known in the black community where Addie's family lived that Addie was his lover. When the man died, he left his two white children his money, but left his property to Addie Mae and their son. Eventually Addie married a black man and together they had my great grandmother, India, who married a black man and had my grandmother Annie Mae, in 1898, who eventually married a black minister, James T. Andrews, Sr. The house, which by this time had become part of a black neighborhood, was passed down three generations to my father and finally sold by Daddy and Uncle James in 1963 after Grandmother's death.

In the year of our Lord, 1963, the centennial anniversary of the Emancipation Proclamation, I went to Birmingham. It was just months before Grandma Annie died. The violence in Bull Connor's city in George Wallace's State had frightened me as we drove to the old wood planked house with chipping paint. Yet once I entered my grandmother's home, I was enchanted. Grandma had a cedar chest at the foot of her bed and I remember asking if I could open it. I was no more than 6 or 7 years old, but that chest fascinated me. Inside was costume jewelry, keepsakes, and an old beaver coat which underscored the full, rich history of not only Grandma's life, but her mother and grandmother's. But it was Grandma's diary and a moth eaten lilac dress which would have the greatest impact on me. The brown leather diary included old photos, yellowing newspaper clippings and love letters given to Grandma by my grandfather. In fact grandma met my grandfather wearing the lilac dress at a "Sadie Hawkins" dance. The way Grandma told it, she asked grandpa James to waltz and upon seeing her in that dress, Grandpa was hers until his death in 1958. As a child I held the dress up to myself in a chipped mirror and pretended. Later, I incorporated the trunk, the diary and the lilac dress in the screenplay not only in tribute to my grandmother, but for all the ancestors who leave a bit of themselves behind for the enlightenment of their progeny.

I worked on the story and the characters for four months, then began writing my play. The process took another ten months. In those days I was using a second-hand typewriter with a bad "c" so every time I typed the word Monticello, it appeared as "Monti ello." I realized I would need a computer or a better typewriter if I intended to submit the play to any professionals. I couldn't afford a computer so I rented an IBM Selectric. Anyone working as a writer during the Jurassic period prior to computers knows that writing and then re-writing meant re-keying every page. Thus typing was the bane of my existence. With my four finger, 35 wpm speed, the script took months. Along the way I missed some payments and the typewriter rental company came to get it.

But somehow, by April 1985, I had my completed play called "The Mistress of Monticello." Now I had to test its merits. Generally I presented my plays through a theater group I was involved with in Los Angeles called "One Flight Up." But by the time I had completed "Mistress," the group had disbanded. I needed a place to workshop the material and thought about Chicago, my hometown. There are great theater groups in Chicago—large and small. Two years earlier, I had been visiting my family and while downtown a man stopped me to say he enjoyed my work on "Days." He handed me a business card and said if I was ever interested in doing any stage work to contact him. He was the artistic director of a writers workshop that was in need of actors to use in their productions of new works. I took his business card and placed it somewhere. But where?

I keep everything, so I knew I still had that card somewhere. Usually I keep business cards in index card boxes. After tearing up the house, I found a box in a trunk and, eureka, located the card. I dialed the number immediately. After four rings I got an answering machine. The voice, thankfully, announced it was Glenn de Costa and I left a message. All I had to do then was wait. Later that night Glenn called me back. I told him who I was and that I had a play I wanted to workshop through his group if he still had it. He was delighted and indicated he had just met a young black woman who wanted to direct theater. Maybe it would be a good match. Send the play…which I did.

The following Saturday, Glenn called to ask how quickly could I get to Chicago? The group was interested in the material. They were shocked by it, provoked by it, and yes, Anita-Joyce Barnes did want to direct it. This was a good sign. But workshopping the material out of town meant staying in Chicago for several weeks. I had bills. I had responsibilities, and remember, I had refused to take any more of daddy's money. When I called my parents that night to tell them the Chicago Dramatists Workshop was interested in helping me work through the play, the first thing daddy asked was if my coming would cause a financial strain. I told him yes, but I'd figure something out. I was surprised by his response. My father told me he was proud of me for setting a goal and meeting it. The fact I'd decided to write serious subject matter, research it and take care of myself while it took so many months to complete, was an accomplishment. He asked how much money would I need in order to stay the three weeks. I was honest with him and told him I felt uncomfortable taking money from him again. He asked if he could "invest" in the play. "That way, if you're successful I get a return and a dividend."

It was an offer I could not refuse.

I sent my father a copy of the play and flew to Chicago the next weekend. Daddy, too, was shocked by the material. He cautioned me when we had dinner that first night.

"Honey, this is incendiary material and this is a racially polarized town. Black folks on the south side, whites on the north side. Where are they presenting this play?"

"Downtown, at the Workshop's theatre on Clark."

"Some folks could be really upset by some things you've got in there. I mean, you've got Sally calling the President a 'coward' and a 'bastard.' Then you've got them kissing and carrying on (translated: love scenes) onstage. Don't you remember what happened to you when you kissed that white guy on "Days." You haven't worked as an actress since. What will happen to you with this?"

"Dad, theater is supposed to make people think. Stimulate them. Provoke them."

"Yeah, but you don't want people provoked enough to burn crosses on our lawn."

After reassuring Daddy that although the project was controversial, I was not in danger of losing my life, he sighed, "You're braver than me. I'd have all that offensive stuff play offstage." I had to chuckle. "Dad, that's already happened in history. The whole relationship between Sally and Tom, which people think is offensive—has played 'offstage.'" Daddy chuckled too. Sure, he shook his head, but he had to agree.

I worked through the material with the group for three weeks. We auditioned actors and were lucky to find an excellent Thomas Jefferson, and, surprisingly enough, my own cousin, Dawn, the product of an interracial relationship between my Aunt Sylvia and a Canadian man, played young Sally Hemings. As with the miniseries, we used a white actor to portray Sally and Jefferson's son Tom Hemings, and my father's own gold pocket watch given to him by his grandfather, served as the gold pocket watch Sally steals from Jefferson to give to her son Tom upon his leaving Monticello.

Response cards were given to the audience to fill out anonymously. Once again, as the lights went down on that very first production of "The Mistress of Monticello," I was backstage pacing and sweating it out. I heard every blown line, every missed joke, every ad-lib. My family was in the audience—which was racially mixed—and I knew that if the play worked here in Chicago, it would work anywhere. Two hours later, it was all over and I was called to the stage. There was that applause and I could clearly see the smiles. Glenn told the crowd there would be a conversation with the playwright and the response cards would be read aloud. I thought, "Okay, here it comes. This is where I'll be bashed in front of my friends and family." Then I thought, "Thank God I am here in Chicago and not in Los Angeles where I live."

But I was pleasantly surprised. Aside from the length—which was considered too long by all, the first thing people commented on was what a beautiful love story it was and why didn't more people know about it. The next thing they wanted to see was more of Tom Hemings. They wanted to see the scene where Tom leaves and is told by Sally to remember his roots. Many members of that audience also said the project was so large in scope perhaps it should be produced for the big screen rather than the stage so that scenes, motivations and emotions could be better fleshed out, examined and expanded. My father and mother were delighted to be a part of the early formulations and suggestions for the material, and daddy, in particular, was surprised no one commented on the interracial aspect of the piece or whether it was true or not. The audience accepted it as a given that Jefferson had the relationship, was conflicted within himself, yet remained a man of his times despite his feelings for Sally Hemings.

I took all of the notes to heart and went back to Los Angeles to start another draft of the play. I thought about how to approach it. I had all of the response cards as well as my notes from the group. But the one suggestion that kept swirling through my head was the idea of turning the project into a screenplay. A filmed version of the play would allow close-ups of Jefferson's inner struggles or Sally's abject frustrations. Many more characters could be used. Passages of time could be presented in a more realistic way. I could utilize the device of flashbacks and really dramatize the conflicts between Sally and Martha, Betty, James and Henry Jackson. It was a challenge, but I wanted to try it.

When I told Dad I was going to rewrite the play as a screenplay, he told me as long as I kept writing projects of importance, he'd be there for support no matter what shape that support took. And he was. Whenever I would call out of career frustration, Dad was there with a word of encouragement. If I was disappointed about something, he found some parable or bible quote that made me feel better, or kept me going. As I look back on it now, I am grateful my dad was there to see the play and the fact I was serious. Writing and rewriting the screenplay took two years on and off. Sadly, my wonderful father died the next June 1987 from lung cancer. Cigarettes were the culprit, and I stopped smoking cold-turkey upon his death. I couldn't help but think, Dad died from tobacco and Jefferson was a tobacco farmer. Funny what the mind puts together as irony. Still, my most ardent supporter and greatest mentor was gone leaving a void in my life which has been difficult to fill even today. It would be two years before I could sit down to finish either "Mistress…" or anything of consequence without crying. The biggest regret I have is that Daddy did not live to see any of my films or the Sally Hemings miniseries produced. He did, however, come to me in a dream a week before I screened the miniseries in Ohio for the descendants. In the dream, Daddy was wearing his favorite green wool overcoat and smiled at me while I was onstage. When I tried to run up to him, he said, "I'm so proud of you" then became diaphanous and disappeared altogether. At the screening, there would be a moment when the spirit of my father communicated the same sentiment to me. It was then I realized I was having a déjà vu experience. Still, I know in my heart my father was there in spirit and these days, whenever I present the play, I dedicate it to my late father, George Washington Andrews. A good man and a great dad.

"The Mistress of Monticello"

Written by: Tina Andrews
Directed by: Anita-Joyce Barnes

The play had its premiere stage reading at the Chicago Dramatists Workshop, June 8, 1985, in Chicago, Illinois with the following cast in order of appearance:

SALLY HEMINGS	Gwen Davis
T. JOHN GERSHOM (TOM HEMINGS)	Doug McDade
YOUNG SALLY HEMINGS	Dawn Deransbury
BETTY HEMINGS	Cecille Collins
JAMES HEMINGS	Michael E. Myers
MARTHA JEFFERSON	Jane Salutz
ABIGAIL ADAMS	Mary Mikva
JOHN ADAMS	Arthur Pearson
THOMAS JEFFERSON	Gary Brichetto

Act Two

THE STRUGGLE

"Thou art white, and I am black: but day must be wedded to night to give birth to the aurora and the sunset, which are more beautiful than either."

Victor Hugo, Bug-Jargal

Performing as an actress in the landmark miniseries "Roots" introduced me to author Alex Haley. Years later, Alex became a mentor and friend who reentered my life at a crucial career point. His own struggles to write "Roots," and sage advice regarding my Sally Hemings script, encouraged me to continue. Wonderful spirits never leave you. Alex's never has.

Chapter Four

ALEX HALEY, DNA, CBS AND OTHER ACTS OF GOD

By 1990 I had married my husband Stephen, and met the person who became so integral to the production of the miniséries…Wendy Kram. Wendy was head of development at Donald Wyre's company at Hearst Entertainment. Donald was a director I had worked with as an actress and Wendy was always looking for good material for him. I was then partnered with a producer named Ira Trattner whom I had met four years earlier at Warner Brothers when he was in business affairs. Ira left Warners to become a film producer and we had another of my scripts, "Frankie: The Frankie Lymon Story" under an option with a production company. I'd sent Ira "The Mistress of Monticello" two weeks earlier and he phoned Wendy to pitch her the idea. After reading the script she set the appointment with Donald for the following Wednesday. Donald Wyre was the perfect director for the project. He handled controversial material and projects starring women very well. He was also sensitive to the needs of actors and writers and had a wonderful reputation. I had loved working with him and I prayed he would take both the project, and me, earnestly.

On occasion, I had experienced a reluctance from directors or producers I'd worked with previously as an actress to consider my screenplays seriously. The presumption being I was writing "vanity" projects designed for me to star in. Ergo, I always had an easier time with individuals who were unfamiliar with my work as an actress. I hoped Donald would view the project with an objective eye and forget I had played a psychotic runaway teenager who participated in the rape of Linda Blair in the controversial TV movie "Born Innocent" which he had directed ten years earlier.

Thank God Donald was an astute man. When we talked about the Sally Hemings material, he just got it. He understood the importance of the project and how incendiary it could become if mishandled. His approach to me was as a professional writer and he commented on the research and the quality of the material. Wendy, too, was a great development executive and ultimately we became professional friends. She had suggestions for improving the script and knew how to communicate her notes to me as an artist. I felt comfortable with them both, and when Ira and I left the meeting, we had a deal at Hearst Entertainment.

Our option was structured for 18 months. I would write, Ira and I would Co-Executive produce, Donald would direct and Executive Produce. During that time Donald and Wendy tried valiantly to set the project up at a network or studio. Inevitably, word would come back that the material, though well written, was too controversial. Without substantive "proof" that Jefferson had a liaison with Sally Hemings, without a letter, scientific data or other incontrovertible evidence, it would be a hard sell. Eighteen months later, Donald and Wendy called to apologize. They could not get it produced. The rights reverted back to me.

This would be the same explanation everywhere I went. Three other companies had read the script, optioned it, tried to set it up and couldn't. I, however, began to attract attention around Hollywood as a screenwriter because of the material and eventually the script ended up on the desk of David Goldman and Bobbi Thompson who, in those days, were agents at the William Morris agency. They asked me for other writing samples. I gave them my Frankie Lymon screenplay and quickly went to work on additional material to show a diversity of literary ability. By Christmas 1990, I was signed by the William Morris agency as a client. I am still with the agency today.

But even with a powerful packaging agency such as Morris at my disposal, setting up "The Mistress of Monticello" still proved difficult. After another two years of fruitless meetings and botched attempts to attach all manner of talent from Lisa Bonet to Diana Ross, to Rae Dawn Chong to Robin Givens, I felt the script would never happen. I spent money I didn't have sending out letters on impressive paper, formed a production company, hired typing services to redraft scripts, and xeroxed script copies to send to everyone to no avail. Eventually, once again, I found myself in financial dire straits. At least I had a husband and a shared life. But our production company, set up with the expressed desire to produce, direct and/or write our own product, was not generating enough income because most of my scripts were always under "free" options, and my husband was shooting mostly three-minute music videos in those days. We really needed two substantial incomes so I had to make another painful decision. Daddy had been dead two years and Mother was not one to send money, especially now that I was married. Stephen and I had continuing responsibilities. So I took another "real" job at Drake Employment as a receptionist.

I had been working at Drake nine months when one day something extraordinary happened. For months I had been fighting depression over the direction my life had taken. I could not understand why everything was so difficult and kept falling apart. I wondered why I had failed to move forward in some substantive way as a writer—and by now my work as an actress had all but disappeared. I had talent, I had a resume, a modicum of personality and I was with a big agency. What was the problem? Why was I worse off than I was when I first arrived in Hollywood? Why were so many answers coming back in the negative. It was as if "no" had become my middle name.

The more I answered phones, the more I hated being there. I remember thinking that being a receptionist was great for some, but could not be what God put me on the planet to do. A trained monkey could recite, "Good morning, Drake Employment." And each day brought some applicant into the office who would recognize me from my soap opera days, *"Hey, ain't you the sista usta play on my stories?"* The embarrassment this brought, and my having to meekly smile and nod while they questioned *"What happened?"* only broadened my deepening emotional depression.

The Drake office was located on Wilshire Boulevard across an alley from The Westwood Memorial Cemetery. This cemetery is where many celebrities are buried— Armand Hammer, Natalie Wood, Marilyn Monroe, Eddie Cantor, Xavier Cugat, Heather O'Rourke and countless others. Every day at lunch I would sit in this cemetery on a bench under a tree and write in longhand. I would make notations in my journal, or rewrite my screenplays or scribble drawings. The locale was not morbid because this particular cemetery did not feature headstones but bronzed plaques on the ground and mausoleums where the crypts are kept. There were trees all around, flower gardens and thoughtfully manicured grass. It resembled a small park and provided a pleasant place of meditation. Let's face it, it was a cemetery—so it was quiet.

One day as I was seated in front of Natalie Wood putting my frustrations down in my journal, I began to weep. "I believe in God," I wrote, "I trust God. I cannot believe God would not want me to be my highest and greatest self." I remember asking aloud, "God, what did I do? Why would you give me so many abilities, and not allow me to exhibit any of them through you? Why would you light my candle, then put a bushel basket over it?"

Then I looked at my watch and realized I should be getting back upstairs to my job. The job God metaphysically arranged for me to currently express myself through. When I reached the office I still had three minutes left. I decided to call home and check my service for messages. That is, if my phone was even still on. But the phone rang. "Great", I thought, "It hasn't been disconnected...yet." Three messages rolled by. Typical stuff. A friend stopping by later to get money I owed them; dry cleaning overdue, come pick up; my JC Penney card past due, please pay; then, lo and behold, a somewhat familiar voice saying: "I hope this is the right number for Tina Andrews, and I hope this is the same Tina Andrews who was in 'Roots.' If it is— this is Alex Haley. Please call me at..." and a number was left. I held my chest. Alex Haley? No. This is a joke. A sick cruel joke some jerk is playing on me.

But curiosity obliterated reason and I dialed the long distance number—on Drake's dime. A female voice came over the line. I asked to speak to Alex Haley, and the voice asked "Who shall I say is calling?" When I told her, she followed up with "Hold on." Now I'm sweating. "Uh oh, this may not be a joke after all," I think, and my beating heart was all I could hear as ten agonizing seconds passed. Finally, the familiar voice came on the line, "Tina? It's Alex. How are you?"

I nearly died. I hadn't seen Alex since I'd taken part as an actress in the most respected, most revered miniseries of all time. Now suddenly I, who can be very verbal, was struck dumb. Words failed me, my voice fell mute forcing Alex to echo, "Are you there?" When I picked myself off the floor and found my vocal cords all I could repeat like a moron stuck on a loop was "Oh my God! Oh-my-God!" Eventually I calmed down enough for us to have a passably intelligent conversation—as the bulk of my end consisted of "uh huh's" He then told me he'd been forwarded "The Mistress of Monticello" script by the William Morris office and had requested other writing samples. He complimented me on the Hemings project and my piece on Frankie Lymon. He felt I had a good grasp on scripting biographies and wondered if I could fly down to his farm in Tennessee to meet with him, perhaps stay a few days and brainstorm a project he wanted to do for PBS called, "Alex Haley Presents: Great Men of African Descent." Again, I nearly fainted. *Brainstorm? With Alex Haley? Me?*

Suddenly, I became nervous. I'd be spending a few days with a literary genius. A true wordsmith whose novel, once dramatized, sat down every man, woman and child in this country for eight nights straight and forced them to examine America and the ills of slavery and racism through the resilience of his indomitable family. It had changed the face of television garnering 14 Emmy nominations. And here he was doing another television series on the lives of great Black men and women whose stories needed to be told. And he wanted *me* to brainstorm with *him*? Where was my father so I could tell him? Oh, yes—dead. Now I'm livid. *"Daddy, of all times for you to be dead. Why now?"*

"Sounds cool," I answered impulsively, then kicked myself. "You idiot! 'Sounds, cool?' You don't say 'sounds cool' to Pulitzer prize winning, nine Emmy awards winning, 32 million books selling, literary icon Alex Haley. But you know what his response was? "Sounds cool to me, too."

I loved it. I then called my mother and begged her to send me enough money so I could buy a laptop. I could not let Alex know I wasn't professional enough to have a computer. Surprisingly, mom sent the money and that Saturday I went to Radio Shack and bought my first computer for a grand total of $500. The following Wednesday, I was on a plane bound for Knoxville, Tennessee. Alex and his assistant met me at the airport. It was great to see him and we hugged and caught up on all the actors who were in "Roots" while he showed me the countryside. When we reached his 127 acre farm in Norris, 20 miles north of the airport, he showed me to one of eight houses on the compound which would be mine for my five day stay. It was called the "Duck House" as everything in it was decorated with all things duck. There were photos of ducks, duck pillows, duck whatnots, quilts of ducks, chairs carved like ducks, and right outside the back window—a pond with, you guessed it—live ducks. I settled in still somewhat disbelieving I was there.

That night over fresh trout and potatoes Alex and I discussed the project, how we'd approach it, who we'd chronicle first. During this discussion I saw an unusual art object on a wall. A nickel, a dime and three pennies were backed against black velvet and ensconced in a glass or Plexiglas container. When I asked Alex about this. He smiled and declared it was all he had to his name the day he was told "Roots" was being published. 18 cents! He had written the story and others using an old typewriter which sat on top of a desk made of a door sitting on top of two metal file cabinets. I had a similar desk. Alex further explained he'd only had wilting lettuce, two catsup packets from McDonald's and a half empty jar of Miracle Whip in his refrigerator. His plan was to have a salad with french dressing made from the catsup packets and mayonnaise leftovers for dinner that very night. As he watched me staring at the coins whose symbolism did not escape me, it was as though he had looked into my soul and seen my condition. He said God doesn't give you more than you can bear, and that you had to keep believing in yourself, for a dream is never placed into your head that you cannot achieve. It's only when you back those dreams with action that they become goals, and goals are attainable—no matter how long it takes.

Alex Haley did not know I only had $165 in the bank. He did not know my Visa card was cut in half in front of my face at Sears. He did not know that the day he called me I quit my job at Drake for the uncertainty of where this working relationship would lead. But when his hand touched my shoulder and he said, "Let's go to work," suddenly, I didn't feel bad about my life. I had far more than 18 cents. I had a mentor. A great Sage.

We did go to work. Turns out Alex hated computers and used his time honored old typewriter. We sat side by side—me with my Radio Shack laptop, Alex clicking away on his upright Royal. Gertie, his housekeeper, prepared meals. On breaks we'd walk his acreage at Haley Farm. He even found an ancient Indian arrow head which he gave me for luck. Alex encouraged me to keep exploring the controversial and not to be afraid of criticism. He encouraged me to be an "artist" which meant being true to ones art. He insisted I not let my enthusiasm for my Sally Hemings project die just because I couldn't get it produced. "Keep working on it. Keep improving it. Write from the heart and don't fear the controversy. A wider audience needs to know this story." He also said the key to success in Hollywood was learning to "get along" with the power structure while at the same time getting your point across—because there would always be differences of opinion. How you handle those differences is what counts. He was inspirational.

By the end of the week, we were well on our way with the pilot for the PBS project which would be on Alexander Dumas. I flew back to Los Angeles with the Indian arrow head in my pocket, and Alex's spirit in my heart. I wrote vigilantly as though Alex was just over my shoulder. I was in touch with Alex once a week for the next month. He was interested in me potentially developing his project on Madame C.J. Walker. He had so many speaking engagements we would not be able to discuss the project for a month. But he promised to have a few people at his farm around the time of my birthday in April and he planned to invite two of his friends who happened to be my heroes—Maya Angelou and Oprah Winfrey. But it was not to be. Nor was the PBS project.

Two weeks later, on February 10, 1992 I arose to the news Alex Haley was dead. 70 years old with so much left to give the world. I was devastated and could not help but think about my father—another wonderful, encouraging man who had so enriched my life.

I've thought about Alex a lot lately. About his legacy and effect on my life particularly as it related to the Sally Hemings miniseries. As a result of working with him on the PBS project, even though it was not produced, I was given story points toward admittance to the Writers Guild of America. Having worked with a writer of Alex's stature gave me a certain cache in Hollywood, which resulted in my first screenplay assignment at Colombia Pictures which led to a working career.

Two months after Alex Haley's death, Los Angeles broke out into a riot the likes of which are still unparalleled. The city was on fire, National Guard was called out and the streets were a madhouse of looting, injury, and fear. All of this was in the aftermath of the jury verdict acquitting white police officers after their brutal beating of Rodney G. King, a black citizen—the action of which was caught on tape for all the world to see. In the wake of the unrest, Mr. King came on camera before the citizenry and with simple eloquence inquired: *"Can't we all just get along?"*

Getting along. Words used by Alex Haley. Words used by Rodney King. Words I've chosen to live by. Recently, in looking back at that day in 1991 when I was sitting in the Westwood cemetery broke and depressed asking God why had he lit my candle yet put a bushel basket over it, the answer came to me...

...Because your faith and belief in self has to be strong enough to burn through it.

During the next seven years, Wendy Kram left Hearst Entertainment but she stayed in touch with me. She would call from time to time to ask about the availability of "Mistress..." whenever she was at a new production company. I would tell her if it was under an option or not. Occasionally we would meet for lunch just to catch up. So much had happened in the intervening years. I had become a produced screenwriter. I had written several scripts for the studios on assignment, sold two spec scripts, and rewrote or contributed to many movies for which I was uncredited—among them, "Sister Act II" and "Soul Food." Stephen and I had moved into a nice house and felt we were in the right emotional, financial and living space to start planning for a child of our own.

But there had been horrible tragedies too. My 18 year old stepdaughter Lucy, my husband's pride and joy, had been murdered in south Los Angeles by gang members. My husband and I had to identify her body in a dumpster, where she had been discarded like trash. It was months before he or I could breathe without crying. Later that year, my favorite uncle and his family were burned to death in Chicago when their house caught fire while they slept. Again, gang violence. We had to sit through a funeral with four caskets bearing all but one of my cousins' bodies. It was unbearable. Three months after that, a routine checkup revealed I needed surgery and would be unable to have children. But I had to keep going. God doesn't give you more than you can bear.

During my four month recuperation, "Jefferson In Paris" was released which incorporated the Thomas Jefferson and Sally Hemings relationship. Though it was written by Ruth Prawer Jhabvala, a screenwriter whose work I greatly admired, it was poorly received and it made me worry about the prospects of my own script on Sally. Wendy Kram relayed her feelings:

"With all due respect to Merchant/Ivory who have made some of my all-time favorite films, "Jefferson In Paris" was not one of them. And very few people saw it. I realized that's the beauty of television. You can do things on the small screen and reach a whole broader audience. A well-received movie for television that gets a 25 share reaches 25 million people. In box-office terms, that's 25 million times $8.50 a ticket which would translate to roughly $200 million at the box office. Very few movies do that. With respect to intimate character dramas, you can have a stellar cast such as "The Accused" with Jodie Foster and very few people go to see it. But put a movie like that on TV, and you can reach a whole new and broader audience. So, I knew we could do that with "The Mistress of Monticello"... So every year from that point on, I would call Tina and ask her... "What are you doing with your script? Is it still available?" And she would answer "yes". This went on for the next seven years."

By the time Wendy called me in early 1998, I was at the tail end of filming, "Why Do Fools Fall In Love" which in another incarnation had been my "Frankie Lymon Story." I was working with a brilliant director named Gregory Nava whom I just adored. Gregory had directed "El Norte," "Mi Familia" and "Selena," and was mentoring me as a director. So I had other plans for my time. But Wendy said she was now a development executive at Craig Anderson Productions, and that Craig had produced some high quality television projects. She wanted to show Craig my old script. I told Wendy that although "The Mistress of Monticello" was available, I had another script I owed Warner Brothers and one due New Regency after "Fools..." so I would not be available for awhile. When Craig finally read "Mistress...", I was promoting "Fools..." and finishing "Dreamgirls" and it was another two months before I could meet with him, but I gave Craig and Wendy permission to send it to CBS.

I was excited about the prospect of CBS because they practically own Sunday night with their line-up of "60 Minutes," "Touched By An Angel," and the CBS movie or miniseries events. They also had a good track record for hiring minorities, which is of great concern to me. As a woman of color I know how difficult it is to get work in Hollywood unless you're very established, very well connected—or very, very famous. But I was also cautious. This would be my first foray into television—an area I was determined to stay out of if at all possible. All of my television writing colleagues always lamented about how much work is involved in writing television long form. There are at least three steps incorporated into your contract—a story outline and two drafts, and the money cannot compare to feature film money. In fact it's generally one-third the average screenplay salary. Also, my concern is to always guard the interpretation of my work and insist on maintaining its integrity. Craig Anderson Productions had produced a number of projects including "The Piano Lesson," August Wilson's memorable play, as a television movie and the company had won a Peabody Award. It sounded like a perfect match. Craig set the meeting for the following Thursday.

Though I was feeling confident the network would be interested in moving forward, that nagging feeling arose every now and then which said, "Yes, but what about the "proof," the "documentation" every other company had wanted all through the years?

Luck and timing prevailed. The Saturday before our Thursday meeting, October 31, 1998, my husband and I were having friends over to play bid-whist when an announcement came on the news. "DNA tests prove Thomas Jefferson fathers child with slave. Film at eleven." We were all stunned. DNA? That's science. That's genetics. Good lord, that's proof! None of us could believe it. At eleven, I had the VCR taping the news broadcast. The report went on to say that Dr. Eugene Foster, a retired pathologist from the University of Virginia, had found a genetic link which connected Thomas Jefferson to Sally Hemings through her youngest son, Eston, in tests conducted in England. By Sunday morning it was on every TV broadcast and front page on newspapers all over the country. I clipped out every article I could find from various papers at international newsstands. I pulled down articles on the DNA discovery from the internet and printed them. I called Craig at home. "Do you believe this?" We then set about xeroxing everything we could find until we had a clipping package to present to Joan Yee, our executive at CBS, in advance of our meeting.

The next week was like an out-of-body experience. By Tuesday afternoon, six production companies called me or my agents asking whatever happened to my script on Sally Hemings and if it was available. Other companies were scrambling to throw together Sally Hemings proposals for the networks. I felt like I was developing a tumor in my ear just fielding calls on the subject matter. And yet, once again, that bitter irony tugged at me. The DNA test proved what black America knew all along. Scientific evidence was all that was necessary for the majority culture to believe the story and for Hollywood to act. Not the words or the oral histories of countless African Americans who have known the story was true for two centuries because they're products of it, lived it, or were an actual part of it.

The science magazine *"Nature"* printed an exhaustive profile on the DNA findings as well as *"U.S. News & World Report."* Historians and Jefferson loyalists, heretofore condemning the relationship as so much conjecture and hyperbole, were scrambling into reverse. Late night jokes were endless and talk show commentaries abounded. But none were as impressive or as thought provoking as "The Oprah Winfrey Show" which aired (and I taped) the day before our CBS meeting.

I sat riveted as Oprah introduced America to a dozen or so Jefferson/Hemings descendants for the first time. It was then I first saw the people who would later become so integral to me and the telling of Sally's story. People who would become lifelong friends. People whose plight for recognition I would later join as a comrade. People like Lucian Truscott IV, William Douglas Banks, Julia, Dorothy and Arthur Westerinen, Michele Cooley-Quille, Billy Dalton, Robert Golden, and Shay Banks-Young, who would prove forever memorable with her snappy retort, "I don't need to be buried on the plantation. I've got my own plot next to my mother's plot right here in Ohio!" Even Robin Williams would mimic Shay on the "David Letterman Show" later. So many actual faces. Living pieces of the puzzle America needed to see to help construct an image of Thomas Jefferson and his relationship with Sally Hemings in the public's mind. We sent the tape and the clippings to Joan, along with a short synopsis of the story and the additional information we would want added as a result of new research.

Then I met Joan Yee the next day with Craig and Wendy. I would write about it in my journal later. I am always struck by how off base I am when I try to visualize the executive I'll be meeting. Even though I do my homework to find out as much as I can about them, they are never quite the personification I have in my head when I actually meet them. In the past whenever I was slated to meet a female executive, I tended to expect some version of Dawn Steel—a producer I had worked with at Disney on "The Power Of No!" Dawn, who'd left an indelible mark on me, was a tough, albeit attractive (great hair), Armani suit-clad, salty-mouthed, hang-with-the-jocks type, former studio president who had fought hard to get to the top spot. She took no prisoners, pulled no punches and had writers (and others) for lunch. I should know. I still have bite marks to prove it (smile), and the project we worked on was my first foray into "Development Hell." But Dawn was coming along at a time when women had to competitively slug it out like a guy in order to gain respect, acceptance and admittance into that most coveted and exclusive "Boy's Club" called "Real Hollywood Power."

The first thing I noticed about Joan was that in addition to having a commanding presence, she was petite and soft spoken. She understood what we all needed out of the production and how we were going to service controversial, incendiary material and present it to the country on a Sunday night at 9. Joan knew what she wanted, how to communicate it, and ultimately how to inspire. I found her to be an intelligent, no-nonsense executive who was sensitive to the material, and I prayed for this deal to work out because I wanted to work with her. Joan's biggest concern (and note) was that we not make the project a stuffy history lesson. I agreed. After all, the company is called CBS ENTERTAINMENT, not CBS UNIVERSITY—even though most people, sadly, get their history from television.

The meeting went well, but I had one concern once I got home. Neither Joan, Sunta Izzicupo, the vice-president of movies, or Les Moonves, president of CBS television, really knew me. I had not written for television before so I was not an "approved" writer which is a writer who had written for them before, a writer they liked, a writer they trusted who delivered the ratings. But if in one sense my being a proven screenwriter was a plus, (television loves screenwriters), my being an African American female writer was definitely an advantage. In fact, politically, the timing could not have been better. The 1998-1999 television season was one of the most dismal for minorities in TV history. According to Sharon Johnson, Chair of the WGAW Committee of Black Screenwriters, of the 8312 active members of the Writers Guild of America, West, only 234 are African American. In 1997, the Hollywood Writers Report confirmed that minorities accounted for less than 7% of the writers employed in television. In 1999, of the 839 writers working in television, only 6.6% were African American with 77% of those writers working primarily on UPN and the WB networks.

These appalling statistics prompted organizations like the NAACP to threaten boycotts and bang the publicity drum loudly if the networks did not agree to more diversity both in front of and behind the camera. One could not pick up a newspaper and not read an item about the lack of minority representation on network television. All three networks and their division heads began working on solutions for the problem—and here, handed to CBS, was a "hot topic" currently in the public's imagination about an African American woman who had been expunged from history by virtue of her relationship with the Founding Father who penned the Declaration of Independence. It was written from that African American woman's point-of-view BY an African American woman who would also be producing it and whose script was already available. It was win-win for everyone. Wendy also describes it:

"Our timing couldn't have been better. This wasn't just a ripped-from-the-headlines story, this was now a story that had contemporary resonance. My personal theory is that in a "Wag The Dog" kind of real-life scenario, Clinton's spin doctors wanted to expedite the results from this long-term debate about Jefferson's affair with Hemings. They wanted to get out to the public the fact that another great president, no less than one of the founding fathers of our country and author of the Declaration of Independence, also had a "dalliance". But a lot of people didn't realize that Jefferson, unlike Clinton, was not an adulterer. Jefferson was a widower who had loved his wife very much, and Sally was his deceased wife's half-sister. Sally probably looked a lot like his wife, and it was not uncommon during those times for a spouse to marry the brother or sister of a loved one who had passed away. In any event, there were so many parallels with what was going on with Clinton, including a Kenneth Starr character back then, James Thompson Callender, who outed Jefferson in the press and caused a huge scandal which nearly cost Jefferson his re-election. With the DNA announcement and all that was going on with the current administration, we had an even greater story than we ever imagined, and we were right there in Joan Yee's office—the right place at the right time."

CBS called Craig…and Craig called me. He was real cute about it saying in a somber voice, "Tina, I'm so sorry…" My heart sank as he continued, "…But all I could get you was a FOUR HOUR MINISERIES for sweeps!!" I screamed. I screamed until I was blue, until I was hoarse, until Alex Haley's voice popped into my head saying, *"Sounds cool to me, too."* What was once a dream had now moved into reality.

The Hemings family quilt begun by the character of "Betty Hemings," played by Diahann Carroll, just after daughter Sally's arrival back from Paris, 1789. From left to right at top: The African matriarch, Captain John Hemings, Betty Hemings, James Hemings, Martha Wayles Jefferson, John Wayles, Sally Hemings, Harriet Hemings, Robert Hemings, Thomas Jefferson Hemings, Madison and Eston Hemings, and Beverly Jefferson Hemings.

Chapter Five

THE DEVELOPMENT PROCESS

CAST OF CHARACTERS

CRAIG ANDERSON	Executive Producer
TINA ANDREWS	Co-Executive Producer/Screenwriter
WENDY KRAM	Co-Executive Producer
JOAN YEE	V.P. Sponsor Programming/Movies/CBS Entertainment
SUNTA IZZICUPO	Senior V.P., Movies and Miniseries/CBS Entertainment
LESLIE MOONVES	President/CEO, CBS Television
REUBEN CANNON	Casting Director

There was a lot of work ahead of us. Craig negotiated for the rights to Fawn Brodie's book, "Thomas Jefferson:An Intimate History," so the production would own the underlying material. Meanwhile, I pulled my old script apart to rewrite it as a four hour. It had to be divided into 14 acts—each needing to progress the story yet concluding in such a way as to allow for commercials and prompt the audience to stay tuned. I had at least an hour's worth of discarded material on my computer which I'd edited out to make the current screenplay only two hours, so I was partially ahead of the game. Still, CBS wanted an "annotated bible" before I could go directly to the first draft of the script. That meant I had to write a story, footnote all my sources and outline each of the 14 acts with all motivations, exposition, action sequences and characterizations. No easy feat. These outlines typically run 50-60 pages. On top of that CBS wanted the project for sweeps November, 1999 at the time, and I was booked with two other commitments which would take me until at least mid January, 1999. That meant a story bible and four drafts including the director's draft in a span of four months if we were to meet our June starting date. Almost impossible. So I hired an assistant to help me research and document the "Sally" bible while I worked on my Warner Brothers and New Regency scripts. But the process took longer than I expected and I did not start on the Sally Hemings outline until the end of January.

I am a perfectionist. Being in a rush to complete the project and meet our schedule, I nearly died during the writing of the story outline. I did not properly look after my health. I spent an average of three nights a week pulling all-nighters like I was still at NYU. I did not go on my usual daily walks in the mountains or on the beach. I did not take my hour breaks to meditate. I gained weight. My world consisted of messengers, faxes and my dear husband carrying me to bed when I'd fallen asleep in front of the computer at three in the morning. Worst yet, I did not eat properly. I downed vitamins after consuming fast food, Thai take-out or Chinese delivery. I drank black coffee like a drug addict. By late January I'd caught the flu during rainy season and just couldn't shake it. I became weak but didn't dare tell anyone. I would stand up and faint, but I continued to work. Three weeks later I was getting weaker and more fatigued, yet I told everyone at the production office I had a bad cold. My girlfriend, Saundra Middleton, knew better. She told me she thought something more serious was wrong with me and gave me the name of her doctor. But I wanted to get the work turned in on time. I had to prove myself to all I was involved with. A schedule was on the line. I would not give them any excuses. To hell with my cold. I turned in the annotated story bible on a Friday. That Sunday afternoon I was taken to the hospital where Saundra's doctor diagnosed me with pneumonia, a 101 degree fever and a cholesterol level at 290. He told me complete bed rest or I'd have to be admitted. My husband put me to bed. I cried uncontrollably because I was scared to death. So close to realizing a dream. Was I going to blow it before it came to fruition? No. I stayed in bed exactly three days before finding an intern from Loyola Marymount who took dictation. I'd talk into a tape recorder and she'd type. This worked out for the first three weeks of the script writing process...and all unbeknownst to the network, the production company or any of my friends, except Saundra.

By April 12, 1999 I had a first draft of a script tentatively titled, "Monticello: The Memoirs of Sally Hemings". On April 23, we had a marathon network meeting on that draft. I was feeling pretty good about the work, and was excited that by Monday morning following the Friday the script was delivered, all involved were responding positively. The meeting was set for Friday at three o'clock. I did not want to delay things by informing everyone it was my birthday and I had plans, so I said nothing and rescheduled my plans for later that night. That is the day I met Sunta Izzicupo for the first time. She was coming out of her office headed for the elevator when Craig introduced us. Her face lit up and she did something every writer cherishes—she quoted my lines. Then she went on to say that she had read the draft on a plane to Morocco where CBS was shooting the "Jesus" miniseries and could not put it down. She called it a page turner. She was so complimentary and expressed genuine enthusiasm that the network was doing the project and to keep up the good work.

Her response underscored why I came to enjoy those early development meetings. We were all committed to the excellence of the project. We all knew what was at stake, and we all respected each other. Very important word—respect. Without it, you're a writer traversing the ocean with no rudder, no support, going nowhere. We'd sit in Joan's office and talk through what worked, what didn't, what could be better articulated and what should be cut. When it came to these things, I left my ego at home...or at least in the CBS lobby. I figured no one consciously sets out to make a bad movie so generally after I've written a draft, I've had my say on paper, so I shut up and listen to the notes and criticism—and try not to take it personally. I always let my colleagues know that I am not insecure or married to anything that doesn't work. If what they really want to say is, "Tina, this section stinks, you blew it here," I encourage them to say it. My feelings cannot be hurt.

By the same token, I do not cave at a suggestion I feel doesn't work. If we can build a better mousetrap, fine. If we can't, let's not reinvent the wheel. By creating an open, honest atmosphere, the working environment is so much healthier and happier. I write better and real feelings are communicated. Not to mention the second draft is generally green-lit.

Writing screenplays is a collaborative process. A lot of talents and personalities, some volatile, most creative, are involved. Jon Voight once used a metaphor that I paraphrase a great deal. We were shooting "Conrack" and I was afraid to ask him to rehearse a scene with me because it was my first film and he was the big star. He said, "Nonsense. Making movies is like making an apple pie. I may be the apples, but without all of the ingredients in their proper proportion, the right cook and the proper baking temperature, you can't ensure the sale of the whole." He was right. When it's a good pie, all slices will sell. The same applies here. When all the pie's ingredients are in proper proportion—the writer, director, producers, script, actors and crew, everyone benefits from all the sold slices. Executives get promotions, networks get big ratings thus better rates for advertising, directors get hired again at inflated prices (same for screenwriters and producers) and audiences come back for more. It's the name of the game.

So with respect to my particular ingredient—screenwriting—I always require network and/or production notes in writing. That way I can go down the list and check off all those we discussed and agreed to while I work on the subsequent draft. Wendy and I always took copious notes during these sessions, but Wendy transcribed hers for Craig, so I asked for her notes to compare them with mine since I have a tendency to scribble in undecipherable handwriting in the margins of my script.

Following are excerpts from the notes I received on the first draft. They represent a working methodology by which I built on the next draft.

Notes on "Monticello: The Memoirs of Sally Hemings" First Draft per meeting, April 23, 1999, CBS - (faxed to Tina Andrews, Monday, April 26, 1999)

[JY – Joan Yee; CA – Craig Anderson; WK - Wendy Kram; TA – Tina Andrews]

JY: The first hour is the most exciting. Chocked full of emotional strands…falling in love, etc. and she goes through the most transformation…it's the most vibrant and exciting part. As we go on, the rest of the movie doesn't have the same evolution and Sally plateaus. We need to continue to give her multi-faceted concerns. The last hour feels like she only has one–Monticello is going to fall and slaves will be sold. We need to find something we're building toward in the second night vs. just being about losing everything. Also, her evolution from young girl to woman and then woman to mother and then mother to Matriarch of Monticello is not as pronounced as they need to be. Example: When Tom leaves, there isn't the sense that Sally wants to find him and that this is an on-going pre-occupation with her. We need to feel more of her longing for her son. This way, the bookends will also become more resonant. Maybe Sally gets a letter, thinking it's from Jefferson and then is shocked and elated when it's from Tom.

When it's time for Sally to be a mother, she needs to take what she's learned from Betty and relay it in a more complicated manner. For example, her reaction to Harriet is an opportunity to bring more to the table. It's not just what Betty told Sally, but it's combined with her own experiences. Also, I'd like to elaborate what it's like from Betty being mulatto to Sally being quadroon to Harriet being virtually white. From Sally to Harriet, going from 1/4 black to 1/8 black – she would have a unique perspective. Sally's ability to provide council as a mother…it feels like she should have greater insight to bear. Betty wanted Sally to have freedom but she didn't want Sally to deny her blackness and try to be white.

Harriet, however, wants to be white and deny her blackness. This is a slap in the face to Sally. If Harriet denies her heritage, then she threatens to wipe out the Hemings lineage. This is something we can elaborate upon in the second night and final hour. The divide is the notion that two of Sally's children went out into the world to "pass" and deny their blackness. The other two went out and fought for abolition, etc. She had to make sure that at least two of her children would be proud of who they are.

CA: Possible arc for Sally – perhaps she might start out, trying not to be black or a slave and comes to the idea that black is beautiful.

WK: This could be good, but we probably shouldn't see this as a characteristic trait from the get-go or it might make her less empathetic. It should also be subtle…and it might be something that might leak in more once she returns to Monticello from Paris and after she has been indoctrinated into a white way of life.

TA: This way also, Henry's reprimand of her is a stronger force of awakening her…of course there's a thin line here, because we can't make her look as though she's completely oblivious to the needs of her people, etc.

JY: Also, James represents the external conflict – he goes North and is still not respected. With Harriet, she suffers from an internal conflict…not accepting who she is internally.

TA: If Harriet were to spurn a slave, Sally might sit Harriet down and say, "There's no difference between you and him…"

JY: Maybe Harriet has an attitude about black slaves. Sally would call her on that as well. Then Harriet would throw back at her mother, "Look at who you wound up with."

WK: That's good…Sally could say, "I didn't raise you to read so you could turn your nose against black people." And then Harriet could say, "But look who you wound up with."

TA: "And I'm the daughter of the President of the United States…I want that royal side. I want that acknowledgement. Why can't I have it. I look white."

JY: Yes. Because of these kinds of specifics, there's the notion of Sally being a mom that's just not generic or universal mom stuff but stuff that's really unique to who she is as a mother of the daughter of the President of the United States and the fact that their daughter is a slave, and that Sally & Jefferson's quasi marriage cannot be publicly validated, etc.

WK: (to Tina) You have such a great line in "born of royalty and slavery" but we need to build more around this to make the idea really impactful.

TA/JY: Harriet has a really good point about being the daughter of the President of the United States. Sally can't discount that. But what can she do about it?

TA: Let's not also forget that Harriet is Martha's sister. A perfect opportunity to convey this is when Martha hands Harriet the tray and Harriet puts it down and says, "Yes, sister."

CA: There should be some kind of warning that if the kids were to go out and say they were TJ's kids, they'd be stoned...the bastard children of the president...We need to heighten the idea of the fear of what's out there...lynching and other dangers.

WK: That ties in with the idea, "We're all safe in Monticello." As a mother, we should heighten the sense of her sacrifice when she makes plans for Harriet and Beverly to go...she had already lost Tom. And even though she wants her children to go out in the world and get their freedom, she will miss them terribly and when they're away, she can't control what others may do to them. At Monticello, at least she feels she does have some control of their physical safety, etc. It's a nest, and she has to push them out.

TA: It's like when Betty pushed Sally to go to Paris. She didn't really want her to go but she wanted her to have a better life.

WK: There's also a different danger for Sally here. The danger for Sally's generation was you might get killed for the color of your skin. The next generation is, "I'll lose you forever...if you go to "pass" in white society, you're going to disappear. This means her family lines will die out...that means the memory of Betty and Sally's grandmother and great grandmother, etc. This is what needs to motivate her with Madison and Eston...it's a step beyond what she's done for Harriet and Beverly. With Madison and Eston, it's the idea that black is beautiful...and don't be ashamed of who you are...your lineage is rich.

TA: Let's see Sally giving Madison and Eston the oral history of Betty and her mother, etc...in essence it should be the "this is who we are" scenario.

JY: Have this dovetail with Sally's relationship with Jefferson because there's a plateau...In hours three and four – let's look at the phases of a marriage. Phase 1 is the courtship. Phase 2 is having children. Phase 3 is the last piece with Jefferson. What roles do the mother and father play in phase 2 & 3? We need to examine how Sally goes through all of this as a mother. What is the legacy for Jefferson and for Sally? What role does Sally play in his last phase? Again, the first phase is the affair. In phase 2, she functions as wife and mother. In phase 3, is she a nurse? She heals him, she helps him preserve his legacy. In the nature of their interactions, what does it feel like? Very comfortable, friendship above all else, still a measure of sparring, much deeper and warmer relationship?

WK: Sally would want to keep him well because the thought of losing him...of life without him...would be emotionally terrifying to her. He's been a teacher, her lover, etc. for over 20 years now. They've had five children, more children who died, Polly's death, Betty's death, the scandal, big brawls, jealousies, etc. He's also been her provider...How will she manage without him? As he's getting weaker, there might be a very touching scene...where he sees the fear in her eyes and he says to her, "I know you're afraid if I die...but don't underestimate yourself Sally, you'll be okay...don't forget, you're the girl who showed up in Washington, you're the girl who taught slaves to read, etc." It would be very touching and beautiful to see him make a list of retrospective of their relationship.

TA: There should be echoes of Paris with the tables turned. We should continue rituals like the discovery and naming of flowers, reading to each other etc.

JY: It would be really nice to show this third phase where they can finally have some peace. There has always been tension in the relationship...conflicts because of politics and kids teetering on the brink. Now, it's different.

WK: They might be less furtive around the house. There are more acceptances from the other household members as well during this phase...

TA: ...Is there? I would think they would remain conscious of their surroundings all the time. All their relationship.

WK: They might take more licenses with each other in holding hands, etc. Some references for this kind of mellowing phase in their relationship—the movie GIANT with Rock Hudson and Liz Taylor. That marriage spanned about 40 years also. Also the opening of the movie FANNY & ALEXANDER where the whole family accepted the father's affair with their domestic.

JY: There can be things like finishing each other's sentences. They both have issues of children leaving. What will happen when the children leave? What is his perspective?

TA: His first son died at 17 months. Let's play this up emotionally with respect to his relationship with Tom. Let's see that he made some plans for him when he ran away—arranging for him to show up at his cousin's plantation. Also we'll need to set up Woodson earlier and the Woodson plantation.

CA: With Harriet also, let's have him manipulate the situation more so that he's more involved in finding a place for her such as a doctor friend in Pennsylvania.

TA: I also want to set up later the idea that Martha is just as equal as Sally in poverty in the very end.

JY: Re: Martha—let's make her more dimensional. Let's clarify that she's officious but not cruel.

TA: I agree. And I'll also lace in the fact that it was Martha who felt slaves should be freed – she was actually very passionate about that...she was just jealous of anyone who had too much of her father's attention...

After those notes and several phone calls for clarification, I went away and wrote the second draft. Although in the course of the movie I would write several more drafts, the second draft is still my personal favorite. There were two areas where Joan suggested possible changes to enhance the script for which I will always be grateful. One suggestion addressed the potential confusion as to the Hemings family lineage and concern whether the audience would really understand how Sally was Jefferson's wife's half-sister. Joan suggested we somehow show the lineage in addition to having Betty Hemings explain it to Sally after Sally's return from Paris. I initially had a sequence where a few slave women including Betty and Critta Hemings were quilting a freedom quilt. The various patterns created within these quilts were once a way in which slaves helped other slaves escape successfully to the river. The quilts would usually be hung out on a tree or a clothesline and went largely unsuspected by slave owners. But since we never showcased any runaway slaves utilizing the quilt, the idea of exchanging the pattern for images of the Hemings family became intriguing. One must remember a slave could be maimed or killed for revealing who their slave owner father was. So for Betty Hemings, on being asked what was "this ornate creation" by Thomas Jefferson, to reveal that the quilt illustrated not only the various Hemings family members, but also Jefferson's father-in-law as Sally's father as well as Jefferson's then children with Sally Hemings, was potential for bodily harm. However, since Jefferson was known for his soft spot for the Hemings family and his aversion to slave beatings and maimings, I had him react with great discomfort at the quilt's contents. It was one of the more humorous moments in the miniseries when he cleared his throat and hurriedly walked away using his wide brim hat to disguise embarrassment. By the way, the quilt now hangs proudly in my foyer waiting to be donated to the Sally Hemings Foundation when it is acquires its permanent location. Thanks, Joan.

The second suggestion was more structural. After being told the last two hours were not as dramatically exciting as the first two, I knew I had to find "dots to connect" which would be compelling to an audience, yet continue to convey a sense of Sally's true life at Monticello. It was inferred that Sally appeared not to be in as much jeopardy as she might have been when Jefferson was away in office. Also relayed to me was the need for more action-oriented sequences, particularly in the last hour, even though the story was working. Ironically, everything in those last two hours had been historically documented and annotated. But, again, we were not doing a documentary, we were presenting a drama and it had to be compelling to keep the audience from switching channels.

So, I prayed on it, as I do everything I want answers to. Then a couple of days later, while flipping through a book on slavery, I came upon an illustration which disturbed me. It depicted a slave woman stripped to the waist, tied to a tree being beaten by her slave master while another white man looked on. Then it struck me. Gabriel Lilly. Lilly was one of the most efficient, but truly heinous and sadistic overseers Jefferson ever hired. He was responsible for the only slave beatings that occurred at Monticello even though Jefferson had a strict policy against beating his servants.

Jefferson's preferred punishment, if a slave was belligerent, was that he or she be sold off and separated from family. Thus only two slaves were ever sold for bellicose behavior that we are aware of.

So when I saw the illustration, I thought about Jefferson being in Washington and Sally and her family at Monticello under the scrutiny and control of Gabriel Lilly. I thought about Lilly's fondness for the whip. I thought about his politics, his southern roots, in fact, his love for a continuation of "the Southern way of life" which interpreted reads "love for the continuation of slavery." Then I thought about how unsafe Sally would have been particularly with Jefferson away. I sat up in bed that night and a vision of Sally being beaten by this man would not leave my psyche. I thought about it all night. Sally was beautiful. What better way to compel Jefferson (should he have also been superficial on top of hypocritical) to break off relations with her than to scar her body. Damage her beauty. Cripple her emotionally forever. Gabriel Lilly once beat Sally's nephew Jamy Hemings so badly, the boy left Monticello never to return.

I simply dramatized the event and with this nugget of truth, created a scene in which Jamy Hemings is being beaten by Lilly and Sally intercedes. Lilly slaps her to the ground and Samuel Carr, one of Jefferson's nephews, witnesses this action and comes to Sally's rescue. Angered and frustrated by his firing, and aided by Peter Carr, Samuel's brother, Lilly concocts a subterfuge by which Sally is abducted and spirited into a barn. There she is stripped and whipped unmercifully requiring her back to later be stitched up by slave women. All the while, the scene is counterpointed with Thomas Jefferson signing the Louisiana Purchase into law increasing the land mass of America which also had the potential to increase the number of slaveholding territories in the country. It became one of the more powerful scenes in the film in that it illustrated just how unimportant and meaningless Sally was to whites intent to keep African Americans controlled and enslaved. It also underscored why some of Sally's children may have chosen to pass for white and bypass the cruel system of America's "peculiar institution" as well as increase the social benefits for their children and themselves.

But I still found I had emotional "dots" to connect. So I decided I wanted to meet and talk to as many descendants as I could find. They more than anyone else would have insights into the story no one else could possibly have.

Co Executive Producer Wendy Kram with the author on location. Wendy kept after me to produce the story.

Chapter Six

DESCENDED FROM THE DECLARATION

From watching the Oprah Winfrey Show, I knew the Hemings/Jefferson descendants would be attending the Monticello Association meeting held in Charlottesville in May of 1999. The Association is comprised of the lineal descendants of Thomas Jefferson through his daughters Martha and Maria. The Hemings descendants had been invited at the behest of Lucian Truscott IV, an Association member descended from Martha Jefferson who felt it was time, particularly in the wake of the DNA revelation, to invite the Hemings descendants into the Association. Lucian has gone on record saying: *"...Even if Thomas Jefferson didn't do the right thing two centuries ago, we can start by opening our hearts and our arms to...all our Hemings cousins..."*

I can only imagine that Lucian must be considered a renegade by some in the Association, but he organized this historic meeting of Hemings descendants, and I had to be there. I wanted the Hemings participation and to include their oral histories and opinions. I felt it would be remiss to treat them as they had been treated by history—like invisible gnomes to be ignored. I couldn't be part of that same hypocrisy.

But I had to get there and the production did not have the resources to send me. So, have plastic, will travel. I had been introduced to the delightful Rita McClenny of the Virginia Film Office through Tim Reid, a producer I had worked with on the Dawn Steel movie. Tim has a wonderful facility in Petersburg, Virginia called New Millennium Studios where he shot the series "Links" and other projects. He was interested in bidding on the opportunity to be our production studio and lot in Virginia and I thought it was a great idea. It would have been a wonderful way to put more minorities to work and give opportunities to people who are invariably overlooked in our industry. He called Rita and when she arrived in Los Angeles with the Governor and First Lady of Virginia, she called me to attend a breakfast and introduced me to them. Once I knew I was coming to Charlottesville, I called Rita and she arranged everything—including the Omni Hotel, a tour at Monticello, a car, and a lovely assistant named Rebecca to show me all the historic sites.

I had been told that we could not shoot our film at Monticello because their policy does not allow filming of commercial programs on their grounds. Accepting that, I still wanted to go back to the little mountain to see how much had changed in the fourteen years since I was there last. What a difference a little DNA makes. Every tour guide answered questions about Sally Hemings. Even the Hemings family history was discussed on the tour. There were three sightings of the name "Hemings", one, a wooden grave marker for Priscilla Hemings; the other a cabin outline on Mulberry Row indicating Critta Hemings' cabin; and a room in one of the dependencies marked as belonging to Peter Hemings. Very different from the "don't-ask-don't-tell" policy of the old days.

The grounds were teeming with people that Saturday, the day before the Association meeting. News crews, reporters and cameramen lurked in every tree ready to thrust a tape recorder or microphone in one's face. On one occasion a reporter mistook me for a descendant and was halfway through an interview before he realized I was a "nobody." He sighed, then walked off in one direction, and I in another. I had to laugh. As I walked the grounds that day, a live costume presentation of life at Monticello in the 1700 and 1800's was going on. Along Mulberry Row, people were dressed as slaves and craftsmen doing whatever chores and duties one did on a plantation like Monticello. I met an interesting fair-skinned African American woman doing one of these presentations and I found myself fascinated by her. She was preparing food the way slaves would have during Jefferson's time. Her oratory was so eloquent and impressive, I listened spellbound. I introduced myself and asked if I could take a photo of her for my scrapbook. She agreed and I took the photo. She then told me her name—Leni Ashmore Sorensen. What is so ironic and coincidental was some months later, when our production required a historian, Craig hired a woman and called me to say how impressed he was with her and couldn't wait for me to meet her. When I got to Richmond for the start of production, I was introduced to this extraordinary woman, and lo and behold it was Leni. We've been friends ever since.

Later at Monticello, I ran into a correspondent from CBS in New York named Randall Pinkston, a delightful man who was there to do a story for his station. We chatted briefly and he wished me luck with the miniseries and asked that I stay in touch with him regarding its progress. I promised I would and we both went our separate ways. As I turned the corner which took me back toward the east front of the house I met two women sitting on a bench in front of the bookstore. I stopped to chat with them as one looked familiar. I discovered them to be Dr. Dianne Swann-Wright, director of the "Getting Word Project" at Monticello, whom I recognized from Monticello's web site, and Beverly Gray, a Hemings family historian. Both women were delighted the story was being done for television and

Leni Ashmore Sorensen at Monticello in 1999. Leni later served as our historian on the production later.

asked me to be more reverential to the character of Sally Hemings than the other film had been. They both felt very strongly about Sally being a mother and the sacrifices she made for her children. Dianne reiterated Monticello's filming policy and assured me it had nothing to do with the subject matter of the piece. She and Beverly wished me well.

Soon, all the cameras began heading toward the west front of Monticello and when I followed them I understood why. Over three dozen descendants were now on the hill. I turned to Rebecca and squeezed her hand. "This is it," I exclaimed, "This is why I came." They were all so different...every complexion from the whitest white to the deepest ebony and all the colors in between. Many of these faces I had seen on television or in newspaper articles and most began giving interviews to news crews. I snapped off a few photos. It was such a historic event. I was witness to the first gathering of the two sides of the family Jefferson—the black and the white—since the slave auction of 1827 when Jefferson's grandson, Thomas Jefferson Randolph sold Sally's family members to offset the third president's debts. I was filled with excitement even though I was not allowed any closer. The little mountain was being closed now to all but descendants, Association members, and sanctioned members of the press. I tried using the excuse I was working for CBS to get in, but I was not on the "list." So, back I went to the Omni and sulked. Rita called later to say don't lose hope, "Most of the descendants are staying right there at the Omni. Just be downstairs before or right after the meeting in the Jefferson Ballroom tomorrow and you'll probably meet them all."

The next day, Sunday, I grabbed my camera and note pad and went downstairs. The Omni lobby was a zoo. The 86th annual meeting of the Monticello Association had begun and the press was out in full regalia. Cameramen, lights, boom microphones, reporters, Association members and Hemings descendants filled the area just outside the Jefferson Ballroom. When I saw everyone heading into the ballroom except press, I knew I'd have to wait until the meeting was over. It would be three hours. During that time we began to hear raised voices—loud enough to waft through the double doors. Evidently, the Association's executive committee had met privately that morning to discuss the prospect of allowing the Hemings descendants to join the 700 plus Caucasian members of the organization. One of the prerequisites of membership is to be a direct descendant of Jefferson which gives one the privilege to be buried in the Jefferson family cemetery at Monticello alongside Thomas Jefferson.

But apparently several on the committee felt the matter needed further study and more proof and they would not be rushed into a decision. Lucian argued that none of the white Jefferson descendants required DNA testing or even birth certificates to prove their ancestry—just their word they were descendants. Then the Hemings descendants were asked to leave the room for a vote on the situation before the dessert was even served. That motion was voted down 33 to 20. On a tape I viewed months later taken of the meeting I saw Shay stand up and announce that she was embarrassed to be related "to you people." One person to leave early was Deborah Edwards, a descendant of Madison Hemings. She indicated she was horrified by the animosity inside the Jefferson Ballroom. *"In days gone by, they wore Wamsutta sheets. Today it's suits. Same scene, different day."* But not all of the Monticello Association members were disinclined to accept "Black cousins." Naomi Nobles had come both for the meeting and to bury her mother in the Jefferson cemetery as was her right as a lineal descendant. She told reporters she felt Sally Hemings descendants should be accorded the same rights and privileges as anybody else in the Jefferson family. *"Clearly, Jefferson loved her. And love is what counts."*

Finally the meeting adjourned and I got the opportunity of a lifetime. One by one I talked to descendants. I got stories, anecdotes, hugs, phone numbers and photos. I was so inspired by the people I had met and the stories they shared with me. So many Hemingses had yet to meet other members of the Hemings family yet they all had similar stories about Sally and her life with Jefferson and her children. I spoke to as many descendants as I could and took notes. Sometimes whole families would give me oral histories—how they learned they were descended from Sally and Tom, and how they were treated as a result of it. I spoke to young Vincent and Troy, descendants of Madison Hemings. Then I spoke with Shannon Lanier, Billy Dalton, Dr. Michele Cooley-

Quille, Nina Boettcher, Byron and Trena Woodson. I also met Julia, Dorothy and Marshall Westerinen, descendants of Eston Hemings who were white and had not known about their black ancestry until 1976 when Fawn Brodie's book was published. These descendants were very embracing of their black heritage and eager to meet and interact with their cousins black and white. I could have stayed all afternoon into the evening, but my plane was scheduled to leave at eight from Washington, D.C., which required I drive from Charlottesville about an hour and a half. So I said goodbye to all, went upstairs, packed and flew home.

When I got back to Los Angeles I was ebullient. I called as many descendants as I could for follow-ups. I discovered that Mary Kearney still had a pair of Jefferson's spectacles handed down for generations. I learned from Michele Cooley-Quille that slaves could be killed for discussing who their white slave owner fathers were. I also learned that Sally walked up the hill to tend Jefferson's grave for many years until her own death in 1835.

Descendants began sending me photos of family members past and present. I thought it would be great to utilize these photos at the end of the film to show the lasting proof in the progeny of the relationship. Some of them turned me on to other descendants who I spoke to at length by phone. People such as Rosemary Ghoston, Priscilla Lanier, Patti Jo Harding and Pat Dalton. What struck me most in both my discussions and in seeing the photos was the fact that so many descendants told me the same stories handed down to them for generations without knowing each other. In fact, many had just met for the first time at Monticello or earlier on the Oprah show. So one cannot say the descendants all drank the same "Stepford Wives" water and devised similar stories to garner publicity and socially elevate themselves. On the contrary, so many have been scorned and several were abandoned by other relatives eager to ignore and denounce their ancestry. I was not surprised by the number of descendants who passed for white or their relatives who protected their choice to do so. There was a lot of pain involved for those refusing to accept their "black" roots while sometimes living in the same household with blood family members who did.

But I was impressed by the number of descendants whose identity and interest in their ancestry was tied to Sally Hemings—and not Thomas Jefferson—of which the press has a tendency to accuse them. These African American descendants are proud of being Sally Hemings' grandchildren, progeny born to strength and survival and not just the fruits of a slave master who may have cared for Sally, but didn't provide for her. Additionally, the number of educators, teachers, professors and abolitionists counted amongst the Hemings descendants is voluminous. This is a family who obviously learned to appreciate and value acquiring and imparting knowledge from both Sally and Jefferson.

So now I was armed with wonderful oral histories, network notes, photos and re-inspired passion, and I went to work. By the end of May, we had a second draft of "The Memoirs of Sally Hemings." With that draft approved, we were greenlit for production with an air date now scheduled for February sweeps, 2000. The significance of this was not lost on any of us as February is also Black History month. At that, we began our search for a director.

Thomas Woodson Jr., (center)
Grandson of Sally Hemings
and Thomas Jefferson, with
two of his sons.

Rachel Cassels
Granddaughter of Thomas
Jefferson and Sally Hemings.

Francis Woodson (1814-1899)
Granddaughter of Thomas
Jefferson and Sally Hemings,
daughter of Tom (Hemings)
Woodson.

George Woodson (1808-1866)
Grandson of Thomas Jefferson
and Sally Hemings.

Sarah Jane Woodson (1826-1878) Daughter of Tom Woodson, granddaughter of Sally Hemings and Thomas Jefferson.

Julia Woodson (1859-1880) Granddaughter of Thomas Woodson, Great-grand-daughter of Thomas Jefferson and Sally Hemings.

John P. Woodson (1822-1853) Grandson of Thomas Jefferson and Sally Hemings, son of Thomas Woodson.

Michele Cooley-Quille, Phd, and clinical psychologist at Johns-Hopkins school of Public Health, with daughter Alicia. Both are Woodson descendants.Michele was very helpful with my research.

The Woodson family has a 200 year old oral tradition chronicling their lineage from Thomas Jefferson and Sally Hemings' first born son Tom Hemings. Most of their family history was researched and published in "The Woodson Family Source Book" by Minnie Woodson.

Francis (Fanny) Butler Chapman,
great-granddaughter of Sally Hemings
and Thomas Jefferson, granddaughter
of Madison Hemings.

Harriet Hemings Butler Spears,
daughter of Madison Hemings,
granddaughter of Sally Hemings and
Thomas Jefferson.

Emma Jane Byrd, (seated in middle next to husband George on the right),
granddaughter of Madison Hemings, great-granddaughter of Sally Hemings and
Thomas Jefferson. They are surrounded by their 10 children. All passed into
white society.

Shannon Lanier, 9th generation descendant through Madison Hemings. Shannon is a student at Kent State University and the first to introduce me to other descendants on my journey to find the Sally Hemings Story.

William J. Dalton, 8th generation descendant through Madison Hemings.

Sharon (Shay) Harris Banks Young, 6th generation descendant of Sally Hemings and Thomas Jefferson through their son Madison Hemings.

The Madison Hemings descendants, shown here and on previous page, are proud of their strong oral history as the progeny of Sally Hemings, who they consider a survivor and teacher. Much of my research was conducted with members of this branch of Sally and Tom's descendants.

Lt. Col. John Wayles Jefferson, (1835-1892) son of Eston Hemings Jefferson, grandson of Sally Hemings and Thomas Jefferson. John fought in the Civil War for the Union, enlisting in 1861 with the Eighth Wisconsin Regiment. He died childless at age 58 and passed for white all his life.

The Eston Hemings descendants only discovered their African American ancestry in 1974 with the publication of Fawn Brodie's book, "Thomas Jefferson An Intimate History." Since then, most have embraced their dual heritage.

From left; Beverly Frederick Jefferson, son of Eston Hemings Jefferson, grandson of Thomas Jefferson and Sally Hemings, with sons: Thomas Beverly, Frederick Arthur & Carl Smith Jefferson.

ABOVE: *Eston Hemings Jefferson descendants at Jefferson's grave at Monticello. Third Row: Justin Boggs, Jeff Westerinen, Art Westerinen, John Jefferson (who gave blood for DNA test.) Second Row: Jean Jefferson, Dorothy Westerinen, Julia Westerinen, Mary Jefferson. Front Row: Becky Westerinen, Emily Westerinen.*

A dusky girl stole my heart
And bore my seed
Yet I denied their inalienable
Rights

I have lived my Life
Enjoyed my Liberty
And pursued my Happiness

But what of them?
And the fruit to follow?

Act Three

TELLING THE STORY

Of all the damsels on the green
On mountain, or in valley,
A lass so luscious ne'er was seen
As Monticellian Sally.

When press'd by loads of state affairs
I seek to sport and dally
The sweetest solace of my cares
Is in the lap of Sally

She's black you tell me—grant she be
Must colour always tally?
Black is love's proper hue for me…
And white's the hue for Sally.

Ballad lampooning Thomas Jefferson appearing
in the Philadelphia Port Folio, October 2, 1802

Kevin Conway as "Tom Paine", Sam Neill as "Thomas Jefferson" and Carmen Ejogo as "Sally Hemings" at the Palace of Versailles. Sally Hemings was at the Palace in her capacity as ladies maid to Martha and Polly Jefferson. Paine suggests Jefferson allow his heart to open again after the death of his wife.

Chapter Seven

"IMAGING TRUTHS MORE THAN SELF-EVIDENT"

"You do what the script tells you. Deliver the goods without comment. Live it—do it or shut up. After all, the writer is what's important..."

Katherine Hepburn, Time Magazine, November 1981

There is an old director's adage in Hollywood..."Directing film is a monarchy, not a democracy." I sometimes wonder if it's not on a banner hanging in the men's room at the Director's Guild. But there is also an old writer's adage, "In the beginning there was the WORD, and the WORD was God." Thus both observations illustrate the ongoing tug of war between directors and writers.

Lesson #1. If you are a playwright, stay in theater for respect. Your words cannot be touched and you have permission to destroy by nuclear attack anyone who so much as tampers with a comma. On the other hand, if you live and work in Los Angeles as a screenwriter prepare to do battle, for anyone breathing is allowed to rewrite a writer in Hollywood. Yes, I know it seems strange because there is nothing for a producer to produce, a director to direct, or an actor to say before the writer has committed pen to paper, but somehow the most witless individuals who would never tell an editor how to edit a film, tell writers how to write one—or worst yet—write it themselves!

Unfortunately, writers are invariably treated like lower level slugs or interchangeable nuts on the bolt of filmmaking and replaced at the drop of a hat. Need better dialogue? Hire a dialogue polisher. Need better action sequences? Hire an action writer. Need more emotional definition within a couple of scenes? "I can do it," shouts a gaffer—and trust me, he'll be hired. If left up to Hollywood, movies would be written by directors, and actors will just make it up as they go along. To hell with the screenwriter. Lesson #2. It cuts both ways. He who rewrites will ultimately be rewritten.

In defense of my literary compatriots, I acknowledge that all too often producers, directors and executives make the mistake of assuming writers do not have a singular, unique voice that sets them apart from each other. Conventional wisdom dictates that film is a director's medium and plays or novels are a writer's. But look at any of Woody Allen, Quentin Tarrentino, Spike Lee or the "Golden Era's" Paddy Chayefsky or Joseph Mankiewicz films and you'll hear a distinctive voice in every role that is the signature of the writer. Naturally, most of the people I just named fought to direct their films to keep those singular, distinctive voices in tact for, if not, the studio machinery would have surely brought in some "rewrite" king. I should know. I made a considerable living earlier in my career as the "African-American script doctor." Need snappy black dialogue? Hire Tina.

So for me to elect to venture into this television project required more than just my being a "writer-for-hire-who-could-be-replaced-or-rewritten," I contracted to be Co- Executive Producer, someone who, in television, was supposed to have a modicum of power. I had nurtured "The Mistress of Monticello" for several years. It had put me on the map. It led me to Alex Haley and thus to a career as a screenwriter. It had been approved, developed by the network, Craig, Wendy and myself, green-lit and on its way to production. So I was not about to allow changes in interpretation, content or intent on the material by anyone who might not be sensitive to the needs and feelings of African Americans—particularly on this project which was so deeply dependant on African American consciousness.

As I've mentioned earlier, the creation of film and television projects is a collaborative process. The nature of the word "collaborate" suggests that more than one person is working together for which each person's opinion is valued and considered. Unfortunately, as we moved closer to production, my opinion began to be the least regarded. On every one of my other films, whether my writing contribution was credited or not, my input on everything from casting to production assistants was not only solicited, but valued. I was present at every production meeting. Every discussion of the material from what was in my head when I wrote the scene, to what color the wall paper should be on a set—included my solicited opinion. Granted, I am a collaborative being so I made it a point to communicate to whomever the director was that the material was now his or her vision--but generally you've chosen that director because he or she SHARES that vision. Even when I was busy working on another project and could not attend all of these meetings, the directors involved made me feel I was needed. And in the case of "Why Do Fools Fall In Love," director Gregory Nava was so insistent I be at casting and production meetings, on the set, and in editing sessions, he would call me and scold, "Tina, we're making your movie! You need to be here! Get over here!" And mind you, I was just the screenwriter on that film—which, as I've stated, can be thought of as the lowliest form of Hollywood slug. So my job as a producer on the Sally Hemings project was to protect the integrity of the material. I, after all, understood and had to service my community, and I knew what had to be communicated in the piece. I had lived with it. I *was* the material.

I turned in the revised draft…which was green-lit. Then we went after a director. I had made a point of suggesting to everyone that we should hire an African American director because of the nature, sensitivity and point of view of the piece and because it was the right thing to do. For whatever reason, I was not present for any of the meetings with the two African American directors under consideration, but I was not and they both passed on the material. Fine. Also, for whatever reason, no African American female directors were considered. I knew that talented, capable black directors were willing and available all over town because I had spoken to several of them who are personal friends who wanted the opportunity. The official response was curious. I was told some were nervous about the material (okay, acceptable, but not the ones I called), some were unavailable (more reasonable) or most could not get approved because they had not directed a four hour miniseries (the best reason so far).

Well, so much for the glare of the NAACP spotlight. One fine day I received a call saying Charles Haid was available and interested in the project. He had done a brilliant job of directing "Buffalo Soldiers" for TNT and several pilots for CBS. But I was also told by several sources that however brilliant, he could also be difficult. Yet in my head no one could be more difficult than Dawn Steel, and I had gotten along great with her even though the project fell through. So I felt if not a black director at least a director who had previously directed black subject matter.

We had several meetings. We came to an understanding about what was needed in the next pass—which would be the director's draft. We knew we were starting in six weeks. Our production designers, carpenters, painters and location scouts were already hard at work in Richmond, as were the costumer, prop people and wig makers. I turned in a draft which incorporated the director's notes on June 22, 1999.

With that draft we got Sam Neill, and a beautiful unknown to play Sally Hemings. We got all three of my first choices--Diahann Carroll as "Betty Hemings", Mario Van Peebles as "James Hemings," and Mare Winningham as "Martha Jefferson." I should have been singing like a lark.

Instead, I began to receive faxes which were clearly script pages, which resembled my scenes, but something was amiss. The words on the pages were not my own. Whole scenes had been rewritten, whole sequences changed, complete content and motivations altered. The work did not resemble my language or tone. I threw a fit. I made angry calls. At the next script meeting, I lost it. "What is this!" I asked the director, "Why are you rewriting me without benefit of consulting me?" I was given all manner of explanation as to why scenes needed to be modified. And as much as I expressed my anger—I must admit I went "black woman" on everyone as my finger went into the air, my head rotated dramatically while I flailed and carried on—the changes continued. Now, attitudes within scenes were being tempered. All the rage and anger the slave characters had at their condition were being systematically toned down. All Sally's scenes where she exhibited a modicum of influence over Jefferson were expunged. A scene where Sally suggests Jefferson go back into politics so that perhaps he can do something about slavery suddenly came back to me with the two of them in bed with Jefferson cooing, "You are my own sweet Sally, let us make the most of the time we have."

Oh, puleeeze!!

I watched scenes, including the one Sunta had personally quoted to me as great dialogue, faxed to me, under my own moniker, as some watered down, impotent version of the socially significant story I had written. I was constantly told Sally was "too strong." I was told I "hit the race card too squarely over the head." Excuse me! Too strong? When Maya Angelou wrote "Still I Rise" she spoke of the endurance and strength of black women. What we had to tolerate, accept and suffer through yet still wake up each day. In the face of chattel slavery nothing Sally did was short of strength. She survived and stayed with Jefferson despite a scandal likening her to Monica S. Lewinsky, Jefferson almost being relieved of office because of her, and, all of America singing ballads and hating her. To raise her children, see that they were all freed and educated, and manage not be killed or sold herself is strength personified. This was an intelligent woman who had to know she had some kind of influence or Jefferson would have moved on to the next sweet young slave thing, or, do what the editor of the Lynchburg Virginia Gazette suggested in 1802 and "married some worthy woman of (his) own complexion."

Sally wanted to make life better for her children. For people to assume that because one was black and a slave, therefore one was ignorant, is in itself racist. Why is it when we depict these kinds of indomitable black women they are invariably called "Too strong" by people who are, well, not African American?

As for race? The whole piece is about race. Race is the reason Sally has not been accepted as the woman in Jefferson's life. Race is the reason the DNA test results are still being refuted today. Race is the reason Jefferson's letter index for the year 1788, the year he began a sexual relationship with Sally, has suspiciously disappeared. Remember, no one so much as raised an eyebrow at Jefferson's relationship with Lady Maria Cosway, a married white woman. Race—is the reason I was willing to suffer through bad commentary or poor reviews for work that was truly of my doing, but not this. I am not a girl to go gentle into that good night. I'm from Chicago's south side. Trust me, I know how to fight. Sally could not (and would not) be some passive, inept slave with no purpose other than the sexual pleasure for an influential white man of power. Oh no. I was not interested in writing that. Sally's descendants have obviously proven that they learned from her generation after generation. So many current descendants are educators, professors and owners of their own businesses. Many, many others in the 19th century became abolitionists on the Underground Railroad for which many Hemings descendants lost their lives. I had a responsibility to them.

So I fought and I rewrote. This went on until the production went to Virginia to shoot. The stress was killing me, and once again I found myself struggling through a second bout of pneumonia. And if my health wasn't enough to put me into the ground, comments on the subsequent draft drove the nail into the coffin.

Actors who knew me began calling, "What happened to the draft we signed on to do?" It was obvious to anyone reading the script that someone other than me had tampered with the material. But I could do nothing. My voice was being silenced and I could not understand why. How can someone go around a "Producer/writer"? So I elected to write letters to all involved stating how unhappy I was with the draft, how far off the mark it was, how it misrepresented my writing, and, more importantly, how displeased the black community would be if certain scenes remained as "written" by me.

I then flew to Virginia for the read through. When I showed up at the Production office, I was livid. Taped to the door of the Directors office was a sheet of paper with the words "Shhhh, Director is Writing" written in magic marker. Now mind you it didn't say "Director is Sleeping," or "Director is Casting" or "Director is Producing." But before I blew a gasket, I heard Alex's voice again and I forced myself to be calm. I did not want to lose it in front of the brilliant cast that had been assembled, many of whom would be meeting "the writer" for the first time. That is NOT the time to come across as a "raving shrew".

So I did the honorable thing. I sat there biting my inside cheek as the cast read from a luke warm script I hated. I cried inside as I listened to a scene where Sally's daughter, Harriet—who should have been expressing her desire to pass for white (which she did in real life), become a scene where the word "white" was not even uttered. Harriet, instead, told her mother she would "never do such a thing." I popped two Motrins and kept copious notes of every scene that had substantially changed, and went back to the hotel where I contemplated calling the network. I had nothing to lose. If this is what the network wanted, fine. But what if they think I have been making the changes? Perhaps they should be told that should the NAACP or the Los Angeles Times gain knowledge that this project, with all the itinerant politics attached, has been surreptitiously co-opted and diluted by persons not of color who've done it poorly, black folks will protest loudly and it would look bad. I was in purgatory. So I decided to light a candle, pray, and go to bed. After all, tomorrow was another day.

As luck (and my prayers) would have it, the next evening after I returned to the hotel, I had a message from the network asking me to call. When I did I was asked if I had been getting their notes. I explained I had not. I then bit my lip and launched into my full scale laundry list of complaints. Sure enough the network had assumed the changes were agreed upon (remember "collaboration"?) and there had been six pages of notes I had never received. And, it turned out, the notes addressed the very SAME concerns I had with the changes. So with new marching orders, I once again rewrote. By the end of principal photography, I had written or rewritten ten drafts of the script.

There were several scenes I could not save from misinterpretation, however, and critics and African Americans nailed ME to the cross (see Chapter Nine). An example is Sally and Jefferson's first love scenes, I had written them in such a way that both of the two principals were nervous, yet drawn to each other. Their attraction had been carefully building and now neither could resist the other, or suppress their feelings. So when their lips meet, nature takes its course. I was very specific in our creative meetings that Sally could NOT make the first move. She was young and I was playing her as a virgin, not sexually manipulative, and did NOT want any interpretations that would represent a black woman as wanton, or sexually aggressive. There are too many stereotypes of this nature depicted in film and, as an African American woman, I would not be party to the perpetuation of such a negative stereotype. I truly felt Jefferson was the only man Sally was ever with sexually. Equally, I did not want Jefferson to be lusty or primal with her or appear to force himself on her. I wanted the audience to see how this relationship developed in the open, social mores of France, into one lasting 38 years. But I sat in utter shock as I watched dailies of Sally pulling off her gown sexually presenting herself to a Jefferson standing at the door, having yet to make a move. And we could not re-shoot.

I had to go on talk radio all across the country to explain how that scene was about as far from what I wrote as one could get.

Equally upsetting was the aforementioned scene with Sally's daughter Harriet, which even after I rewrote it, somehow, magically, went back to the version I disdained. The day I saw those dailies, I knew I had to write this book. As wonderful as the miniseries was, and as proud as I am of it—and I am monumentally proud of it—there will always be those scenes I wish I had the power to reverse.

But I also, quite honestly, must be fair. All artists can be eccentric, unnerving and temperamental, and God knows I am as eccentric as the next creative type. And I will also admit there were ideas and visual elements added to the production that were truly emotional and strikingly beautiful. Many times in watching the movie I found myself caught up in the sheer pageantry and grandeur of the piece—which must all be credited to the director. I just wish that one day somewhere in our creative future, the visual artists that are directors, and the literary artists that are writers, can find a collaborative communal synergy born of mutual respect which will lead to more powerful, provocative and innovative productions. Until then screenwriters will always feel abused and identify with that great line from Joesph L. Mankiewicz's "All About Eve":

"When will the piano realize it has not written the concerto."

The blood of Africa and Europe
Of Slave and Slavic, Black and British
Coursed my veins to create
The high yellow lie which became
A historical reality

I am an American truth...
...To be self evident

And when history books are written
To reflect subservience or bowed head
Remember from wince those tomes come
For strength, endurance and survival
Were my inheritance and my legacy

I am an American truth...
...Who shall not be denied

Chapter Eight

PRE-PRODUCTION

The search for the actress to play Sally Hemings was tantamount to the search for Scarlett O'Hara. First of all, we thought we would require a name actress for the role or the project would not move forward. CBS suggested if we did not find a star name for "Sally" then definitely a star name for "Jefferson" would be paramount. But it would prove much easier to find a "star" Jefferson than the right unknown to portray Sally.

Foremost, the actress was required to be beautiful. Sally's beauty has been very well documented and we all felt America would be far more understanding of Mr. Jefferson's interest in Sally if our actress was attractive to our audience as well. Of course finding pretty actresses in Hollywood was the least of our concerns. They poured forth from the rafters. However, the actress had to also be biracial or so light skinned she could pass for a quadroon (the racial classification of the 19th century for a person who was one-quarter black as Sally was). She had to be able to play from age 14 to 53 years old convincingly, she had to be able to speak in unlettered slave dialect in the earlier sequences before her training in France, and later become an educated and sophisticated lady. She had to have the natural bearing and carriage of a woman of gentry to show contrast to the other slaves at Monticello upon her return from France. Additionally, she had to speak French.

Names were bandied about—Halle Berry, Vanessa Williams, Thandie Newton, etc., etc. Halle was finishing "Introducing Dorothy Dandridge," Vanessa was filming "Don Quixote," Thandie was wrapping "Mission: Impossible 2." Once CBS assured Craig that we could go with an unknown, the floodgates opened. Our capable casting director, Reuben Cannon, who had been responsible for so many roles I received when I was an actress, came onboard early on. He had loved the first draft, which he later told me was his reason for taking the job, and both Craig and I were fond of him. Reuben pre-screened most of the actors before they auditioned for either of us or our director.

We read some three dozen girls. They came short, tall, cream colored, beige, tan and golden brown. They came with straight, curly, long, short, fine, bushy, real—and not-so-real hair. They came with real and not-so-real green, hazel, brown and blue eyes. And they came equipped and ill-equipped for the role. As we would watch actresses come and go, one thing became clear: many of the women were missing some crucial element necessary for Sally Hemings. Most gave adequate but very contemporary readings of the scenes. In several cases heads would bob in a very "angry-black-woman/Sapphire" characterization. Several were too old to play the young, naïve Sally. Several were far too young especially when Sally became "Matriarch of Monticello" in night two. Still others couldn't handle the role's range of emotion which ran from A to Z. It got down to four girls, all of whom tested, but none made the final cut. So we were back to the drawing board.

Reuben then had a suggestion. Why not go out to the world? After all, Thandie Newton had played Sally Hemings in "Jefferson In Paris" and Ms. Newton is British. So Reuben contacted his associate in London, Carol Dudley, who asked me to e-mail the script to her. Within a week, she had screened several actresses and called Reuben with news. She had found four wonderful choices and wanted to put them on tape and send the videos to us. Needless to say we were concerned because we were set to begin principle photography in six weeks and had no "Sally." Costumes had to be fitted, wigs built, prosthetic make-up created for "old Sally." It was imperative we find the actress. Soon.

The tapes arrived. Reuben saw them first. He called us. *"There are some fabulous girls on the video, but one, in particular, is fantastic. Her name is Carmen Ejogo. I'm sending the tape immediately."*

I asked him if Carmen had done any work here in the States. Reuben said yes, but small parts. She had been in "Metro" with Eddie Murphy and "The Avengers." Then it dawned on me. Carmen was the actress with the cute English accent who played Eddie's girlfriend. She was adorable in the film with her corkscrew hair and affable personality. But the role in our miniseries was a lead. Sally was in every scene except four. What is wonderful in twenty minutes of screen time may not necessarily hold up for four hours.

The messenger arrived at my house with the tapes. I watched the tests. The first girl was lovely and capable. Same for the second. The third girl was excellent but only reasonably attractive. The fourth actress was Carmen Ejogo. I lit up immediately because she was so bright and articulate in her pre-interview, and stunning. "But her accent" I thought, *"What will we do about her accent?"* It had been so cute and infectious in "Metro" but inappropriate for "Sally." I had only to wait a moment. Carol Dudley had given each actress the five most difficult scenes in the film for their audition. Carmen's first scene was one in which she discovers Jefferson has been escorting a married, white female friend around Washington. Sally's jealousy and anger spills forth and she challenges Jefferson by telling him she, too, has been seeing someone else—a slave. Though it's a lie, she and Jefferson bitterly argue. Carmen handled this scene with such depth and maturity, such dramatic skill, I stood up and held my chest. "My God," I exclaimed to my husband, "She's Sally" and there was no trace of British accent. Bravo! Each of her successive scenes was better than the last and obviously she impressed Les Moonves. Carmen Ejogo was cast immediately, and we were never happier.

Carmen would later tell me she felt a certain connection to the character even though she is not of African *American* descent. She, like Sally, is of mixed race—Carmen is Scottish and Nigerian—and she has been ridiculed for not being black enough for some people and not white enough for others. Carmen said, *"Understanding who Jefferson was as a man helped me determine what kind of personality Sally may have had that would attract Jefferson to her and allow the relationship to occur and continue." She also said, "The way I chose to portray Sally was partly defined from what I assumed Sally's life may have been like in terms of being a slave and a woman in those times. Even women of gentry lacked many rights and obviously for a slave it was compounded. She (Sally) had to have been a woman of great strength to have gone through the scandal. She probably had enemies from all quarters."*

Carmen insists her most difficult scene was laying in mud for hours in the aftermath of the savage beating from Gabriel Lilly. But my concern for Carmen was her health. I had written her into every scene and eventually, during the rainstorms and Hurricane Floyd, she became ill and it shut down production. No Carmen, no shoot. But I'm pleased to report, she came through like a champion, many times working ill, and went on to finish the film while continuing to exhibit the class, dignity and sheer talent I've come to so love about Carmen Ejogo. What a talent.

And what about Sam Neill? Just the idea of Sam as Jefferson was exciting. He was quite simply—perfect. Tall, patrician bearing, handsome and a marvelous actor, Sam Neill's career has included some of Hollywood's best, most memorable films— "Jurassic Park", "The Piano", "My Brilliant Career" "Dead Calm," and TV's"Merlin."

Even though the project was primarily about Sally and her travails, early on, we all felt the Jefferson role should be beefed up to accommodate Sam. I love Sam's work. I had seen every project and knew his nuances. He is likable—which was so necessary for Jefferson—and Sam could be vulnerable yet strong concurrently. Not to mention he is terribly attractive and let's face it—if you're selling a love story you want to see two attractive people on screen for four hours. Sam is also an actor known for doing his homework and accepting a number of challenging and diverse roles. We knew if the Jefferson role were expanded, Sam might just say yes. And he did.

Born in Ireland but a resident of New Zealand, Neill immersed himself in the role of Thomas Jefferson trading his Irish-by-way-of-New Zealand accent for Jefferson's soft Virginia Piedmont's. Sam read up on Jefferson and many times came in with some interesting Jefferson quote or anecdote he thought appropriate to a scene and asked if he could incorporate it. He also commented that one of the great things about playing Jefferson was that Jefferson was wildly contradictory. Said Neill, *"If you take, for instance, Jefferson and slavery—and that is, in large part, what the film is about—this was a man who was avowedly against slavery and attempted to introduce legislation that would do something about it. At the same time, this was a man who had hundreds of slaves and only emancipated five or so of them. This was a complicated life with a lot of complicated little areas that were sometimes kept separated from one another."*

Sam played Jefferson's contradictions with such subtlety his thoughts could be read from his face. An example is one of my favorite moments when Sam comes through the door to Sally's room in Paris knowing he's drawn to her—that he wants to make love to her, but hesitates and closes his eyes. In that one quick moment you can read his mind. It's as if he's praying, "take away this cup from me." Sam also captured so many of Jefferson's purported quirks including Jefferson's soft voice, his penchant for wearing wide brimmed hats and the practice of soaking his feet in ice water to ward off colds. His performance was richly textured and so beautifully nuanced, that I was miffed by comments from those who maligned us for using foreign actors to portray two very American historical figures. With Sam Neill's portrayal of Jefferson, I feel Jefferson himself would have been pleased.

I could go on about the brilliance of all of the actors, many of whom we cast from New York who were accomplished stage actors. The production was blessed by the divine Kelly Rutherford, Mario Van Peebles, Zeljko Ivanek, the wonderful Rene Auberjonois, Paul Kandel, Klea Scott, Amelie Heinle, Kevin Conway, Jessica Townsend, Larry Gilliard, the incomparable Mare Winningham et al. But, I could not imagine making this movie without Diahann Carroll.

Miss Carroll was the quintessential Betty Hemings and added such strength and dignity to the role, I still stand in awe of her. When I wrote the play, I had her in mind as I constructed "Betty." Diahann's life had formed her, her career had developed her, indomitable will has sustained her, and her beauty is legendary. The woman is a true pioneer. She and I sat down to lunch before the shoot and as it turns out, she had tried to produce a Sally Hemings project in the 80's. She had the same difficulty I had mounting it. People just wouldn't believe it was a true story. In fact, Miss Carroll told me producers and studio heads laughed in her face for even suggesting the story to them. I commiserated with her, given my own journey with the material, then told Miss Carroll how her being who she was had made such an impression on me growing up in Chicago. Diahann was the first African American actress to star in her own TV series "Julia" in the late 60's. I watched this program religiously and saw an attractive, hard working mother with a good job who was intelligent and funny, and I thought "I can do that. I can be an actress too." Diahann inspired and motivated a generation of young African American actresses, not to mention opened doors for minorities behind-the-scenes. I have said to her that if not for women like her kicking down the doors then, women like me would not be so able to walk through them now. For Diahann Carroll's presence in the film, and for what she has meant to me personally, I am truly grateful, and the production was much benefited.

PRODUCTION DESIGN

The cost to recreate our "Monticello" ultimately exceeded a million dollars and resulted from our inability to use the real Monticello as an exterior. The Thomas Jefferson Memorial Foundation, which owns and runs Monticello, has rules that forbid filming non-documentaries there. So we took our production to Richmond and built our own version of Jefferson's cherished home. We were lucky to have Production Designer David Crank to recreate Monticello as well as all our sets. One must remember Monticello is one of the most famous historical landmarks in America. All one need do is look on the back of a nickel to see a rendering of it, so we had to be careful. We felt, since we were building the mansion from scratch, we would make the interiors high enough as well as durable enough to accommodate cameras, cast and crew, and still pay attention to the detail for which the real Monticello is so well known. We would also need to find acreage large enough to house the structure as well as several outbuildings which comprised Mulberry Row and the slave work areas.

We shot most of the project at Tuckahoe Plantation, which curiously enough was once owned by relatives of Thomas Jefferson. It had fields, a large land area suitable for the sets, and we shot there five weeks out of the nine-week schedule. David Crank said, *"Monticello is more than a set, it's a character. Unlike many productions where facades of buildings are created for exterior shots and the interior scenes are done in studios, the Monticello structure was built for filming both inside and out."* We also made sure to include some of Jefferson's memorable inventions like his swivel chair and writing desk and tried to match paints and wallpapers. Our production team, headed by Crank, only had eight weeks to build Monticello. When filming wasn't taking place at Tuckahoe Plantation, we shot at the Centre Hill Mansion in Petersburg, Virginia to act as the exteriors and interiors of the Hotel de Langeac, Jefferson's Paris residence and the Executive Mansion much later called The White House.

COSTUMES

Michael Boyd, our costume designer found we would be dealing with not only two different time periods but also very obscure time periods as it would affect our costumes. As a result, of the five thousand plus costumes for the principals and extras, Boyd could only rent about 10 percent. The rest were designed and manufactured by Boyd and his team of 10 seamstresses, tailors, dyers and milliners. Boyd also found himself designing the differences in Jefferson's fashions from two different countries. Jefferson dressed differently in the States before he went to Paris. His clothing became more ornate and stylish while in Paris. Then when he came back to America and ultimately became president he tried to dress like a man of the people. I had both Thomas Paine and Dolley Madison comment on Jefferson's dress at the White House in the script.

Michael also successfully showed the various levels within the slave labor force at Monticello. Slaves working in the house, particularly the Hemingses who were at the pinnacle of the slave hierarchy at Monticello, had access to the master and the master's family and therefore access to cast-offs which were of quality. They would be better dressed than the artisans and craftsmen, who would invariably be dressed better than the field hands. Boyd did a great job of differentiating between the three groups by showing the degree of ornamentation, the materials, and the levels of deterioration that made the difference in their looks.

As for Sally's lilac gown for the party at the Palace of Versailles in Paris, four had to be constructed for the production. Two for Carmen and two for Amelia Heinle, who portrayed Harriet Hemings, Sally's daughter, because the two actresses were different sizes. In the script, Harriet finds Sally's dress in an old trunk and puts it on to serve at a party Jefferson has almost twenty years later at Monticello. The dress symbolizes Sally's fondest time in her life and the beginnings of her affair with Jefferson, and in the sequence Harriet attracts William Alexander, a DuPont nephew while wearing it. The dress had special meaning for me because as I've explained, in visiting my grandmother, I looked through her cedar chest as a child and pulled out a moth-eaten lilac dress which grandma explained was the dress she was wearing when she met grandpa. So as I wrote the play and the screenplay I was always inspired by the idea of Grandma wearing that dress and driving grandpa to distraction. Michael Boyd will tell you when I first saw the lilac gown for the movie, I held my heart. It was so gorgeous—exactly what I had in my head as I wrote the scene. And, yes, I did hold it up to a mirror and envision myself in it. Some things are okay to re-live.

PRINCIPAL PHOTOGRAPHY

Just before the production went to Richmond for principal photography, I was told the film would exceed the budget and was asked if I would give up my bonus. Writers make their living in hopes of receiving their production bonus. But since others were giving up theirs, I did not want us to shut down. We had come so far. So I acquiesced. Certain sacrifices one makes for material they believe in.

We began shooting on August 8, 1999 in Richmond, Virginia. Cast and crew gathered around our director and prayed for a good shoot. I was still rewriting the script and making entries in my journal. I wanted to record every emotion, every feeling I was experiencing about this oh so important day in my life. How I wished my father had been alive to be there. How I wished Alex Haley could have been there wishing us well.

The first scene was one in Paris where Sally is coming to the Hotel de Langeac for the first time and seeing that her brother James was doing well and was in charge of the residence. We were shooting interiors at Centre mansion that day and I was so excited to actually watch my words coming to life in front of an 80 member crew. The sound man, Jay Patterson, gave me a set of headphones and I listened and watched behind the monitor as Carmen and Mario Van Peebles went to work. Mario was so grand as James. He was polished, dignified and exhibited James' well-documented volatility. Mare Winningham was also in this sequence and her performance throughout was one of finely textured lace. What a pro. Half the time I found myself just staring at her—looking for some line of demarcation between her performance and reality.

Later, after lunch, while we were setting up the next scene, an older woman was asking around and finally someone pointed to me and she came over. She introduced herself and took my hand. *"I'm 78 years old. I've lived in Richmond all my life. I've grown up to revere the many contributions Thomas Jefferson has made to this country. Please don't write anything that will destroy the dignity of our Mr. Jefferson. After all, you people from Hollywood will be gone and we'll still be here dealing with the aftermath of your storytelling. Please be conscientious."* She then put a hand to my face and continued. *"You seem like such a nice girl."* I smiled and tried to be respectful of her feelings, *"But I think Sally Hemings was a nice girl too."* The woman frowned then quickly left. We never saw her again. But this happened quite a bit. Jefferson lovers showing up and asking that Virginia's favorite son not be vilified by "Hollywood."

One day, I was given the message that Shannon Lanier, one of the Madison Hemings descendants, would be in Washington D.C., and wanted to drive down to watch us filming. He wanted to know if he could bring Jane Feldman, who was photographing the book they were writing together on the Hemings/Jefferson descendants. I was excited. Shannon is one of the sweetest, most well mannered young men I've ever met. A guy whose visit I was truly looking forward to.

Mare Winningham, and Sam Neill with descendants Julia Jefferson Westerinen, and Dorothy Jefferson Westerinen on the set.

That Wednesday, Shannon and Jane arrived on the set. I didn't know Jane and vice versa, but something clicked. I loved her instantly. We talked like two old sorority sisters who hadn't seen each other in years and I knew I had made a special friend for life. Jane took photos while Shannon met the cast. Everyone embraced him as a living testament to the story we were telling and I promised him that in the next month, if we could arrange it, we'd have him back to actually be in the movie as an extra. Then we watched the scene being shot and our director let Shannon stand behind the camera with the producers to watch the monitors. The scene was one in which Martha Jefferson (Mare Winningham) tells Thomas Jefferson (Sam Neill) she wants to be a nun while Lady Maria Cosway (Kelly Rutherford) is resentful of Jefferson's seeming preoccupation with anyone but her. Kelly was the most divine Lady Maria Cosway and Shannon got autographs, photos with the cast and the chance to watch a movie being made about his ancestors. In many ways Shannon's presence on the set really made the experience all the more real for all of us.

Not long after Shannon and Jane left, I extended invitations to other descendants to come to our set and watch filming. Julia and Dorothy Westerinen from Staten Island, and William Dalton from Columbus agreed to come and their visit was a three day party. The first night they arrived Wendy and I took them to dinner and we all shot video of the event. Over the next two days, Julia, Dorothy, Billy and I bonded. In fact, Billy, Wendy and I closed down many a night spot in Richmond and some of my fondest memories of the shoot are those days on the set with them. But one moment was very emotional.

We were watching the scene where Jefferson is coming home to Monticello from Paris and all the slaves run up to greet him. I started to pay attention to the slave "extras." During a break we started talking to them and discovered the African American extras had given up days of work to participate in the filming of what they thought was an important story. It turns out, there were several teachers, two nurses, an accountant, a writer, several bankers, and 40% of them were college graduates. But when they donned the costumes of their ancestors and dramatized the slave mentality of the downtrodden, they, like me, became emotional. Much like the scene I played in "Roots" as Kunta Kinte was beaten and all of us who played slaves actually cried, I cried. I cried because these educated, articulate, intelligent people would not be who they are now, had not their African ancestors gone through a living hell and survived to build a lasting bridge to the future. A future allowing all of us the opportunity to succeed. Julia and Dorothy shared their discovery of their African-American ancestry in 1976 and the impact it had on their lives. They told us how they have embraced their mixed heritage and how they view the world from both sides of the coin. Dorothy Westerinen recounts:

My name is Dorothy Jefferson Westerinen and I am the great-great-great granddaughter of Eston Hemings Jefferson, who was Thomas Jefferson and Sally Hemings' youngest child. My uncle, John Weeks Jefferson, supplied blood in 1998 for Dr. Foster's DNA test, which resulted in proof, for the first time in 200 years, that Jefferson and Hemings did indeed have an affair that resulted in at least one child, Eston. My branch of the family had "passed" into white society long ago, and knowledge of our African-American heritage was lost to us until 1976.

News about the DNA results broke nationwide and my family was deluged with media attention. This ultimately resulted in an appearance on the Oprah Winfrey show, where we met our African American cousins from Thomas Woodson and Madison Hemings branches for the first time. The historical impact of this meeting paled in comparison to the blessing it has been to reunite with family members after a 150 years separation.

When Tina Andrews called to ask my mother Julia and me to come down to Virginia and visit the set of "Sally Hemings: An American Scandal," we were thrilled to participate. To watch a movie being filmed about our grandmother was a special treat.

Ever since I learned of my African-American ancestry, I wondered about Sally and what she was like. I couldn't wait to see how Tina would present her story.

I didn't expect the emotional impact of meeting Carmen Ejogo as Sally Hemings. Though I knew she was acting a role, it was inspiring to watch her in costume, playing a woman about whom I'd admired, dreamed and thought about for years. There are no portraits of Sally Hemings in existence today, and seeing Carmen filled a void I didn't know was present in my heart. It was terrific at last to put a face to Sally's memory.

As we watched the movie unfold, my mother and I were delighted with Tina's image of Sally as an independent, strong-willed woman who stood up to Thomas Jefferson and forced him to take responsibility for their children's well being. I was glad that Tina didn't portray Sally as a slave without free will or influence, and that she made Sally's independence and courage live.

The character of Betty Hemings, Sally's mother, was beautifully played by Diahann Carroll and echoed this matriarchal strength. Betty's story reinforced the point of how tough one would have to be to survive slavery, much less triumph over it the way her sacrifices enabled her descendants to do. I was pleased Ms. Carroll was chosen to play this part. I trusted that her portrayal would be powerful, and I was not disappointed. In addition, to have the opportunity to meet someone of Ms. Carroll's stature was a great pleasure, and we found her to be as warm and gracious as her public image.

Meeting Sam Neill was also enjoyable. He listened to my mother's stories of our family history with real interest. I thought he did a great job as Jefferson, showing his struggle to balance his knowledge of what was morally right with the cruel reality of slave ownership. Since my discovery of my African roots, I have had difficulty coming to terms with my great-great-great-great grandfather's hypocrisy. The way Jefferson was depicted in the movie didn't let him off the hook, but gave us a glimpse into this complicated, tortured man.

Because of the way Jefferson has been turned into an American icon, history has not been kind to Sally Hemings. For countless years, historians who want the story of her affair with Thomas Jefferson whitewashed have smeared her name. But when I think of my grandmother, I see her as Tina imagined her - standing up for her own rights and for the rights of others. I see her raising her children to look to the future and overcome the burden of slavery. I see her as a strong woman who turned her affair with Jefferson into a ticket to freedom for her children. Now, America will see her that way too.

During the course of filming, we encountered many obstacles. We had tried to utilize some of the descendants as extras, however, daily changes in the schedule made it impossible due to cast illnesses and weather. It was my biggest regret. In fact, the weather proved to be the greatest impediment. From the beginning, because of the 100 degree heat and humidity, carpenters building the Monticello set could only work six hours a day. Then, if we weren't dealing with heat we'd suffer through rain. In fact Hurricane Floyd blew onto the eastern seaboard and in addition to the terror and destruction it wreaked on the inhabitants in Virginia and other states, our set and the roads leading to it were flooded halting production from September 15th through the 17th. As a result we went over budget and over schedule, Craig put up his house and some of his own money and somehow the actors held on and our valiant crew held up. Finally, on October 17, 1999, we wrapped. That is when our capable post production team went into high gear. My second regret was that we could not use the photos the descendants sent to me at the end of the film.

I was not on the set when we wrapped. I was in Los Angeles finishing my obligation to Warner Bros. I felt bad about it because the production represented so many years of my life and I was not there to say goodbye to cast and crew, the good people of Richmond and everyone who had made it possible. But Warners had been patiently waiting through the production and could wait no longer. They, too, had a production schedule. Shortly thereafter, our "Monticello" was dismantled. Craig videotaped it for posterity and all of us were just a little bit saddened. Tuckahoe Plantation went back to normal as did Centre Mansion, and the actors went on to other employment. All that was left to do now was wait for our director to deliver his cut of the project.

Line Producer Gerrit van der Meer and Executive Producer Craig Anderson on the set in Petersberg, Virginia. Both are in front of Centre Mansion which served as our "Paris" location.

My favorite photo of Mare Winningham in a quiet moment on the set. Mare's work in the difficult role of "Martha Jefferson" was like fine lace--subtle, textured, beautiful

Chapter Nine

A MINISERIES AIRS - REACTIONS, REVIEWS, AFTERMATH

On late November, 1999, the first cut of "The Memoirs of Sally Hemings" was delivered to my door. It was unbelievably beautiful and poignant. Aside from a need for additional voice-overs for historical clarification and context, or to better understand motivations, the miniseries was an emotionally moving experience, and I was for the most part pleased. The network was estatic and began pulling out the promotional artillery. Before it was over, Sally Hemings and Thomas Jefferson were on the sides of buses and billboards from Maine to California.

Then, in early January, while we were editing and scoring the final cut, I received an e-mail from one of the descendants who told me there was going to be a press conference in a few weeks and to expect good news from the "folks at Monticello." The person could not go into detail as they were sworn to secrecy, but I was told to make sure I bought a nice dress for the premiere screening I was planning in Columbus, Ohio on February 5. Well, on January 26, 2000, I arose to wonderful news for the descendants of Sally Hemings and Thomas Jefferson. The Thomas Jefferson Memorial Foundation released its findings after a year long investigation into the facts after the DNA. Daniel P. Jordan, president of the foundation, made the announcement and had written copies of the report available. In it he said:

"...Although paternity cannot be established with absolute certainty, our evaluation of the best evidence available suggests the strong likelihood that Thomas Jefferson and Sally Hemings had a relationship over time that led to the birth of one, and perhaps all, of the known children of Sally Hemings. We recognize that honorable people can disagree on this subject, as indeed they have for over two hundred years. Further, we know that the historical record has gaps that perhaps can never be filled and mysteries that can never be fully resolved. Finally, we stand ready to review any fresh evidence at any time and to reassess our understanding of the matter in light of more complete information. But for now, we will move forward to implement the findings of the research committee in a way that reflects the Foundation's ongoing commitment to scholarship..." Jordan went on to say that, *"Whether it was love or lust, rape or romance, no one knows, and it's unlikely that anyone will ever know."*

I personally regretted that the report did not include the Woodson's as descendants of Hemings and Jefferson's first born son Tom, but the Woodson DNA test findings resulted in a negative match. But as so many of the Woodson's have privately lamented—until someone exhumes Thomas Jefferson's remains and tests his actual DNA against any of the descendants', one cannot dismiss the Woodson's 200 year oral history. The omission of the Woodson's was also a shame to me because more Woodson descendants I'd interviewed felt the relationship between Mr. Jefferson and Ms. Hemings was one of affection.

On Friday, February 4, 2000 I left for Columbus, Ohio. With the announcement of the TJMF report, the Eston Hemings DNA results, a miniseries I felt good about, and a new dress, I boarded a plane headed for a private screening for the descendants of what we were now calling, "Sally Hemings: An American Scandal."

I had no idea I would be as nervous as I was. I've been on stage, on television, and a public speaker all my life, but nothing had prepared me for the feelings I was now experiencing in presenting this project to the public for the first time. On the flight I began to mentally backtrack over the preceding year of production and my reasons for wanting to present the story in the first place. But as the plane taxied to the gate, I was shaking. Everything suddenly became a bad omen. The fact the plane was an hour late leaving Los Angeles was an omen. We almost missed the connection in Chicago where mother and "aunt" Ann were set to join us—another omen. The fact my luggage was lost and didn't show until an hour before the screening the next day—omen three. Everything from missed cabs to lost hotel reservations portended doom and gloom. I kept checking my horoscope and going over my karma. *"Had I inadvertently screwed over anyone to get here?"* I asked myself.

Thank God my mother, Ann and Stephen were there for support because I seriously considered flying back to Los Angeles. It would be easier for me to await my fate with the television critics whose bows and arrows would be pointed my way the next week anyway. At least I could hide from them. I would not be face-to-face, up close and personal with reviewers. I could always tear up their opinions, fling them to the wind, or burn them in my fireplace while shouting obscenities if I chose. But a public screening of this story? A screening specifically organized for the descendants of Thomas Jefferson and Sally Hemings whose story I was telling? Was I crazy? Was I just inviting insult? Creating it? Attracting it? Where was my mind?

I had always wanted the premiere screening held in Ohio. The state has the largest concentration of Hemings/Jefferson descendants in the country. Ohio is where brothers Tom Hemings (Woodson), Madison Hemings and Eston Hemings moved when they left Virginia, Monticello, and the ownership of Thomas Jefferson. Their offspring and generations of offspring to follow still live in the southern regions. Chillicothe, in particular, still has a huge faction of descendants. I thought it only proper to pay homage to this enormous group of people who continually find themselves ignored, maligned by the press, or reconciled to history as the progeny born of sexual favors between a president and his slave property. And that is if they are even acknowledged at all.

Over 600 invitations had gone out. I had been working for months on the screening when I should have been writing my next two projects. But I wasn't working alone. Shay Banks-Young, a Madison Hemings descendant, and Julia Jefferson Westerinen, an Eston Hemings Jefferson descendant, had been working hard too. Julia alerted as many descendants as she was aware of throughout the country and urged them to send lists of their family member's addresses. I hired an assistant to start compiling the lists so we would know how many invitations to send. Lists began to arrive in late December. The Woodson list was the first to arrive. The family is very organized. They have a web site (www.woodson.org) and knowledge of the whereabouts of nearly every member of their prodigious clan. Their list came alphabetized and, thankfully, on mailing labels which was extremely helpful since there were at least 350 of them alone.

Shay, too, had gotten word out to all the Hemings descendants in Ohio. Though Shay and I differed on my approach to the story, we discovered we had someone in common who had encouraged and inspired us both in our separate journeys toward the Sally Hemings truth–author Alex Haley. Shay went out of her way to arrange for the auditorium on the campus of Ohio State University once we realized we had more descendants than expected planning to attend. She contacted Edwin "Ed" Clay, the dynamic director of WOSU, the university's public broadcasting station, who agreed to host and underwrite the entire event including catering the food in addition to providing the 500 seat auditorium at the Fawcett Center. Ed's Director of Publicity, Don Scott, a charming man with impeccable taste, coordinated the press releases and organized two local PBS presentations on the subject of Sally Hemings and Thomas Jefferson which would spotlight several of the descendants along with myself. On top of that, Shay arranged for her son Doug (actually, the Reverend William Douglas Banks) from Pennsylvania, to fly in and give the sermon at Abiding Faith Baptist church that Sunday. It would be a spiritual treat for all who were staying overnight after the screening. A larger church, Ascension Lutheran, located next door to Abiding Faith also agreed to lend its sanctuary to accommodate the large crowd wanting to worship. Shay and her church arranged for many organizations to come onboard to help make the event possible. Food and drinks were donated, State Representative Ray Miller would speak, Pastor Raymond Caruthers would officiate, and Columbus City Council member Charleta Tavares also agreed to speak. So there was no backing out now. Music had to be faced. The proverbial fat lady was singing. I had waited 16 years to see this project on the air and we were ready for launch. The countdown was on. Five, four, three, two, one…

… Lift off.

We arrived at the Fawcett Center Hotel in Columbus around 6:30 that Friday evening. I was furious because my luggage was God knows where and all I had were the clothes on my back. I didn't have toothpaste or a hairbrush. I had no idea when my luggage would arrive, and I had to appear on the WOSU PBS program the next morning at nine o'clock. I also knew I was having dinner with Julia, Shay, Billy Dalton and their families that evening. A lack of clothing wasn't my only concern; as mother and I checked in, Aunt Ann was having a problem with her room. They hadn't made a reservation and the place was packed with descendants. While she was working out the details with the desk clerk, I called Shay to tell her I had arrived.

"Tina, are you ready for this? The descendants are out in full force. Hundreds are here and we're all going to meet in one of the banquet rooms downstairs for dinner."

"How many "hundreds?" I inquired in shock.

"You haven't heard? At least 800 people are here for the screening tomorrow night. Almost everybody sent in their RSVP's and more."

I hung up the phone and started trembling again. Eight hundred people? That was more than the auditorium could hold. When did so many RSVP's arrive? At last count on the Wednesday before that Friday there were slightly over 350. Turns out when the invitations had run out, descendants got the RSVP response number and called in. No one wanted to be left out. Finally, after calling Ed Clay, I was informed that after 800, they simply had to stop accepting requests. As it stood, WOSU would have to provide two overflow rooms just to accommodate the crowd. Naturally, I was excited, nervous, overjoyed… and scared to death.

When I finally got to my room, I prayed to God to just give me strength and protection. (Prayer is something you've heard me call upon quite a bit throughout my experience with this project.) Prayer, and trust in higher power, is all I have sometimes to comfort, console, and reassure me during trying times.

The hotel sent up toothpaste and toothbrushes and I borrowed a scarf, a hairbrush and some red lipstick from my mother. Then, after freshening up, I went downstairs now in my same but accented traveling clothes. Shay introduced me, and as we entered the banquet room I held my chest in utter amazement.

The room was filled with black, white, beige and tan Hemings family members ranging in age from Michele Cooley-Quille's infant, Alicia, to an eighty-four year old woman who only wanted to grab my hand and squeeze it. "Thank you for telling this story," she said in a voice quivering with age, yet as ebullient as a child's, "I don't care what you've got in it. You're telling it and America is gonna know who we are now."

The number of Woodson descendants who attended also struck me. Most of us were feeling frustrated for the Woodson clan after the release of the Thomas Jefferson Memorial Foundation's findings which had rejected their strong oral history of decendance from Tom Hemings. I was also nervous about the descendant's concerns over the title change. I had received more than a few calls before I left Los Angeles from those who threatened not to attend the screening for fear it was "some whitewashed CBS propaganda."

Initially, the miniseries was announced and promoted as "The Memoirs of Sally Hemings." But a month before the official press tour and the scheduled airing, the network made the decision to change the title. We were all understandably worried about our competition on ABC, "Who Wants To Be A Millionaire" which was eclipsing everything in its path and we were scheduled to go head-to-head with it the first hour of the first night. The thinking was if people were flipping through the TV Guide looking for something to watch on Sunday night and saw "…Millionaire" or a project called "Memoirs of… someone-you-didn't-know-connected with-a-dead-President,"— which would you watch? I was asked to come up with a title that included both Sally Hemings' name and the word "Scandal" in it. People love watching scandals unfold on television. They react to the word "scandal." The country was just emerging from quite a salacious one in the White House and this would be the presentation of another one— only some 200 years earlier. I was also encouraged not to use Thomas Jefferson's name in the title for fear people would dismiss the project as a documentary-style history lesson. All understandable, acceptable suggestions.

But naturally my personal concern was that Sally Hemings not be portrayed (thus condemned) as the sole blame for a scandal. There were two people involved in the relationship, one of whom was Thomas Jefferson. So I felt compelled to protect Sally's name. I had written the project from the slave woman's perspective because someone had to give Sally a voice. I did not want her to be the sole voice associated with a negative. So, again, I prayed on it and thought about America's inability to accept Sally for who she was and what she meant to Jefferson, thus, an *"American scandal"* kept running through my head. Jody Frisch, head of publicity for Craig Anderson Productions, and I came up with a few suggestions, then after calling Michele Cooley-Quille, (I was concerned about acceptance of the change), we signed off on "Sally Hemings: An American Scandal." However, even with all our care, I knew there would be dissenting voices and I found myself repeating the reason for the title change several times in interviews all over the country, as well as at dinner that night at the Fawcett Center.

But this proved to be minutia in comparison to what lay ahead. The appreciation, support and acceptance I received from the entire Hemings family that night, and what transpired thereafter was powerful, emotional and inspirational. I was embraced by the whole family—sight unseen, film unseen—and as the one night magically turned into the next, I somehow knew God would take care of the outcome.

That Saturday night my luggage finally arrived an hour before I was set to go downstairs and present the film. My husband held me close and whispered, "Remember, it's only a movie, not your life. Keep things in perspective and ask God to walk you through this." But I couldn't tell my husband this *was* my life. It had consumed a third of my life. I couldn't tell him how important it was that this screening go well. But I did take his advice. I closed my eyes and asked God to walk me through it. The answer I received almost in the instant I prayed was, "Trust yourself and the work." I then looked at myself in the mirror, smiled, then ala Bob Fosse, let out a resounding, "It's showtime!"

When I arrived downstairs, the lobby was filled with descendants. A table was set up with the names of every guest and color dots for each branch of the family were placed on each name tag...red for Madison, yellow for Woodson's and blue for Eston Hemings descendants. Then everyone went into the theater or the overflow rooms.

I found I could not sit in the audience with everyone else as the theatre went dark. I was too nervous, so I was pacing in a small projection booth in the back like a playwright opening night on Broadway. My heart was in my mouth and forced deep breaths were ineffective. I had Kleenex stuffed into my pockets so I could keep the sweat from forming on my face. I didn't want to look a nervous wreck for the news media which had gathered en masse in the lobby. I kept perusing the crowd. There was not an empty seat in the house. Present, amongst others, were the descendants themselves along with Dr. Eugene Foster, Annette Gordon-Reed, Dianne Swann-Wright, director of special programs at Monticello; and Lucia Stanton, senior historian at Monticello. As the credits rolled I couldn't help thinking, "Okay, at least you did it. It's on the screen. You got the story made. Now turn it over to higher power." Then as the credits rolled, I saw my mother nudge my husband and grin.

So far so good.

There was a joke in the first act and when the audience laughed at it, I let out a sigh of relief. Maybe this wouldn't be such a horrible experience after all. Finally I felt comfortable enough to go into the lobby and give an interview to the news crew there to tape a segment for the national broadcast of the CBS Evening News. You better believe there was no hint of the jitters I felt inside exhibited on the outside while I was "on camera." There could be no vulnerability or the media would attack like vultures. Fortunately it was Randall Pinkston, a correspondent at CBS News, New York, who was doing the interview. Randall had been following my journey on this project for a year. He and I met at Monticello in May 1999 when the black descendants were first invited to meet their white Jefferson cousins. Randall had mistaken me for a descendant of Sally Hemings and when I told him I was doing a miniseries on the story he asked me to keep him posted. Now he had the exclusive for the news division and wanted to know how it felt to finally see Sally "live" after 16 years of trying. I told him "pretty darned good."

Just as the interview was wrapping the doors to the auditorium opened and the crowd came spilling out. It was intermission between night one and two. The crowd was enthusiastic, effervescent, vocal. Microphones were instantly shoved into faces.

"What did you think?"

"Do you like it?"

"How factual is it?"

I kept an ear open while I signed autographs, took pictures and gave interviews to local news. I shook hands, hugged people and eavesdropped on reactions which were so wonderful, so positive. I also met Dr. Eugene Foster who had conducted the DNA tests which helped the miniseries get off the ground after such a long struggle. But still the devil was at work poisoning my mind. There was that eerie, lingering feeling a shoe was about to drop somewhere. The movie wasn't over yet. There were still two more hours to go before reactions to the film could really be assessed.

But halfway through the conclusion my fears were allayed. A moment transpired

The Descendants of Sally Hemings and Thomas Jefferson at the World Premiere of "Sally Hemings: An American Scandal" in Columbus Ohio, February 5, 2000. Over 800 were witness to the story of their ancestors.

onscreen that caused an unexpected reaction from the audience. It was so spontaneous and emotional it brought me to tears. Sally Hemings was now an older woman of 52. In her younger years she had made a wish to a slave conjure-woman to see her first born son Tom again and she wanted to rid herself of James Thompson Callender, the man who originally caused the scandal by revealing her relationship with Jefferson in the press. Callender was found drowned not long after Sally made the wish. But in this scene, years later, Sally sees a white man on a horse in the distance and starts running toward him. As she got closer she recognized the man and the music swelled to a crescendo. When the red-haired white man said "Hello, mama" the entire auditorium cheered. Woodsons howled. They felt validated that their oral history was on the screen and a part of television history despite the Thomas Jefferson Memorial Foundation report to the contrary. Their tradition had held that Tom Hemings ran away to a nearby plantation owned by a Jefferson cousin named Woodson. There, he changed his name to Woodson and took Jemima, one of the Woodson slaves as his wife. And all of this was right there on screen.

It was a defining moment for me as well because it showed just how powerful words on a page can become when translated to the screen. How they can elicit such deeply felt emotion. When I witnessed the descendants' reaction, I broke down into tears of joy because I somehow knew everything was going to be alright.

Finally the miniseries concluded and the lights came up. The descendants gave me a rousing standing ovation, and the spirit of my father, now dead, came to me. I heard his presence clearly say, "I'm proud of you." To this day I could not tell you what I said to that audience when I found my footing and was able to walk to the stage through my tears. I do however

remember thanking father/mother God and asking him to allow me to be the portal through which his words flowed for I, at that moment, had none of my own. All I do have—is the memory of that night and the feeling it would be the triumph and the apex of the project, and that a goal set many years ago had been realized.

On Sunday night, February 6, 2000, I returned from the screening in Ohio glowing with a sense of accomplishment and satisfaction. Before I went to bed that night I wrote in my gratitude journal, "Thank you God, for all the blessings you have bestowed on me this past weekend. Thank you for allowing me to come through production and emerge with product the people for whom the project was intended appreciated. Thank you Lord, for my health and happiness and for allowing me a mate who always reminds me of the joy when sometimes I forget." Then I went to sleep. A peaceful, restful sleep.

I had no idea it would be the calm before the storm. My world was about to explode the next week, this time in a very public, professionally challenging way that by the following Friday, I would be incapable of getting out of bed. I received a call from Wendy Kram. "Do you believe that review from *USA Today*?" I flew to my car and drove to the nearest newsstand where I purchased the paper then stood there stunned as I read it. It was the most venomous, hurtful, unworthy personal attack, and suddenly I felt like Sally Hemings herself…misunderstood and deprecated. Tuesday brought a fresh round of interview requests and radio talk show invitations. Unfortunately it also brought a fresh round of gut wrenching reviews. I began to analyze them. It seemed reviewers were becoming Jefferson affectionadios who had lost all objectivity with respect to good drama as it related to history. I compared the reviews to the "Joan of Arc" miniseries and noticed that no one commented on whether that writer was actually in the room to hear God speak to Joan or what exactly God said to her. It was an interpretation. A dramatization. But with this story, once again, everyone wanted irrefutable proof that Sally danced with Jefferson in Versailles or that she taught her children French (despite the fact her son, Madison uses the word "enciente"—meaning pregnant—in his memoirs), or that Sally helped slaves escape to freedom in the North. They called it "soap opera" completely misunderstanding that my acting on one did not constitute my writing one. Wednesday brought more interviews including one I'll always treasure with Army Archerd for his Morning Report column in the Daily Variety. He was delightful. But even that once-in-a-lifetime interview could not make up for the whammy I received on Thursday.

Bright and early, a phone call awakened me. It was my aunt in Philadelphia. "Tina, they're picketing in front of the CBS station, talking about your show." Shortly after I hung up the phone, a network publicist called me. "There are protesters picketing the Philadelphia affiliate station and two newspapers want your comments. You're going to have to give them a statement." I called Byron Woodson, one of the descendants who lives in Philadelphia. I asked him what was going on. He told me there were 20 to 25 people who were upset by the ad campaign by CBS heralding, "The Greatest Love Story Never Told," as well as the tone of the piece being presented as a "love story." I asked Byron if he had spoken to anyone at the newspapers as he was a descendant and it would be interesting to get a descendant's point of view. He said no. I asked him if I could have them contact him as well. He said absolutely.

I then called the CBS publicity people and told them I would be happy to speak to the press and to give me the number. I spoke to the Philadelphia Tribune, in fact I was honored to. The Tribune is one of the oldest black newspapers in the country. I recounted some of my research, my experiences being thrown off the air and my accounts from descendants. I cannot say for sure if I disswayed any concerns or objections, but I did state my case sincerely as an African American dramatist and asked that everyone hold their comments until after they watched the miniseries because we did a pretty good job of presenting all political points of view.

After that, I took to my bed. My husband gave me the only thing that works in times of depression—vanilla Hagen Daz. It's hard to be depressed when you've got two tons of ice cream in your gut. I called mother and asked if I could fly in the following day. I wasn't sure I wanted to be at home in California or with her in Chicago when the miniseries aired given what I was going through that week culminating with the picketing in Philadelphia. I told her for all I knew crosses might be burning on my lawn. Mother laughed. "And what about that gown you bought for the Image Award you're presenting tomorrow? Bring that home too. I'll look great in it at my next dance." I slapped my forehead. "You can't go home, dummy. You've got the Image Awards tomorrow." It also signified a halt to the ice cream if I intended to get into that dress.

Later, both Sunta and Joan called to say "good luck." Sunta, added that if I needed network presence on any of the interviews I was giving in connection with the controversy, she'd be willing to give an interview. All I had to do was ask. I appreciated the offer deeply because it isn't often network executives are willing to put themselves on the line to go public for their choices or fight for a writers' interpretation. The good folks at CBS must have known I was feeling a bit like Salman Rushdie, so that vote of confidence came as a welcomed bastion which I will always esteem.

But as luck would have it, my heart was lifted in joy by Saturday. Most of the reviews and commentaries were in from around the country and instead of being dragged through a deluge of negatives, I was pleasantly surprised. Following are a few excerpts:

"...Indeed An American Scandal argues against the view of Hemings as the helpless victim of Jefferson's advances. Here, she defends her children and her household perquisites with an intelligence and ferocity that are seldom attributed to slaves in the movies." "Sally Hemings: An American Scandal is a breakthrough film that offers a convincing even visionary portrait of the relationship while broadening public awareness of details that are primarily known only to specialists."
Brent Staples, TV GUIDE

"...Controversy alone does not equal artistic success. Even if it were pure fiction, Sally Hemings: An American Scandal would stand as a beautifully crafted, seamlessly acted movie. It bleeds with such emotion that clever salespeople at CBS should have wangled a little money from the Kimberly-Clark company for stimulating heavy use of Kleenex..." "Sally - feisty, beautiful, intelligent - could have stepped out of a Danielle Steel novel, if Steel imbued her characters with the kind of depth that Tina Andrews includes in her script..."
Jonathan Storm, THE PHILADELPHIA INQUIRER

"...Its Sally is no passive victim. Her beauty is matched by her intelligence and force of will, and she often confronts her lover on matters of importance to her family and to her people, pointing out the dissonance between Jefferson's words and deeds..."
Barbara D. Phillips, WALL STREET JOURNAL

"...The gold mine itself is the convincing portrayal of Jefferson and Hemings together at Monticello. For nearly 38 years they lived a double life: as husband and wife and as master and slave... A major achievement of An American Scandal is to graphically show us how it probably happened. As in a Jane Austen novel, everyone knows the truth, but everyone also agrees that it cannot be spoken. The powerful effect of this film springs from its ability to appeal simultaneously to our hearts and our heads. It's a bittersweet love story that...effectively symbolizes the covert racial mingling we always suspected, and it allows us to visualize and personalize the central paradoxes of American history, the chief one being the awkward coexistence of chattel slavery and human affection..."
Joseph J. Ellis, TV GUIDE

But there was one memorable pan that called us to task for the love scenes that pretty much summed up all the others:

"...Most accounts that have been handed down of unions between slave owners and their female property suggest that these were pretty one-sided relationships—owner forces himself on slave, who has the choice of submitting, dying or being sold. Here, Sally Hemings submits willingly, slipping off her robe before Jefferson has so much as kissed her..." "...How could they make a teenage Sally the initiator of this liaison? To suggest she was making a conscious choice to become her master's concubine?..."
Megan Rosenfeld, WASHINGTON POST

But then, glory hallelujah, on Sunday we aired.

What gives all of us solace—particularly those of us who were there from the beginning, and what allows me personally to rise in the morning even to this day—was the audience response. My agent called at 7 am Monday morning to say congratulations, we were number #1. Even though "Who Wants To Be A Millionaire" won the first hour, our ratings had gone through the roof! 20 million people had watched the first night. We had a 20 share. It meant we were a hit! People called the network with congratulations. My phone did not stop ringing. My fax machine churned out congratulatory faxes. Florist deliveries were non-stop as were offers for meetings and subsequent employment. Notes and cards arrived daily for the whole week. Before the CBS "Jesus" miniseries which aired in May, "Sally Hemings: An American Scandal" was the highest-rated, most watched miniseries of the season. And how could I begrudge "Jesus" for topping us—let's face it, the "Son of God" does have a few fans.

On Thursday, after the second night aired, and our success was solidified, a thoughtful thing happened. Julia Westerinen called to say she wanted to fax me a letter she had received right after the screening in Ohio. She felt I should have it even though it was intended for her and she asked Mary for my permission to reprint it here. She wanted me to know the miniseries was having an impact and I cherish the following excerpt:

Dear Julia,

What a wonderful weekend this was. I came home feeling spiritually refreshed and my faith restored that there is a world of good people out there. I heard so many times people say that this weekend experience had changed their lives for the better. One person even told me, "I'm not hard-core racist but I've always been prejudiced toward whites, but this weekend has been a life-altering experience for me and I'll never be able to feel the same way I used to again." This, to me, is the heart of this movement. To be bringing the races together on common ground and healing the chasm that has divided us is the miracle, and I'm humbled to be a part of it. And none of this would have happened if it hadn't been for you and Shay and your determination and hard work to make this come about. So I want to thank you again for making this weekend happen and especially for including us. We don't even know if we're family, and yet you include us. Thank you.

I was so impressed with the movie. I must confess that I had fears at first. I feared that Jefferson would be portrayed as a rapist and a buffoon and that it was going to be just another incendiary issue that would anger the white population and not serve any other purpose than to drive the races apart. But when I saw it and saw how well it was done and how believable it was, my fears were laid to rest. I thought, "This is the way it really could have happened." I think the movie gave all of us a way of viewing the relationship in a realistic way, which is what we needed to be able to understand it. I was very pleased with it and thought Tina did an exquisite job with an extremely difficult topic. And what a terrific woman she is! I've thought many times of her story about being a lit candle with a bushel basket over it and how when she prayed for answers she realized the message she got was that she was meant to burn through that bushel basket! What a beautiful and inspiring story. Truly, this experience has changed me, too...

With Love, Mary Hemmings

By Friday of that week, the network sent us gold pocketwatches. Documentaries on the subject of Sally Hemings went into high gear. Interest in the Thomas Jefferson/Sally Hemings story was rekindled. The web site for Monticello received over three million "hits" the week we aired, and newspaper commentaries were far kinder than the previous week. The miniseries struck a chord and letters from around the country started pouring in to me. Correspondence came through my agents, the Writers Guild, newspapers, the network and the internet. One woman from Duluth, praised me for *"Telling the truth."* A man from Mill Creek, Indiana wrote: *"I can understand Jefferson's dilemma because I've fallen for a black woman in the town where I live and my family is upset by it. I don't know what to do about it..."*

But it was the letters written to Sam Neill from a class of inner-city "at risk" students at Pueblo High school in Tucson, Arizona that impressed me the most. They really understood what we were trying to communicate with the project. Sam was kind enough to share them with me, and I felt compelled to share two of them at the end of this chapter. Their English teacher, Ms. Cynthia Dagnal-Myron wrote, "... these kids are acutely aware that huge chunks of American history are left out of most textbooks..."

I also received a letter from a woman from Cleveland whose letter was revealing. She wrote: *"I don't know how much of what I saw in the program was actual fact, but I didn't care. I saw another side of Thomas Jefferson that made me understand how he could have been in love with Sally. But he also made me angry because he didn't free his slaves. It has made me want to read more about it... It also makes me want to get in touch with my own personal ancestry for I now believe for many of us if we go six generations back we probably have African or Indian or something not purely white in us. Thank you for presenting your program. It must have been hard for you. Incidentally, I had all but given up the idea of being a writer for fear of failure. Now, because of your journey* (well chronicled in the press by this time), *I think I want to try again."*

I wrote her back. "Don't 'try'. Do it. When you put action in back of a dream, it becomes a goal—and a goal is attainable." I also told her that a lot of shared creative talents went into the making of the miniseries in addition to the script. Besides the incomparable cast, we had a great director of photography in Donald M. Morgan, the aforementioned David Crank and Michael Boyd as production designer and costumer respectively, a wonderful editor in Andrew Doerfer, and a music score from Joel McNeely which still haunts me. Plus none of it would have been possible without Craig and Wendy.

As I travel the country these days lecturing on screenwriting and on Sally Hemings and Thomas Jefferson, I always tell students never to give up on their dreams. To never let life put a bushel basket over the candle of your desire. Burn through it. No matter the circumstance, how long it takes, or what they may say, make your determination to succeed burn through it.

The author with the young cast of "...American Scandal" on the set in Richmond, Virginia.

Dear Mr. Neill:

I thought that the miniseries "Sally Hemmings" was well played out. I felt that it showed how some Americans felt about not only slave and owner relationships but also black and white relationship. I see this movie as a view to what we have grown from, how Americans today changed from Americans of yesterday. The performence that you portrayed as Thomas Jefferson was very unique. I felt that it was a character that many people felt angry toward, I, on the other hand thought that the role was very courage to be able to play a role that some people really hate. I learned from this movie that things in history are not always as they appear or how society wants it to be. When you get down to the real facts every thing is really different.

Thank you for giving us a great movie

Sincerly,

A handwritten letter to actor Sam Neill by Rebecca Slayton, a junior at Pueblo High School in Tucson, Arizona after the airing of the miniseries.

To my darling children and grandchildren,

      I am Sally Hemings, your mother and grandmother. I'm writing to inform you, my little darlings, about your curiosity relating to my relationship with Thomas Jefferson. I am aware that you, my children, question why I choose to spend 38 years living with a man who could not give me my freedom or even acknowledge his love for me and you, our children. Yes, I admit that it hurt very much knowing that I could never be seen as more than a black slave and never being able to marry Mr. Jefferson. I loved him all the same. I ask you to understand that our relationship could never have been better. There is nothing that could have brought us two closer together.

      In the beginning, I am sorry to admit, that I never once thought or foresought what our relationship would do to your lives. I know it's selfish, and I'm sorry again. Mr. Jefferson, the wonderful man that he was, also never thought about it. I guess I just didn't want to face the fact that my children, our children, would never "fit" in. I remember the time when my oldest darling daughter fell for a white man. He not knowing her "original" origin fell for her also. But when he did find out that she had posed as a white woman and lied to him about his family, he grew very angry and turned very ugly towards her. This was the start of the questioning of who she was, of who you were. I'm sorry my dear, I did not know the pain you felt and the confusion with you being Mr. Jefferson's child but could never be his daughter. I know you have endured much pain in your confusing life, but it has only made you stronger and more aware, less naïve to the reality of human nature. Don't feel outcaste, your free my child!

      As for me, I too was free, am free. Mr. Jefferson freed me right after we left France. I choose to stay with him out of love, I would and could never leave him, our love is everlasting and eternal. After his withdrawal in his presidency we became even closer to each other and spent much more time together. It was a cherishable time, and will be missed. You see with Mr. Jefferson I had more freedom than I ever needed. He provided me with love, security, and you, my children. He gave me the means to take care of you and provide you with an acceptable prosperous life. With Thomas Jefferson we were safe from a lot of racist people that would like nothing but harm to come our way. In our land America, emancipated black woman, black people in general, are not seen as equals. On our plantation is where the whites wanted us to stay, too pick food and to do as we were told. You must understand that our life with Mr. Jefferson was a blessing compared to other slaves and our "freedom" from slavery.

      I led a harmonious life and regretted only giving you more freedom. I was content and happy with my life and couldn't have asked for a different setting. I love Mr. Jefferson and I love you. Please understand why I did everything I did. It was all out of love for you and for my love for Mr. Jefferson. Don't ever deny who you are or where you came from, don't be ashamed of where you came from. It is equal to any "normal" family, because love is all you need.

Love, Sally

A letter by Angelina Thierry, a junior at Pueblo High School in Tucson, Arizona, writing as "Sally Hemings." I was moved by this one.

Epilogue

"…I have a dream that one day…the sons of former slaves
and the sons of former slaveholders will be able to sit down
together at the table of brotherhood…"

Dr. Martin Luther King, Jr., 1963

The author, center, with Hemings/Jefferson descendants from left: Jean Jefferson, Mary Jefferson, Michele Cooley-Quille, Nina Boettcher, Shay Banks-Young, and Shannon Lanier surrounded by Sierra Truscott, Lucy Boettcher, Lilly Truscott, Emily Westerinen and Becky

CAN'T WE ALL JUST GET ALONG?

"...The souls of black folks are divided
by their blackness, by their Americaness..."

W.E.B. Dubois

In what has been called the ultimate "irony and tragedy" of Sally Hemings life was that she and her two sons were listed as "white" by an Albemarle County census taker in 1830. After a lifetime in search of acceptance as a person of color, Sally died considered a Caucasian woman and an enigma. When she passed away in 1835 at age 62, she was buried in the backyard of the house she shared with Madison and Eston on what is now Main Street in Charlottesville. These days that land now houses the Hampton Inn, and, sadly, scientists believe that somewhere under it is Sally's final resting place.

After the miniseries aired, Lucian K. Truscott IV invited me to attend the next meeting of the Monticello Association as one of his guests. At this meeting it would be discussed (again) whether the Hemings descendants would be allowed admittance into the Association as well as burial at Monticello. I agreed to attend. On Saturday, May 6, 2000, I stood in front of the Hampton Inn and quietly paid homage to the spirit of Sally Hemings whose life story had so inspired me. Later I went to Monticello for a reception for the Hemings and the Jefferson descendants and I could not help but experience another sense of irony. First, the sons and daughters of the former slaves of Monticello, who had on so many occasions brought wine in crystal glasses to serve the white guests of Thomas Jefferson, were themselves being served glasses of wine and hors d'oeuvres by the sons and daughters of slaveholder Jefferson at the table of brotherhood. I recall raising my glass to that bit of progress…and a dream of Dr. Martin Luther King.

Second, as I walked down Mulberry Row, where once the slave artisans and crafts people carved furniture, forged iron, smoked meats and poultry, and grew vegetables, I thought about Sally and her family. The family who was responsible for most of these chores. I thought about Peter Hemings who smoked the meats and prepared the food for the Jefferson table. I thought about Robert who tended the horses and drove Jefferson to and from the White House. I thought about Sally's sisters Critta and Thenia, dusting, sweeping and cooking for the master; of Betty Hemings doing the laundry. And I thought about Sally's brother John Hemings, Monticello's most prized furniture and cabinet maker. So much of John's magnificent furniture, particularly his campeachy chairs, has survived and is still on display at Monticello. It was John Hemings who made Thomas Jefferson's coffin—and that, in itself, presented for me the final irony.

As I reached the end of the Row, I came upon the great Jefferson Family Cemetery with the Jefferson shield and initials, "TJ" in gold leaf on the padlocked wrought iron gate. It meant something different to me this trip as the cemetery is such a source of contention and symbolism for both the Hemingses and the Jefferson's. The large obelisk which so eloquently and simplistically proclaims: "Here was buried Thomas Jefferson, author of the Declaration of American Independence, of the Statute of Virginia for religious freedom, and the father of the University of Virginia," cannot compare with the absolute nothingness which distinguishes the final resting place of Sally Hemings— the principle object of Thomas Jefferson's affections for almost four decades. I thought about Sally a lot that day as I stood at the foot of Jefferson's magnificent tomb. I thought about how she was listed on the slave inventory after Jefferson's death as worth $50.

I thought about Sally's humble little house in Charlottesville and how it stood until 1934 before another building was constructed in its place. Then I thought about how her remains may have been meaninglessly dug up and scooped away in the bowels of some John Deere earthmover and dumped God only knows where. And if her remains survived that, then she probably did not survive the building and construction of the Hampton Inn presently on the site. I thought about her legacy. What she means. What she represents for so many people all over the world. How she fits in the diaspora of African-Americans. The fact she has no marker, no ceremonious final resting place, and no acknowledgement of her existence beyond that of seamstress at Monticello is indicative of the supposed value of most slaves to America—which is no value at all.

There is no surviving slave cemetery at Monticello. The place where Betty, Priscilla, Harriet and the unknown daughter Hemings were buried along with favorite slaves like Jupiter and Sukey is unknown. Archeologists have been digging in several areas trying to locate any one of a probable four slave cemeteries on the property. These once hallowed grounds of the work force which built not only the great house on the mountain and the University of Virginia, but tilled its land, picked its tobacco, wheat and corn and ran its industry, was most likely razed by subsequent owners for whatever fleeting purpose they deemed fitting. I could not help but notice that even the Levy family, who bought Monticello after it had been purchased by Dr. Barclay to raise silkworms, still had a burial site on the grounds of Mr. Jefferson's former home. Not so Monticello's slaves...not even the Hemingses, purportedly Jefferson's most beloved servants. Yes, John Hemings built the coffin that houses the remains of Thomas Jefferson beneath the most famous headstone in Virginia. But where, pray-tell, is John Hemings himself buried? Again, final ironies.

At nine-thirty Sunday morning, May 7, 2000, I attended a memorial for Lucian's father, Lucian Truscott, III., on the burial grounds at Monticello along with the Hemings/Jefferson descendants. At this most beautiful service, as we were all gathered together to honor the deceased Mr. Truscott, once again I couldn't help thinking about bitter ironies. There in the graveyard amongst the Oak and Juniper trees were the tombstones of many members of the lineal descendants of Thomas Jefferson through his daughters Martha and Maria. And yet, also there, holding hands and tearing up at the touching remembrances of a life gone by, were black, brown, tan and white faces belonging to another lineal Jefferson family. A family, who, as of this writing, cannot be buried in the sacred burial site. Jefferson's "bastard" family, as the Hemingses would be referred to later that very day at a meeting to vote on their possible membership, were likened to the illegitimate children of Edward the Seventh. *"...Sure they may exist..."* one of the white Jefferson descendants quipped, *"...but they'll never be King, and they'll never be buried in the Royal burial site."*

I sat in astonishment with members of the much maligned Hemings family at that meeting. I thought about who carved the headstones, who dug the graves, who made the coffins and carried them to the "royal" burial site, who tended the graves, who fed the mourners afterwards, who washed their dishes and cleaned up after their horses.

Just the day before, a fringe faction of the Monticello Association attempting to call themselves The Thomas Jefferson Foundation, whose missive is to discount the DNA evidence, the TJMF report, and the entire relationship between Jefferson and Hemings, barred the Hemings descendants from a private press conference (is there such a thing?) at the Omni Hotel. This group is not to be confused with the Thomas Jefferson Memorial Foundation who conducted the investigation into Jefferson and Hemings and came forth in January 2000 with their TJMF report supporting a relationship between the two. The mock "Sergeant-at-arms" posted at the door of the conference room told the Hemingses if they were not "invited members of the press," or did not have press passes or badges, they could not attend. Lucian remained outside the doors with the Hemingses even though he was doing a story for American Heritage magazine. Still harboring my old hippie sensibilities, I suggested we all stage a sit-in. Any member of the press to emerge from that room had to see all those descendants sitting there disgruntled and frustrated, and have to ask questions. The real story was in the hall—not what was going on in the conference room. Though we never actually "sat down" we did stand there en masse and the media took note and reported the whole story and not just the bias at the news conference.

But I would be remiss if I didn't note that not all of the Monticello Association members are opposed to the Hemings descendants' admittance into the Association. In fact most were appalled at the racist way in which they had been depicted by the media the year before. So many of them are willing to let a bygone era remain past and open the door to an inclusive future. Still one can't help but wonder what is the point? Why so much emphasis on being buried where someone doesn't want you? Why stay in the fight? I asked one descendant, Dr. Michele Cooley-Quille, whose father Robert's dying wish was to be buried at Monticello—and who was denied that wish at the time of his death. Her answer was eloquent and powerful:

"I owe it to Daddy and every previous generation to fight for equity in rights and privileges due us ...due them! Martha (Wayles) and Sally bore Thomas Jefferson seven living children. The cemetery was established for his descendants. No one has the right to choose who among Jefferson's great-great-grandchildren may be buried alongside him but each of us descendants ourselves. It is our birthright. Being buried there is symbolic of achieving the equity long-due our ancestors." I also asked Michele why she felt the Sally Hemings story has such lasting impact. She said: *"Although Sally had no choice, Thomas Jefferson chose to have a 38-year relationship with her. Was it love or was it rape? Only Thomas and Sally truly know. The greater effect of Sally Hemings' story is exposing people to the girl-who-became-the-woman who captivated such a powerful, ingenious man's attentions and buoyed him so that he could make the innumerable contributions to our country that he is revered for today. Sally raised their five living children to be cultured intellectuals who made tremendous contributions in their own right. Her accomplishments are even more awe inspiring given that she was a slave."*

My take on the Sally Hemings story has received much the same reaction as the Hemings family story. We all suffer the slings and arrows of public attack. In the

Hemingses continued quest for simple recognition, they endure all manner of ridicule from people who don't realize they did not choose this fight. They were born into it. In a letter to the New York Times, a woman complained about a comment a white Hemings descendant made in an article about a street in Charlottesville being named for Sally Hemings which was before the city council. The comment stated in part: *"We want our family to recognize us, to embrace us."* The complaining woman's commentary was that she was saddened to see Sally's descendants acting *"like grateful supplicants at the prospect of being recognized by the master's family." The descendant's response to the complaint was indicative of most minorities concerns in this country today that, "If we Hemings and Jefferson's cannot heal the racial rift at the family level, what hope does this nation have?"*

Hope for this nation indeed. In April of 2000, I took part in a symposium on Thomas Jefferson and Sally Hemings at the University of Richmond. I had been elated to participate for I felt it would be a lively, serious, thought provoking discussion and I would be in good company. Professors Jan Lewis, Annette Gordon-Reed, Clarence Walker and Thelma W. Foote would be on the panel as well as Dr. Eugene Foster, writers Henry Wiencek and Barbara Chase-Riboud; and Dianne Swann-Wright and Lucia Stanton from Monticello.

Above: Dr. Eugene Foster, 3rd from left, performed the DNA test linking Thomas Jefferson and Sally Hemings through son Eston. He is flanked by Stephen Gaines, Mrs. Jane Foster, and the author. This photo was taken after the Klan was escorted from the University of Richmond at a Jefferson / Hemings symposium. Obviously we were all relieved.

Well, so too, were members of the Ku Klux Klan in attendance. They came, not donned in white sheets and hoods like the Klan of yore, but with their confederate pins, racist attitudes and misplaced anger concerning "the continuing systematic defamation of Thomas Jefferson." And, as it turns out, several of the same people who were so unpleasant and disruptive at the Monticello meeting I attended in May, including a man who stood up and announced to all that Jefferson was "the best friend the American slave ever had," were also present at this symposium. This suggests to me an organized attempt to keep the truth silenced whatever that truth may be. I was understandably nervous and once more called on God to move his hand of tranquility over the auditorium. He did, and after lunch the panel was informed the Klan had been removed from the campus grounds.

But oddly, shortly after I returned home from that symposium, I received an anonymous package. It had no return address, no note. When I opened it, it was a book entitled: "The Interracial Dating Book For Black Women Who Want To Date White

Men." At first I was amused—because naturally, if you write about an interracial relationship and you're a black woman, your burning desire—is to date white guys. If you've played a character on television who was in an interracial relationship, of course, your real life quest—is to date white guys. If you speak out against discrimination and feel there can be interracial relationships between equal partners manifesting equal affections, quite naturally—you've set your sights—on dating white guys. Understand, I have nothing whatsoever against Caucasian men—some of my closest business associates and best friends are Caucasian men (smile). Yet for 15 years I have been happily married to a smart, humorous, attractive African-American man who is possessed with the patience of Job to be married to me.

But then I stopped being amused. I became annoyed. I was sent this book to make a point. And as unenlightened and insipid as the point was, it was based on misconceptions people still have about race and race relations. Fallacies steeped in centuries of ignorance and misguided intent that become divisive, insulting, and perpetuates the dissonance between us. It is too simplistic for people to assume because African-Americans are interested in being included in the American Dream, which is so willingly accorded the majority culture, that their ultimate interest lies in aspiring to, emulating or *becoming* the majority culture. It is the equivalent of Sally Hemings being deemed *"white"* near the end of her life when her goal was equal access as who and what she was…black.

America's garden is beautiful. Can we not learn to appreciate all the flowers in the garden, not just roses, and expand our experiences to include and accept all cultures and hybrids which derive from that shared experience? Can we not learn to live in a country where the Jefferson inspired credo "All men are created equal" can be lived in thought and deed despite the internal hypocrisy of the man who penned it?

In the aftermath of the miniseries, I went to my quiet place and thanked Higher Power for allowing us to tell a story which piqued the interest of our viewers, pro and con. My hope was to get Americans thinking and talking about race and race relations. Perhaps we will come to understand that after all is said and done we, as Americans of African, Asian and European descent, do not live in an America with independent pasts. Our histories, whether we wish to accept it or not, are intricately entangled and interdependent.

Sally Hemings currently occupies a distinctive place in popular culture, history and current politics. Though denied her place in Jefferson's life during her own lifetime and his, Miss Hemings has come to symbolize the by-product of America's almost fanatic preoccupation with race, the racial divide, and racial ambiguity. Andrew Hacker calls it "Two Nations, Black and White, Separate, Hostile, Unequal." Alex Kotlowitz refers to it as "The Other America." But I find I am an eternal optimist, and it was Rodney King whose simple observation in 1992 best sums up my own sentiments:

"Can't we all just get along?"

FADE OUT:

The Hampton Inn on Main street in Charlottesville, Virginia, is believed to be the burial site for Sally Hemings. The house she shared with sons Madison and Eston once stood on this location. There was a proposal before the city council to rename the cross street "Hemings Road" or "Hemings Way," but many African American citizens of Charlottesville were uncomfortable with the idea and it was voted down.

The grave of William Beverly Hemings, (1847-1910) son of Madison Hemings, grandson of Sally Hemings and Thomas Jefferson. William fought in the Civil War for the Union and died in a Kansas military home. He is buried in Leavenworth National Cemetery.

Since William was a direct male line descendant of Madison Hemings, it has been suggested that DNA tests be conducted on his remains to further prove (or disprove) Thomas Jefferson's paternity of Madison. This suggestion has been rejected by Hemings descendants since no one is willing to exhume Thomas Jefferson's remains for similar DNA testing.

SCREENPLAY OF:

Sally Hemings: An American Scandal

A Four Hour Miniseries

Written by

TINA ANDREWS

Formerly entitled: "The Memoirs of Sally Hemings"
Formerly entitled: "The Sally Hemings Story"
Formerly entitled: "The Mistress of Monticello"

REVISED FINAL DRAFT

MAIN TITLE AND CREDITS IN OVER:

EXT. JEFFERSON FAMILY CEMETERY - DAY

CLOSE ON...the headstone on Thomas Jefferson's grave.

> SALLY (V.O.)
> ...I do not know how history will treat Thomas
> Jefferson, I pray his legacy will not be defined by
> me...

PULL BACK TO REVEAL...SALLY HEMINGS, 53, a still beautiful, graceful
mulatto woman, turns from the grave and walks away, revealing...

EXT. MONTICELLO - DAY - ON YOUNG GIRL'S LEGS   (FLASHBACK, 1787)

Dangling from a swing in the f.g. Behind her the large mansion is an
impressive masterpiece, rich in red brick and white columns and backed against
the picturesque Blue Ridge Mountains.

> SALLY (V.O.)
> I was born Sarah Sally Hemings in the year of our
> Lord 1773. I was conceived in love, born to
> slavery, but destined to scandal...

CUT TO:

EXT. MULBERRY ROW - DAY

A slave hand belonging to Nance rings an iron bell hanging from the "Birthin'
Tree"—a large mulberry tree on the row. The bell rings at passing—into life or
into death.

EXT./INT. MONTICELLO MANSION - MORNING

CLOSE ON BETTY HEMINGS, a beautiful mulatto whose long, graying hair is
unraveling as she barks out orders to several light-skinned slaves of various ages on
her way out of the house.

> BETTY
> Hannah? Isabel! Hear the bell! Critta's havin' her baby!

Two slaves, followed by several children, come running from various parts of the
house— all heading out, all laughing and yelling, and down the steps toward the
great tree.

> SALLY (V.O.)
> ...My family, the Hemings, were unique in that we had
> last names and comprised most of the house servants. At
> Monticello, we were never referred to as slaves.
> And my mother, Betty, was its matriarch.

                                BETTY
        Sally...?!

EXT. MONTICELLO - MORNING

The young legs belonging to SALLY HEMINGS, a beautiful, child/woman of 15
with dark, waist-length pigtails, hears her mother's call, jumps off the swing and
runs after the group.

                                SALLY
        Comin', mama. Baby's here. Sister's baby's here!

They are joined by a very pregnant ISABEL as they continue down the road.

                                BETTY
        Don't you be runnin', Isabel. You'll have your
        baby now the same as Critta!

As Sally laughs we can see the plantation is abuzz with activity. Betty rushes
down Mulberry Row finding sons PETER and ROBERT HEMINGS, 18 and 24,
coming from the smokehouse. The two carry chickens ready for plucking. More
slaves join the group heading for the far end of the row.

                                BETTY
        Robert! Peter! G'on leave them chickens in the
        kitchen!

The BELL RINGS again! Betty looks up. So do the others.

                                BETTY
        Ring that bell Nance, ring that bell!

EXT. MULBERRY ROW - DAY

The now-large group reaches the last cabin as slave midwife, SUKEY, comes out
in a sweat. Holding the newborn over her head she yells to the excited group.

                                SUKEY
        It be a boy... Critta's boy child Jamy Hemings!

The crowd shouts and cheers then turns to see: Riding up through the row on horse
back is the baby's father, PETER CARR 18, and his brother SAMUEL 19,
Jefferson's white nephews.

                                PETER
        Well, another one of my pickaninnies. Oughta
        fetch $800 one day.

                                SAMUEL
        Another pretty little Hemings, no thanks to its papa.

BETTY

Massa Peter, Massa Samuel, you git them horses out
the row! An' you mind your business about my Critta!

Betty swats at the young man as Peter, laughing, spurs his mount and they go.
Sukey hands the infant to Betty as they enter —

INT. BETTY'S CABIN - MORNING

Critta Hemings, 20, is sitting up as Betty places the infant in her arms. She
smiles at her mother and sister Sally.

SALLY

Oh, Sister, he a sweet little thing. I'm gon' help
you look after him.

But Betty frowns and motions to Sukey to see after Critta. She pulls Sally away
and out the doorway. She doesn't know how to start.

BETTY

Sally, Isabel's baby is due any day. She can't go.
So you takin' Polly.

SALLY
(instantly upset)
To Paris? No! Git Hannah or Ursula. I don't wanna go!

BETTY

Honey, I'm sendin' you — cus your brother
James been writin' me an' he say Negroes is free
over there. So that's where you gon' be.

SALLY

Mama, I don't wanna leave you—or Henry. I
don't care 'bout bein' free.

BETTY

Don't you never let me hear you say that. Bein'
free is a precious gift. Now pack your bags, Chile.

Sally is in tears as Betty then starts gathering Sally's meager things together.
Sally keeps putting them all back until she sees something, a small iron bell.
She holds it flopping on the cot. Looks at Critta and her baby.

SALLY

I wus gon' jump-the-broom wit Henry.

Betty holds Sally's face in her hands and speaks softly.

ument0   BETTY
You think cuz you jump-the-broom wit Henrythat
mean somethin'? Masta Tom done sold three
slaves the last two months jus' to pay his bills
over there. Time you turn around, Henry be sold
too.
         (sincerely)
What I'm doin', I'm doin' for you, chile. I want
you to have what ain't none o' us got here.

ISAAC "HENRY" JACKSON 17, appears... He is a proud dark-skinned carpenter
carrying an exquisite pigskin leather trunk and a brass key. What Henry may lack in
refinement, he makes up in charm.

              SALLY
     Oh, Henry.

They hug. Henry shows her the trunk proudly...

              HENRY
     Look what I made for your trip.

Sally frowns at him. How did he know she was going?

              BETTY (O.S.)
         (calls from inside)
     I tol' him...' fore I tol' you.

              HENRY
     I made it for Isabel. But when Betty tol' me the
     trunk wus for you now, I lined it with fresh cedar.
     Every time you smell it, think o' me, Sally.

Sally hugs him. Henry holds her tighter.

              SALLY
     It's beautiful. It ain't never had nothin' so
     beautiful in all my life.

              HENRY
     An' I ain't never lost nothin' so beautiful in all
     mine. I love you, Sally.
         (pained)
     What I'm gone do without you?

              SALLY
     You act like I ain't comin' back.

              HENRY
     You ain't.

EXT. MULBERRY ROW - DAY

Sally's eyes fill with tears as POLLY JEFFERSON, a gangly adolescent, approaches along the road from the house also in tears.

                    POLLY
        Sally... Sally... Sally, I don't want to go...!

                    SALLY
        I don' neither, Polly...

                    POLLY
        Oh, Henry, please jump the broom with Sally so
        we don't have to go.

The girls hug each other. Henry stands embarrassed. Betty appears in the doorway of the cabin. As they walk up the road, Sally wipes Polly's eyes.

                    SALLY
        ... At least we got each other.

                    POLLY
        Promise we'll always have each other?
        Betty always says, 'A Hemings and a Jefferson. It
        always was and it always will be.'

Sally nods. The girls hug each other again. Betty looks on heartsick at losing her daughter.

INT. CARRIAGE - CLOSE ON GIRLS - DAY (PARIS, 1787)

Still holding each other. Sally and Polly look out, taking in their new surroundings.

EXT. JEFFERSON'S PARIS RESIDENCE - DAY

Their carriage pulls up to a magnificent structure, flaunting cobblestone and a huge, fenced courtyard, sumptuous in foliage. ADRIEN PETIT, 45, Jefferson's effeminate valet, opens the door. Speaks in French.

                    PETIT
        Ah, Mademoiselle Maria. Allow me to introduce
        myself, I am Adrien Petit, Monsieur Jefferson's
        valet, and I am at your service.

                    POLLY
        What did he say?

                    SALLY
        I think he called you by your grown- up name,
        Polly. "Maria."

Out the front door of the mansion steps JAMES HEMINGS, 23, Sally's handsome educated brother, and three white servants.

> JAMES
> Mon Dieu, Sally! Is this my sister?

> SALLY
> James, oh, James.

They hug. Sally looks at the mansion. Impressed.

> SALLY
> This where you an' Massa live?

James cringes at the use of "Massa," but nods as he shows her the residence.

> JAMES
> The Hotel de Langeac. Fabulous, no? Very
> old, very grand. Very expensive.

James instructs the white servants, in French, to take Sally's luggage — and they obey him beginning to remove the luggage from the carriage.

INT. JEFFERSON'S PARIS RESIDENCE - CONTINUOUS - DAY

Sally is led by James up a staircase and into the grand entrance room.

> JAMES
> What are you doing here?

> SALLY
> Isabel is having a baby. Mother sent me to
> care for Polly.
> (then)
> Them white folks listens to you?

> JAMES
> Of course. Petit and I are in charge and I'm head
> chef. Now come on. Let me show you upstairs.

He begins a tour.

> JAMES
> This is the entry hall, it connects to the
> diningsalon, here. It is called the east salon. One
> of three. Mr. Jefferson serves wine and tobacco in
> this one. It is also used for gaming—chess, cards,
> baccarat...

Sally looks in wonder.

JAMES

These are Ambassador Jefferson's private
quarters—only enter when requested to do so. His
library is extensive—volumes in English, French,
Latin and Greek.

A French maid walks quickly through. James greets her in French.

JAMES

Bonjour, Madame Grandeille.
(to Sally)
Madame Grandeille is in service to Lady Cosway
from England. She is the Ambassador's
houseguest and some say more than that—these
things are not spoken of by the staff.

SALLY

I wish Mama and Henry could see this.

JAMES

How is Mama?

SALLY

The same. Still runnin' the plantation like it's hers.

James then takes her to another room across the hall. Polly is being settled in by Petit.

POLLY

Sally, Sally, isn't it beautiful?

JAMES

This room is Martha's. Madame DuPre conducts
her classes here as well. The oils were painted by
Francois Boucher.

Sally marvels at the paintings.

SALLY

No wonder he always needin' money.

JAMES

On loan, no doubt, darling girl... My God, Sally.
You've grown so. Not at all what I expected.

SALLY

You neither. You so... 'French- actin'."

JAMES

You'll be 'French-acting' too. Oh, Sally, you're
going to love it. The things you will

JAMES (Cont'd)
learn. Now come. I want to show you your room.

INT. SALLY'S ROOM - DAY

The servant's room is done in striped wallpaper and oriental rugs. There are two
four-post beds, armoires, and a writing table as James leads a disbelieving Sally
into the room.

JAMES
Voila! Here it is. She shakes her head, then
suddenly bursts into tears.

SALLY
This mus' be Polly's. It can't be mine. I don't
deserve it. I's jus'...

JAMES
... A slave? Not anymore. Here in France, you
are 'La femme de chambre.' That's French for
'maid.' And look...

James goes to an armoire, opens the door. Fabulous serving gowns and maids
uniforms are in abundance. Sally comes over, touches the dresses in shock.
James pulls out a couple, then selects one.

JAMES
Yes. Wear this. You'll be serving Mr. Jefferson's
best friends — Monsieur Lafayette, Mr. Paine,
Monsieur Du Pont.

SALLY
Serve? Wearin' this? 'Spose I fall? Or say
thewrong thing? Or don't understand what
theyesayin' to me? I don't know no French.

She flops on the bed.

SALLY
Lord, what was mama thinkin'?

JAMES
She was thinking you'll learn French, and how to
read and write, Speak proper English so you can
take advantage of opportunities she's never had.

Sally holds the dress up to herself in the mirror as James unpacks her trunk frowning
at her things — except the bell — which he remembers with a smile.

JAMES
Now get dressed, cheri. The journey of a thousand
miles—begins with the first step.

He hands her a new pair of shoes, kisses her, leaves. Sally looks at the fancy shoes. Sighs.

INT. DINING HALL/SALON - EVENING

We hear VIOLIN MUSIC as servants are setting the lace- covered table with fine china, silverware and crystal befitting an elegant dinner. Tapered candles are lit. Napkins are placed. Jefferson's guests are in the first- floor salon, visible through the doorway. All are delighted to meet Polly dressed with ribbons in her hair. But Polly is uncomfortable around these new faces and she fidgets. CAMERA FINDS each guest — LADY MARIA COSWAY 27, a beautiful, haughty English woman with white makeup and red lipstick, chats with MADAM de LAFAYETTE 29, whose hair is tousled, and a mole painted on her cheek.

> LADY COSWAY
> ... Yes, but Thomas and I went to see the Mozart
> and I must say, as rumored, the tenorwas anything
> but in good voice. We had just seen Dechampes in
> January and he was so wonderful, so you can only
> imagine our disappointment.
> (turns to Polly)
> Madame, Marquis de Lafayette, jevous presents
> Polly Jefferson.

> POLLY
> Thank you, Lady Cosway.

MARTHA JEFFERSON 25, a tall, awkward, auburn-haired woman, steps up boldly.

> MARTHA
> Polly, you must curtsey to the Marquis and
> Madame... mustn't she, Papa?

THOMAS JEFFERSON, 44, a tall, red-haired man with an aristocratic bearing belying a simpler soul, answers from the side of the dinner quartet where he is in discussion.

> JEFFERSON
> As you will, Martha.

He approaches THOMAS PAINE, 49, and PIERRE SAMUEL DU PONT, 50, as they enjoy a variety of delicate canapes served on silver. Jefferson's right wrist is bandaged.

> JEFFERSON
> My daughter has become an authority on
> continental etiquette in just three years. You have
> a choice of music at dinner, gentlemen, French or
> German?

DU PONT

Can you believe France is bankrupt? The King
told me he tried to buy the hotel Rambouillet,
went to Calonne for the money - and found the
treasury empty.

JEFFERSON

Du Pont, how could Louis even think of sucha
purchase with his people deprived of freedom and
starving.

DU PONT

I caution you to not speak so boldly outside these
walls, Ambassador. On the streets perhaps, but I
recommend restraint of pen and tongue in loftier
circles.

PAINE

Restraint of pen and tongue! You're in the wrong
house.

Laughter all around. Jefferson glances toward the stairway as James and Sally appear
coming down the landing.

JEFFERSON

James, who is that?

JAMES

It's Sally, sir.

Sally walks down the stairs. She is stunning in her new serving dress. Everyone
looks at   her including Jefferson, charmed by her somehow. He moves over to
her. Lady Cosway frowns, curious—as does Martha when Polly runs over to
Sally wrapping her arms around her. Sally's arm goes around Polly as well.

JEFFERSON

Sally Hemings?

SALLY

Yes'm, Master.

JEFFERSON

My goodness. Betty's little girl. Last time I
saw you, you were this tall. But why have
you come? I specifically instructed Betty to
send Isabel.

SALLY

Isabel's havin' her baby, so...

Jefferson's hand lifts up her chin and calms her down.

JEFFERSON
And you accompanied Polly all this way?
Speak up child. No one will hurt you.
She looks directly at him for the first time and something transpires between them.

SALLY
Is I in trouble, Massa?

JEFFERSON
No, Sally, you have done very well indeed.

SALLY
Thank you, Massa.

Paine excuses himself from friends. Comes over.

PAINE
Thomas, you really must do something about
those slave endearments.

JEFFERSON
My dear Mr. Paine, the girl's speech merely
reflects Southern life.

PAINE
Southern slave life. Remember, dear boy, she's
now in France where she's as free as she was not
in America.

Sally reacts to her being "free." Jefferson shakes his head.

JEFFERSON
I cannot believe Sally's speech is of such concern.
Thank you, Sally.

Sally walks away awkwardly.

PAINE
Forgive me. I just think, since the girl is nowhere,
you could tutor her — and in turn she would help
you complete your observations on Negroes which
you started in Notes On The State of Virginia.

Lady Cosway's been left alone far too long. She comes over and flirts with
Jefferson.

LADY COSWAY
Gentlemen, can we not postpone this discussion
until after dinner? After all, Thomas's youngest is
here at last.

JEFFERSON

My apologies, Lady Cosway. Now, the best food
and tobacco in Paris awaits. So let's enjoy
ourselves. You sit to my right...
          (turns to Polly)
... And you, my little angel, you shall sit to my left
and tell me all about your trip... Life has been so
bleak without you.

MARTHA

What about me, Papa?

JEFFERSON

Oh, and you, my loveliest jewel...

PAINE

...You shall sit to my left, my dear.

Martha, grateful for attention, smiles. Takes Paine's hand.

MARTHA

Oh thank you, Mr. Paine. I'd be honored.

As she rambles on to Paine, Jefferson leads everyone from the room and they
make their way into the dining room. Sally trails behind them, still in awe.

DU PONT

...That the monarchy is so debauched, so filled
with disregard for the proletariat that many fear
insurrection, even revolution.
          (in French, to himself)
And then what...and then what?

JEFFERSON

You're right, monsieur, as long as your queen
insists on her present course of extravagance, I see
nothing but bloodshed ahead.

EXT. STREET IN PARIS - DAY

Peasants crying, "Liberte, Liberte" block the street. Sally and James approach in
the carriage and watch as an angry spokesman, JEAN MICHEL, 18, incites the
crowd in French.

JEAN-MICHEL

...Are we to stand here and allow Marie Antoinette
to bankrupt the very souls of the people?

The people shout "No!" Sally turns to James.

SALLY

What is he sayin'?

James explains as Jean-Michel continues in the b.g.

                    JEAN-MICHEL
          (in French)
     We have no food, no work and no say in our
     government! We cannot sit back and be crushed
     by taxes. We cannot let our children beg in the
     street and die of starvation while the queen basks
     in luxury! We must fight

                    JAMES
          (to Sally)
     He's saying the poor people have no food and no
     say in their government. That they should not sit
     back and let their children starve because of high
     taxes while the king and queen ignore their plight.
     They want to fight.

The crowd cheers. Sally is stirred by the people's emotion. James suddenly
becomes serious. Studies his sister a moment.

                    JAMES
     He's right. Freedom is a right. It's why I want you
     to stay. It's why Mama sent you. So you'd be
     free.

                    SALLY
     How'm I free when French folks ain't?

                    JAMES
     'Aren't.'
          (then tries to explain)
     Well, French people are free in body, but not in
     opportunity. They want to make sure all of them
     — aristocrats and peasants—have their opinions
     and grievances dealt with fairly. That is why they
     march.
          (beat)
     Back home Negroes are not citizens at all by law,
     Sally. We are not afforded any opinions. That's
     why I am arranging for you and me to work in
     other homes after Mr. Jefferson goes back home.

                    SALLY
     You an' me, here? By ourselves?

                    JAMES
     We are family, Sally. We should be together—you
     and me—here, where we are free to be ourselves.

Sally frowns, looks back at the people shouting "Liberte!" A few turn to see
their fine carriage and run over, shouting obscenities until Petit points his finger
at them cautioning:

PETIT
Mssr. Jefferson's servants! Negres!

The dissidents back away, realizing Sally and James are no better then they are. Both Sally and James look away.

INT. HALLWAY - DAY

Sally and another maid are bringing linens through the hallway outside Jefferson's room. She stops, hearing the sound of a VIOLIN PLAYING and follows the sound down the hallway where, through the doorway, she spies Jefferson playing a lovely and sad tune. She listens a moment then hears a sound from behind her in the hallway. Martha speaks from behind her.

MARTHA
Albinoni. It was Mother's favorite. He misses her
so and promised her on her deathbed that he would
never remarry. You remember, don't you, Sally?

Martha moves to the open doorway and, looking at Sally with little expression, closes the door.

INT. POLLY'S ROOM - NEXT DAY

Sally and Polly are learning French from MADAME DuPRE, 50, a petite instructor whose job is to teach them French, charm and manners. Sally and Polly repeat each phrase she instructs.

DUPRE
Repetez apres moi. 'Bonjour Madame.'

SALLY AND POLLY
Bonjour Madame.

DUPRE
Commentallez vous?

SALLY
Commentallez vous?

CROSS FADE TO:

INT. POLLY'S ROOM - DAY

Sally and Polly have books on their heads as they walk around the room grace fully, repeating French phrases.

INT. PARIS RESIDENCE - JEFFERSON'S BEDROOM - DAY

Sally is sweeping the floor and humming. Jefferson enters looking for his gold pocket watch. Hears her humming, smiles. He finds his watch, and attempts to attach it to his waistcoat but his wrist is killing him.

> JEFFERSON

Sally, help me, please.

Sally affixes the pocket watch to his coat. She's still humming.

> JEFFERSON

What was that you were humming?

> SALLY

Somethin' Jupiter sings back home.

> JEFFERSON

I miss my little mountain. Give me some news from home.

> SALLY

Well, them grapes—I mean those grapes you planted, the hi...

> JEFFERSON

...Hybrids?

> SALLY

Yeah. Well, the hybrids all died an'-

> JEFFERSON

—No. Not that news. Mr. Batiste writes me of
those. I mean, what is going on, on the Row, in
the kitchen?

> SALLY

Oh. Well, Martin and Peter was ready to kill each
other over Hannah, whose baby ain't neither
o'theirs, but Joe Green's from Massa Lee's place.
>   (as Jefferson laughs)
> ...an' Esther ain't never been the same since Davy
died of the yellow fever. An' Great George an'
Ursula married last May.
>   (finishes his collar)
> Now. You all caught up and ready for dinner.

> JEFFERSON

So I am indeed.

Jefferson smiles at her. She finds herself smiling back.

INT. HALL/DINING ROOM - LATER

Sally and Polly come down the stairs toward the dining room. Polly is eating
chocolate candy.

> POLLY

Sally? When we grow up, we should have our
babies at the same time, so they can play together
like we do. If I'm ever strong enough to have any
babies.

SALLY

Oh, you'll have lots of babies.
(then)
You know you shouldn't have candy before
dinner. You'll become ill again.

POLLY

I know, but don't tell?

They come into the dining room where Martha, Lady Cosway and Jefferson are
awaiting dinner. James carries a tray of vegetables as Sally helps with the serving.

MARTHA

Papa, since coming to France I have begun to
admire the piety and humble nature of the Church.

LADY COSWAY

The 'church'... indeed, Martha...

MARTHA

Are you aware the best primary education in Paris
can be obtained in convent schools?

JEFFERSON

Yes I am, dear.

Lady Cosway leans into Jefferson, pulling his attention way.

LADY COSWAY

Pretty, isn't she?

JEFFERSON

(looking toward Sally)
Beautiful... indeed.

LADY COSWAY

(a beat; hurt)
I was referring to Polly.

Jefferson registers a moment of embarrassment as Sally puts carrots on his plate.
Martha, once again, vies for attention.

MARTHA

Cardinal Le Halles has referred to the people of
Paris's great hunger for the spirit.

JEFFERSON

The people are hungry for food! You know my
position on organized religion. Let go of the
nonsense...

MARTHA

But, Papa...

Sally can see Lady Cosway is still miffed by Jefferson's earlier faux pas.

> LADY COSWAY
>
> Thomas, I've accepted that you weren't over your
> wife's death. But I had hoped when you were
> ready to open your heart again, it would be to me.

> JEFFERSON
>
> Maria, you know how I feel, but this is not the
> right...

> MARTHA
>
> ... Papa...

> POLLY
>
> Martha wants to study with the Catholic nuns,
> Papa.

> LADY COSWAY
>
> ...No. I don't. I've been seeing you eight months,
> I've been willing to leave my husband, my
> religion, England. But except for your letters,
> you're always withdrawn and aloof...
> > (a look to Sally)
> ... lately, more than ever.

> JEFFERSON
>
> No, Maria, don't judge me by...

> MARTHA
>
> Papa... you're not listening...

> JEFFERSON
>
> What, is it!

> POLLY
>
> Papa!

> LADY COSWAY
>
> Pay attention to me, Thomas.

> MARTHA
>
> Don't take up for me, Polly. It's always like this
> when I want something.

Martha runs out of the room, crying.

> POLLY
>
> You have made Martha weep, Papa.

Polly runs from the room. Lady Cosway suddenly grows cold.

LADY COSWAY

This talk of religion brings to mind the recent
censure by my priest.

JEFFERSON

Your priest?

LADY COSWAY

The church has refused to annul my marriage. And
I fear that under the circumstances, I'm going to
try to work things out with Richard. I shall return
to London.

JEFFERSON

Maria, please...

LADY COSWAY

Thank you for your hospitality, Thomas. Tell Petit
I'll be ready to embark at dawn. Good evening.

She leaves, hoping Jefferson will stop her. Instead, he drops his head to his
hands. She goes. James enters, followed by two servants carrying his culinary
masterpiece. But no one is there but Sally and Jefferson.

JEFFERSON

I'm sorry, James. Apparently no one is hungry.

James leaves the tray and walks out. Jefferson and Sally stare at each other a
moment—then Sally begins to laugh. So does Jefferson. It's a shared moment.
Then it settles. As Sally goes to get Jefferson's plate, she finds him staring at
her... in total captivation.

FADE OUT:

END ACT ONE

ACT TWO

FADE IN:

EXT. CANDY SHOPPE - MARKET SQUARE - MORNING

Sally and Polly, along with other wealthy patrons, shop. The OWNER fills their bags with candy. Suddenly, a crowd of peasants swarm in, crowding them. A WOMAN accosts the girls and the Owner.

> WOMAN
> (in French)
> You sell chocolate to the rich and outside the poor
> cannot find a even a loaf of bread.

> OWNER
> Get out! I must survive too!

A rock hits a shop window, BREAKING the GLASS. Polly is crying. She holds Sally as the woman grabs at Polly's chocolates. Sally, though frightened, yells.

> SALLY
> (French and English)
> Leave her alone! She is a child!

> WOMAN
> And you, whore to the aristocracy! How do you
> pay for your food?!

> OWNER
> Get out. Get out. All of you.

As others begin stealing candy and toss it to the hungry, angry crowd, the girls flee while the rage escalates.

EXT. STREET - MARKET SQUARE - MORNING - SAME TIME

Sally and Polly run into the square. Lady Cosway's carriage, filled with her luggage and trunks, rounds the corner and speeds through the crowd.

> POLLY
> Lady Cosway! Lady Cosway!

But the carriage speeds on and Lady Cosway turns her head away, leaving the girls in the street. Polly hangs onto Sally as they make their way through the growing turmoil.

INT. JEFFERSON BEDROOM - DAY (LATER)

The study is crammed with books and papers. Sally dusts over to Jefferson's desk, then notices his gold pocket watch on top. She flips open the lid and reads:

SALLY

'To Thomas Jefferson, student and friend. From
George Wythe.'

She snaps the lid shut and suddenly pretends to be Jefferson, strutting around
with arrogance. Jefferson enters and watches her. Highly amused. Finally, he
clears his throat.

SALLY

Massa Jefferson, I'm sorry.

She polishes the watch with the kerchief in her bosom and returns both the
watch and kerchief quickly. Scared to death.

SALLY

I was admirin' it. Not stealin' it.

JEFFERSON

It's quite alright. It was given to me by my law
teacher and mentor. Do you know what 'mentor'
means?

Sally shakes her head.

JEFFERSON

It means a trusted teacher or guide. My instincts
tell me you have a good mind worth mentoring.

Sally smiles. Jefferson's wrist throbs. He tries to unbandage it, but has difficulty.

SALLY

I'll do that.

JEFFERSON

I slipped on ice last winter and I'm afraid my
wrist just hasn't healed properly since.

As Sally unbandages his wrist Jefferson flinches but finally relaxes. Becomes
reflective.

JEFFERSON

All I think about lately is going home. Paris is lovely,
but if anyone thinks that kings, nobles or priests are
good conservators of public happiness, send them here.

SALLY

I hear French folks talkin' 'bout that queen. They
ain't happy.

Jefferson corrects her with great exaggeration.

JEFFERSON

TalkingG. TalkinG. Please put 'Gs' on the end of
your words. NothinG is more debasingG than the
slurrinG of the English language.

SALLY

I is getting the point, Massa.

JEFFERSON

"Am" getting. And stop calling me "massa."

SALLY

Why? Ain't you my massa no more?

JEFFERSON

Aren't. Call me Mr. Jefferson or sir or
monsieur,but please no more 'massa's and
'Yes'm's.' It is imperative you speak the language
correctly.

SALLY

Yes, sir. I'll be more imperative.

Jefferson chuckles—then an unnatural quiet permeates. He stares at Sally.

JEFFERSON

Right now you look exactly like my wife. The
resemblance is uncanny.

SALLY

I don't remember too much about her, 'cept
she gave me a bell—just 'fore she died. She
was kind.

JEFFERSON

She was kind. I miss her. She was clever and
funny. And she told the worst limericks I've ever
heard.

SALLY

What do 'limericks' mean?

JEFFERSON

A limerick is a five-line poem. Meant to be
humorous. For example...

He recites one.

JEFFERSON

'A man from Virginia said why, "Can't I sit on my
lap if I try?" So he turned round and round. Till he
fell on the ground. And finally gave up with a
sigh.'

SALLY

Oh, I knows one.
    (recites)
'I once knew a girl from Trevizes. Whose feet
were of two different sizes...'

Jefferson knows this one, too. He chimes in.

SALLY AND JEFFERSON

'... The right one was small and of no use at
all.But the left won her several prizes.'

They laugh.

JEFFERSON

Thank you, Sally.

SALLY

Mr. Jefferson.

She curtseys. Leaves. Jefferson looks after her a long moment.

DISSOLVE TO:

EXT. BOOK STALL MARKET - DAY

Jefferson, Martha, Polly and Sally are looking through the stalls, accompanied
by Petit and the driver. Jefferson is picking out books for the girls.

JEFFERSON

Books are wonderful repositories of learning. You
can lose yourself completely in the philosophy of
Locke or Rousseau, or a Shakespeare sonnet.
    (pulls one down)
Polly, this is yours.
    (He hands her another book of Shakespeare
    sonnets)
Oh, and here's Greek Myths and Legends You'll
enjoy this one.

He places both in Sally's basket. Martha frowns, moves away to another area of
the shop. As Jefferson continues finding books for them, Sally notices a rattily
dressed peasant boy take a book off the shelf and stuff it into his pants. The boy
leaves quickly. Sally looks up. Jefferson has seen the boy stealing, but says nothing.
Martha sees the boy, too.

JEFFERSON

Never mind, Martha...

Jefferson moves to another section of the bookstore and finds a leather book with
blank pages. Gives it to Sally.

JEFFERSON

This is a journal. I find keeping one is an excellent
way to chronicle one's thoughts over time. Try it,
Sally. Write whatever comes to mind and do not
censor yourself. No one will ever read it but you.
(indicates her books)
And you must read one of these by next week.
Try the story of Pygmalion.

CROSS FADE TO:

INT. SALLY'S ROOM - NIGHT

Sally is writing in her diary, surrounded by books. We see "Greek Myths and
Legends".

EXT./INT. KITCHEN COURTYARD - DAY

Sally has on her apron and places a tray of fresh-baked rolls on top of the table
as she accepts a delivery of fish from the fish monger. She leaves the door open
as she brings the fish over to the table, dripping water.

An intruder peeks into the open back door and comes in with a knife. He
attempts to steal a bag of grain and some rolls. But Sally turns and sees him.
She grabs her own knife.

SALLY

Who are you! What do you want!

The intruder panics and runs out the gate, but he slips on the damp cobblestones
of the courtyard. Sally runs to him, knife in hand. She pulls off his hat. It's
Jean-Michel Salveaux, the young protestor she saw with James. She gasps.

SALLY

I've seen you in the square.

Jean-Michel frowns. Doesn't understand all she says in English. Sally speaks to
him in rudimentary French.

SALLY

I agreed with what you said — about liberte. But
you're just a thief!

JEAN-MICHEL

No. No. Please. Every day your butcher comes
with meat and poultry. I have son I can't feed.

Sally looks at him. His sincerity grips her. She picks up the bag of grain and hands
it back to him. Jean-Michel is surprised by her generosity.

JEAN-MICHEL

Aristocrats are... selfish.

SALLY

I'm not an aristocrat. I work here.

JEAN-MICHEL

(frowns)
You are American?

SALLY

No — I'm a slave.

She can't believe what she just said.

JEAN-MICHEL

Does that mean you are not an American?

Sally can't answer.

JEAN-MICHEL

I know about American slavery. In many ways
it's no different from peasants here. You should
join our cause. Stand for something.
(re: the food)
Merci beaucoup. Tonight my son will eat. Thank
you—Miss "not American."

He walks out the gate, leaving Sally to reflect on their conversation.

EXT. FOUNTAIN LAKE ROAD - DAY

Jefferson, Martha, Polly and Sally ride in a buggy —side by side — along the
lakeside.

EXT. FOUNTAIN LAKE PROMENADE - DAY

Martha and Polly walk ahead, followed by Jefferson and Sally as they promenade
near the water's edge, a man tips his hat to Sally when he passes them.

SALLY

Mr. Jefferson, if one is a slave in America are you
an American?

JEFFERSON

What a curious question. Of course you are
American.

SALLY

When you wrote the Declaration of Independence,
you wrote it for all Americans, right?

JEFFERSON

Yes. What are you getting at?

                    SALLY
    Well, if 'all men are created equal,' that would
    mean all Americans?

                    JEFFERSON
    All men everywhere. All human beings.

                    SALLY
    Including slaves?

Now Jefferson is on the spot. He looks at her. Says nothing.

                    SALLY
    It's... imperative... you answer. Because in
    America — I'm a slave.

Her correct use of a word he taught her and her ability to reason, staggers him a
moment.

                    JEFFERSON
    Sally, if you ask for my opinion, slavery is an
    abomination, a cruelty against human nature, that
    must end.

                    SALLY
    No, I wish to know how it is that documents that
    are written for all the people in a country, and then
    —some people aren't included... because of laws,
    documents... I'm confused.

Jefferson's caught off-guard, tries to explain, but struggles.

                    JEFFERSON
    Yes, well, sometimes one document cannot cover
    the concerns of every citizen. Sally. This is a
    complex dilemma. There is no easy solution, but I
    pray to be part of one.
              (then)
    I, um, have a pamphlet I want you to read. It's
    called Common Sense by Thomas Paine. He asks
    these same questions and provides some answers.
    Yes. Mr. Paine may help shed some light on this
    complicated subject.

                    SALLY
    Better than you can?

Jefferson can't answer.

INT. POLLY'S BEDROOM - DAY

Sally and Polly are practicing the minuet.

POLLY

Mademoiselle, you dance so well.

SALLY

Thank you, Miss Polly. You do as well.

Madame DuPre comes in with two servants carrying dresses.

DUPRE

Voila! I have your dresses and not a moment too
soon. I want you to look your very best when you
meet the King and Queen tomorrow.

She presents a dress to Polly... and one to Sally. Sally is in shock.

SALLY

For me?

Polly holds her dress up to herself. Sally follows and holds up her lilac chiffon
gown. Gasps.

DUPRE

Monsieur Jefferson wanted youto wear something
decent to the Palace—even if you were help.

Martha enters.

DUPRE

Now. We must practice our minuet.

MARTHA

Polly and Sally seem much more accomplished
than I. Besides, for one who has chosen the
cloistered life, it would not be proper to be seen
dancing at Versailles.

DUPRE

To the grand disappointment of every nobleman in
Paris.

EXT. GATES TO VERSAILLES - LATE AFTERNOON

Hungry people are gathered, their poverty in stark contrast to the arriving guests.

EXT. GARDENS OF VERSAILLES - LATE AFTERNOON

An elegant garden party is in progress, replete with powdered wigs, satin waist
coats and silk gowns. Members of the aristocracy stroll through the king's
gardens as a string quartette plays. People chat and/or gossip about the trouble
brewing outside the gates.

Arriving guests are announced as they reach the top of the grand staircase and
other guests comment on them. Sally, James and Petit follow "at service" to

Jefferson, in a white powdered wig, and his daughters as they approach the head of the line. James gives a running commentary to Sally on the guests.

> ANNOUNCER
> Madame Necker, Baroness Bonette Helvetius, and
> the Prince de Conde...

> JAMES
> The Baroness corresponds with Mr. Jefferson. She
> and Madame Necker praise the virtues of the
> domestic woman, yet are anything but...

> ANNOUNCER
> Monsieur Pierre Samuel Du Pont de Nemours and
> the Marquis de Condorcet.

> JAMES
> The Marquis wrote a passionate indictment of
> slavery which Mr. Jefferson translated, but has
> yet to lend his name to...

Martha overhears and snips...

> MARTHA
> James, Sally, retain our coats for the introduc-tion.
> We're next. Monsieur Petit, see to father...

> ANNOUNCER
> ...The Minister from the United States of America,
> Thomas Jefferson and Mademoiselles Martha and
> Maria Jefferson.

Jefferson bows as he and the girls begin to walk down the long stairway. Sally watches their gowns from behind.

EXT. GARDEN OF VERSAILLES - AFTERNOON

Du Pont finds Jefferson and kisses him on both cheeks, then greets his daughters.

> JEFFERSON
> Du Pont, good tò see you, mon ami.

> DU PONT
> Bonjour, Mr. Ambassador.
> (sees James)
> Ah, James, greetings to you, too.
> (to Jefferson)
> Thomas, you must let me borrow James for one of
> my parties. People are still talking about the
> divine food at your gaming salon in March.

MARTHA
We'd be lost without him.

We PICK UP James and Sally.

JAMES
(sotto voce to Sally)
Then they'll just be 'lost without' me. For the
days of the Queen's extravagances and Mr.
Jefferson's spending are numbered and we shall
both be gone.

Thomas Paine calls from the bottom of the stairs.

PAINE
There you are, Thomas!

Jefferson and the others turn.

JEFFERSON
Ah, Mr. Paine, I see you decided to join the
festivities after all. I won't breathe a word of
your proximity to the Royals.

PAINE
Only for you Ambassador. I cannot bear this
King or his silly wife.

JEFFERSON
Then let us create more distance between you.
(as they pass Sally)
Sally, should anyone ask, Mr. Paine and I are off
to admire the gardens.

Sally looks at Paine, awed.

SALLY
'Weak mean cannot see and prejudiced men
will not see' and 'We have it in our power
to begin the world again.' Oh, Mr. Paine, such
wonderful, powerful words you wrote, sir.

Paine and Jefferson are transfixed for a moment. Paine bows.

PAINE
Why thank you, my dear.

As he and Jefferson move off. Paine stares back at Sally.

PAINE
Extraordinary girl, Thomas. Extraordinary.

EXT. PALACE GARDENS - EVENING

The night glows with candlelight and torches as couples dance under a vine-covered walkway. A quartet plays. The theme is indeed, blue, white and gray. Jefferson and Paine stand apart from the crowd on a parapet, talking, drinking, watching the guests dancing.

> PAINE
>
> So tell me, will you accept Washington's appointment?

> JEFFERSON
>
> If you must know. I am going to retire.

> PAINE
>
> Indeed. That is what one does when one is ill, or an old lion in the December of his years. Now where is your tobacco? I know you brought it.

Jefferson pulls out a tobacco tin from his waistcoat. Offers it to Paine who savors its aroma.

> PAINE
>
> Ahhh, Virginia.

> JEFFERSON
>
> I am a reluctant politician, Paine. I see myself more as a scientist or educator. Yet I am constantly coerced into office because people confuse and tangle my ideas, forcing me to express them myself. But my heart has never been in public office.

> PAINE
>
> Where, pray, is your heart?

Jefferson sips his brandy, becomes reflective.

> JEFFERSON
>
> I am not a religious man, but Monticello is the closest thing to God on Earth. There is no place more majestic. And I long for her.

> PAINE
>
> But she is not a woman. And once you're in the bosom of Monticello, into whose arms will you keep warm?

> JEFFERSON
>
> Since my wife's death, I've done nothing but immerse myself in work, knowing my heart has been dead... until recently.

Paine's interest is now piqued as he smokes.

>   PAINE
>   Oooh. Then there is a new intrigue?

A butler has a tray of whiskeys. Jefferson quickly tosses one back, realizing he's said too much. Paine throws him a mischievous look — then guesses.

>   PAINE
>   Of course. That stunning mulatto you obviously
>   gave my pamphlet to.

>   JEFFERSON
>   You're mistaken, Paine.

>   PAINE
>   Well, if ever there was a reason to accept
>   Washington's appointment and push an anti-
>   slavery bill through Congress, dear boy, she is the
>   best.

>   JEFFERSON
>   (dismisses him)
>   Paine...Paine, please...

But Paine motions for Jefferson to follow him. They look out at the party — and at Sally as she waits on Martha and Polly.

>   PAINE
>   When I was here less than a year ago, that young
>   girl could barely speak. Now she's quoting, well,
>   me. Look at her. She exhibits your taste, your
>   tutorship, your style. Does she not represent the
>   thousands of slaves who can be productive
>   members of society were it not for slavery?

>   JEFFERSON
>   Well, Sally is quite unique, but...

>   PAINE
>   ...She is indeed. What are you waiting for?

Paine walks down the steps and approaches Sally.

JEFFERSON'S POV

Paine bows and asks Sally to dance. Sally shakes her head "no." Paine bows again. Extends his hand. Sally looks around. Finally accepts.

JEFFERSON

Slowly walks down the steps, mesmerized.

NEW ANGLE

Sally minuets with Paine — who winks at Jefferson.

JEFFERSON

approaches the dance floor, still looking at Paine and Sally. He sees Martha and asks her to dance. Martha, thrilled to be asked, accepts. But she dances awkwardly.

> MARTHA
> I'm sorry I don't do this well.

> JEFFERSON
> Nonsense, my darling.

But Jefferson's eyes are on Sally and Paine.

> MARTHA
> Papa. What do you care if I enroll in the abbey?
> You have so many other preoccupations, it seems.
> I would hardly be missed.

> JEFFERSON
> No, my angel, you would be missed. I would miss
> you. You're the biggest part of my heart, and I
> need you. Please don't take that for granted.

> MARTHA
> Oh Papa.

He pulls her head to his chest. She feels accepted for now. Paine takes Sally's hand and grandly promenades her over to Jefferson and Martha.

> PAINE
> Mr. Jefferson, I realize I haven't had the pleasure
> of chatting with Martha since I arrived. Do you
> mind?

Martha, not sure if she's relieved by the interruption, leaves with Paine. Jefferson and Sally look at each other. The music is lovely, other couples are still dancing. Jefferson extends his arms. Sally hesitantly enters them... ... and they dance as if the world around them has disappeared.

Finally, when the music ends, Jefferson bows. Sally curtseys. Jefferson courte ously kisses Sally's hand... in front of all eyes.

Suddenly, the moment is broken as a fanfare plays and MARIE ANTOINETTE, dressed as Diana, Goddess of the Hunt, replete with bow and white dog, bewigged and all in white, is led down the long covered corridor by six children dressed in Greek Revival costume waving sparklers in her path. The crowd applauds. King Louis XVI follows, encouraging the crowd.

But Sally Hemings and Thomas Jefferson have eyes only for each other.

DISSOLVE TO:

INT. JEFFERSON'S RESIDENCE - STUDY - NIGHT

CLOSE ON a washbowl. Jefferson dips his hands in the water, wipes his face. Looks in the mirror. Looks at himself again — a 45-year-old man. Closes his eyes.

But when he opens them again, Sally is in the mirror's reflection, standing in the hallway with towels. They silently look at each other. We hear the sound of RAIN OVER.

CUT TO:

EXT. JEFFERSON'S RESIDENCE - DAY

It's pouring rain as luggage is carried out of the hotel and placed into a carriage by Petit and James. Martha, Polly and Jefferson emerge from the hotel, followed by Sally. Both girls kiss their father good-bye. Polly runs to Sally. Hugs her.

> SALLY (V.O.)
> ... The same week Martha and Polly were enrolled
> in the Abbey Royal de Parthemont, Thomas made
> arrangements for James to cook for the Du Pont's.

> JEFFERSON (V.O.)
> ...Perhaps I was too rash. She kept begging me to
> let her go. And so now she has her wish...

Martha and Jefferson embrace and he gives Polly a tender kiss before the girls get into the carriage. It takes off. Jefferson looks at Sally. She finds herself staring back.

> JEFFERSON (V.O.)
> ... I can only hope I've done the right thing by
> sending her to a convent school. After all...

INT. JEFFERSON'S MASTER SUITE - EVENING
Sally is kneeling before Jefferson massaging his temples.

> JEFFERSON
> ...she was correct. Convent schools do offer the
> best education here.

> SALLY
> Why are you looking at me like that?

> JEFFERSON
> I find I enjoy looking at you, Sally. I so love your
> touch when you massage my temples. I find I
> want your touch when I'm perfectly sound.

He takes her hand and their fingers have been intertwining. Jefferson almost kisses her, but...

JEFFERSON

Sally, you're...
> (suddenly conflicted)

I think it proper you go.

Sally's heart breaks as Jefferson turns. She leaves.

INT. HALLWAY - NIGHT

The hall is empty. Sally's door is open enough to see her sitting in front of the fireplace gazing into the flames. We can still hear RAIN. Further down, sounds of a DOOR OPENING cause Sally to look over.

INT. SALLY'S ROOM - NIGHT

INTO FRAME, OVER HER SHOULDER, Jefferson appears. Still conflicted but compelled. He sits next to her in front of the flames. Looks at her. She looks at him. He takes her hand. Sally folds her fingers across them.

They never break eye contact. Finally, with his other hand, Jefferson traces her cheek, her nose, her mouth...until neither can suppress their feelings. Jefferson kisses her, then undoes the buttons of the dress. Sally isn't afraid. Rather, she accepts the inevitable...

SALLY (V.O.)

... And so we began...

...and nature takes its course.

FADE OUT.

END ACT TWO

ACT THREE

INT. DINING ROOM - MORNING

Jefferson sits at the table awaiting breakfast. He stares at the day's work ahead of him. He thinks. Sally enters with a tray of food and places it in front of him. It's awkward between them. Finally, Jefferson tries to speak as she goes.

> JEFFERSON
>> Sally...

Sally stops in the doorway.

> JEFFERSON
> ...what happened last night, forgive me...we can't...it can't...

He can't go on. Sally goes to him and looks into his eyes. He is overwhelmed by her. They kiss—and can't stop.

> DISSOLVE TO:

EXT. HOTEL FORMAL GARDENS - DAY

They walk arm in arm through the gardens, Jefferson pointing out the various varieties of flowers.

> JEFFERSON
> Soleirolia soleirolii — creeping babies, rosa
> glauca, rosa macrantha, and this is Ajuga neptans,
> thyme and these—centaurea macrocephala and
> day lilies which bloom in late summer.

INT. JEFFERSON'S BEDROOM/STUDY - NIGHT

They make love by firelight.

> DISSOLVE TO:

EXT. GARDENS - DAY

Sitting on the garden bench, Jefferson ties a small, silver locket around Sally's neck. We detail their intimate moments.

EXT. LONG ROAD - DAY

Their carriage moves along a lovely Parisan lane.

EXT. HOTEL DE LANGEAC - FORMAL GARDEN - DAY

Jefferson and Sally walk arm in arm thru the formal gardens. Her head is on his shoulder as they pass thru the flowers.

                              SALLY
Mr. Jefferson...

                            JEFFERSON
Perhaps under the circumstances these last three
months, you'll call me "Thomas?"

                              SALLY
Yes... yes... Thomas. I love you...

He stops in his tracks. Then quietly —

                            JEFFERSON
You must not.
         (a pause)
I have felt what you are feeling now... long ago.

There is a long silence as she searches for meaning.

                              SALLY
You are frightening me.

                            JEFFERSON
I too am afraid. My head and my heart have
wrestled with the consequences of this. My head
implores, 'Take caution, Thomas, for, though
lovely, she is too young, too vulnerable, she is in
your service, and she is...'

                              SALLY
... your slave.

                            JEFFERSON
...but my heart counters, I am happy. Happier
than I have been in years. When I am with you, I
feel again, and I only feel joy.

She touches his face.

                          SALLY (V.O.)
And as the weeks turned into months, Thomas
became my respite from the world— and I his...

EXT. MARKET PLACE - CLOSE ON FACE OF THIEF - DAY (1789)

being dragged through the streets by the military. The crowded market place is
teeming with resentment. Sally, accompanied by Petit, is pushed against a stall
as an argument turns into a fracas as she tries to shop.

Jefferson's carriage, pushes through the swelling crowd. Jefferson calls out to
Sally.

JEFFERSON

Why are you out here alone? Don't you know the
streets are no longer safe? The city is filled with
mobs running blind. I've sent for Martha, Polly
and James. We leave tomorrow.

SALLY

Tomorrow? No.

She shakes her head and bursts into tears.

JEFFERSON

I know it's sudden, but we...
(then)
Sally, what is it? What's wrong?

SALLY

Thomas. Je suis enceinte.

INT. JEFFERSON'S STUDY - NIGHT

James and Sally are packing Jefferson's belongings into trunks and bags. James
is infuriated.

JAMES

With child! My God, have you lost your mind? How
can you bring another slave bastard into this world? How?

Sally is weeping.

JAMES

Now he's trying to force us home. Well, you tell
him you're staying. Revolution or no, you and I
and your child are free here!

SALLY

But I love him, James.

Suddenly Jefferson appears in the outer hallway.

JEFFERSON

James, I wish a word with you.

JAMES

Whatever you have to say, you can say here in
front of Sally and your unborn child!

JEFFERSON

James, I'm very fond of you. But under our
present circumstances...

> JAMES

> Sir, I'm sorry, but I'm staying in France and my
> sister is staying with me.

Sally looks over at him. She never agreed to this.

> JEFFERSON

> Sally...

James turns to his sister.

> JAMES

> I did not come all this way to taste freedom alone.
> If you decide to return, I would only go because
> you're family and must be protected. But you
> must be careful. Your choice affects us all,
> especially your child.

> JEFFERSON

> But you're in danger here.

> JAMES

> We're in more danger in America sir.

> JEFFERSON

> In America, you are under my protection.

> JAMES

> We'll be slaves under your protection.

Sally can't take it and screams out:

> SALLY

> Stop it! Both of you! Have I no choice in what
> becomes of me?
> (to Jefferson)
> I will not give birth to a slave. I'm free now and I
> want my child free. I'd be foolish to wish
> anything else.

> JEFFERSON

> Please, Sally, come back with me.

> SALLY

> Why?... Why should I?

> JEFFERSON

> Because... I...

> JAMES

> You see, you see you're nothing to him. He can't
> even tell you he loves you.

JEFFERSON
(to James)
That's enough!
(to Sally)
I cannot return to Monticello without you. Tell me
what I must do?

At that moment a VOLLEY of MUSKET FIRE is heard from below. They rush
to the window to see:

THEIR POV

A carriage enters the front gates followed by a mob. The military is FIRING into
the crowd as they try to climb the fences. Du Pont and two military men exit the
carriage and rush to the front door.

INT. VESTIBULE - NIGHT

Jefferson, James, Sally and Petit run into the entry hall. Petit runs upstairs.

PETIT
Put out the candles and lamps. They're at the
gates. Madame DuPre, bring the girls down to the
kitchen.

We hear DuPre from the girls' suite as the lights are blown out leaving the rooms
in an eerie darkness.

DUPRE (O.S.)
Martha, Polly, come quickly.

Martha and Polly are coming down the stairs. Polly is weeping.

POLLY
But my dress... from the palace.

DUPRE
Come, come. Your dress is in the trunk, my
darling. Now we must go!

Martha hugs her father in fear.

MARTHA
What will happen to us, Papa?

James steps up to help the girls down the stairwell, leaving Jefferson and Sally
alone for a moment in the semi-darkness.

SALLY
Freedom...for me and my child. A promise from
you, Thomas. In writing.

JEFFERSON

You shall have it.

EXT. KITCHEN COURTYARD - NIGHT

Jefferson gathers them all and they enter into the inner courtyard. Jefferson turns to James, who hesitates.

JEFFERSON

James Hemings, return with your sister to
Monticello and you and any children you shall
have shall be freed. That is my solemn oath.

Jefferson offers his hand to James, who takes it. The driver cracks the whip as Jefferson rides beside him atop the coach. The gates swing open and the mob runs to the side to avoid the horses. They shake the carriage from side to side in anger. Ahead, the Jefferson party can see bodies on the pavement, dismembered heads of aristocrats exhibited on pikes. Sally holds Polly's face from the sight as the crowd shouts, "Vive la nation!"

Suddenly, a man we recognize runs up with two flaming torches in his hands. He blocks their path. It's Jean- Michel Salveaux the young man from the kitchen. The horses rear in fright and the coach is halted in the entranceway. Jean-Michel yells over the crowd.

JEAN-MICHEL

(French)
Halt in the name of the people! Aristocrats! Pawns
of the monarchy! Your day has come to an end!

As the crowd presses in, the coach door opens and Sally leans out. She recognizes Jean-Michel. He recognizes Sally as well.

JEAN-MICHEL

You!

SALLY

Monsieur, I beg you. Let us go home.

There is a moment as the crowd quiets, awaiting their leader. He looks to Jefferson.

JEAN-MICHEL

(to Jefferson)
You are the Ambassador, Thomas Jefferson from
America?

JEFFERSON

I am.

JEAN-MICHEL
Sir, I remember this of you. 'The tree of liberty
must be refreshed from time to time with the
blood of patriots and tyrants.' Because you are a
defender of liberty, you shall not this night join
the natural 'manure' you have eloquently written
about.
 (backs aways lightly)
Safe passage, monsieur. Vive la nation.

JEFFERSON
Vive la nation.

Sally acknowledges Jean-Michel as he orders an escort of two revolutionaries
with torches to accompany them. The carriage continues on. The mob moves
aside, chanting "Vive le nation" as the carriage passes into the night and freedom.

CAMERA PUSHES IN TIGHT ON Sally. She realizes she's leaving her life in
Paris forever.

FADE OUT:

END OF ACT THREE

ACT FOUR

EXT. RIVANNA RIVER

Three boats — Jefferson and his daughter in the front, followed by James and Sally in another, followed by a baggage boat — glide up the river.

CLOSE ON SALLY AND JAMES

as they look at the beautiful countryside. Row upon row of tobacco and corn fields attended by slaves boiling in the hot sun.

Some of the slaves on shore recognize Jefferson, and they remove their hats and bow. Children run along, trying to keep up with the boats.

SALLY
is painfully aware of their separate positions.

EXT. MONTICELLO PLANTATION - VARIOUS SHOTS - DAY

Two carriages approach Monticello plantation. The fields are filled with slaves who rush from all over to greet the returning Jefferson and family. They are cheering and waving their arms or kerchiefs. On the porch several slaves have taken up a song in greeting. It is a celebration.

CLOSE ON Jefferson in the first carriage, almost in tears at the sight of his beloved home.

CLOSE ON Martha and Polly, overwhelmed by the greeting.

CLOSE ON Sally and James with mixed emotions.

ANGLE

Jefferson's nephews, Peter Carr, now 22, Samuel Carr, now 23, and JACK EPPES, 18, come charging across the fields on horseback. As they approach the carriage Jack calls out.

> JACK
> Welcome home, uncle, cousin Martha, and who is
> that pretty Parisian lady? My goodness, it's Polly.

> MARTHA
> That is your cousin, Young Jack Eppes.

> PETER
> Sir, all of Virginia has sent messages of welcome.
> Even the President has posted a letter to you.

Samuel rides up to the second carriage, looks in.

> SAMUEL
> And our James is back too with...
> (then)
> ...can this beauty be Sally? Peter, will you look at
> Sally now.

> PETER
> Time enough for that, brother.

He laughs and spurs his mount toward the house. Suddenly the group surround
ing Jefferson's carriage unhitches the horses and despite Jefferson's protests
begin to pull the carriage the last 25 yards to the house.

EXT. MONTICELLO ENTRANCE - VARIOUS SHOTS - DAY

When the carriage reaches the mansion, Sukey, Critta, Robert and Peter Hemings
and many house staff and their children crowd the porch. The welcome is highly
emotional.

The carriage is opened and Jefferson emerges followed by Martha and Polly. The
slaves literally lift Jefferson in their arms and joyfully carry him onto the porch.
James helps Sally climb out. She wraps her coat around her big stomach.

Sally and James come through the crowd receiving hugs and kisses. Sally sees
Sukey, Critta and...

... Henry Jackson peering through the crowd at her, smiling, but Sally is immediately
swept into hugs by her family.

> CRITTA
> Oh, Sally, we's so happy to see you.

> SALLY
> Oh, I've missed you all, too.
> (then looks around)
> Where's mama?

> SUKEY
> Betty be in her cabin, mad. You bes' go there now.

INT. BETTY'S CABIN - AFTERNOON

Critta helps Sally unpack her leather trunk, impressed with all the beautiful
French clothing. Critta pulls out the lilac chiffon gown and holds it up to herself
in a cracked mirror.

> CRITTA
> Real French fabric — look at this!

> SALLY
> Would you like to try it on?

BETTY (O.S.)

Don't you dare!

Sally and Critta turn to find... Betty in the doorway.

SALLY

Mama!

But Betty snatches the dress from Critta.

BETTY

Don't you dare start wantin' fine things, Critta.
They traps.

CRITTA

But I only wanted to try it on.

BETTY

An' I'm sure your sister only wanted to 'try it on'
too.
(re: Sally's stomach)
But look what it got her. Now git!

Critta leaves. Betty turns to Sally.

BETTY

I'm mighty disappointed in you. You was 'sposed
to stay over there an' be free. James was gon see
after you. Now yall both back here—an' you
blowed up big as a house, by Masta Tom.

SALLY

Please, Mother, enough of this.

BETTY

(mimics)
'Please, Mother, enough of this.' My, my. We got
such class now, don't we? Such style an'
sophistication. Well let me tell you somethin',
missy. You comin' back here wit' all your proper
English an' French clothes don't make you nothin'
but a fancy slave!

SALLY

I made a choice, Mama. The same choice you
made—with Master Wayles.

Betty slaps Sally hard across the face.

BETTY

I didn't have no choice!
(then)
Sally, you ain't nothin' but a damn fool!

Betty walks out leaving Sally hurt and confused.

EXT. MONTICELLO - DAY

A party on the plantation grounds honoring Jefferson's return. Jupiter plays the fiddle and slaves are singing and dancing. Jefferson, Jack Eppes, Martha, Polly, Peter and Samuel Carr are tapping their feet on the porch enjoying the festivities.

Another Jefferson nephew, THOMAS MANN RANDOLPH, 22, dark haired and brooding, hitches his horse. Jefferson's arms spread to him. Randolph bows.

> JEFFERSON
> My dear nephew. How good of you to come, Mr.
> Randolph.
>> (to his daughters)
> Martha, Polly, you remember your cousin Thomas
> Mann Randolph?

Martha shakes Randolph's hand. She's curiously infatuated. Randolph smiles back equally intrigued.

> RANDOLPH
> Uncle, I have brought an urgent personal
> correspondence from President George
> Washington himself.

> JEFFERSON
> Thank you.

Jefferson opens the letter. Reads it. He's resigned.

> JEFFERSON
> The President has asked me to become Secretary
> of State.

> MARTHA
> Oh, Papa, how wonderful.

> RANDOLPH
> Hear, hear.

But Jefferson is clearly conflicted.

EXT. MONTICELLO - UNDER OLD TREE - AFTERNOON

Sally, in one of her fancy dresses from Paris, has distanced herself from the others on the swing under the old oak. She is writing in her diary when Henry Jackson approaches. Two slaves on their way to the party pass her, commenting on her dress, her pregnancy.

> SALLY
> Oh, Henry. Hello.

They hug. He pulls her back. Touches her stomach. Sally looks away. Henry is caring.

> HENRY
> Don' you worry none, Sally. You needs a man to
> take care o' you an' the youngin' when he git
> here. I'll do that.

So much love is in his eyes. Sally tears up.

> SALLY
> But it's not like that, Henry. The baby's got a papa.

She looks at Jefferson dancing to Jupiter's fiddle music. Henry follows her look.

> HENRY
> Ah naw. Naw, Sally, naw.

> SALLY
> I'm sorry, Henry.

EXT. MONTICELLO - PARTY - AFTERNOON

Critta is dancing with other slaves to Jupiter's music when Peter Carr approaches
her lustily.

> PETER
> We'll make that later this evening, girl.

> CRITTA
> But, Masta Peter, my sister's home.

> PETER
> More reason to celebrate.

EXT. MONTICELLO - UNDER TREE - AFTERNOON

Betty comes up with a basket of cookies and little cakes, sees Sally and comes
over. Mother and daughter sit quietly for awhile still painfully aware of their earlier
argument. Finally...

> BETTY
> ...After mama wus brought over from Africa, ole
> Captain Hemings, he took her, and she had me.
> Then he turn 'round an' we was both given to
> Masta Wayles. Masta Wayles started in with me, I
> had the six of yall, an' he turned 'round an' we all
> ended up here. That's how it be wit' us. See, me
> an' mama jus' assumed we be protected cus our
> mastas wus wit us.
>> (a beat)
> Now here you got a baby comin' for Masta Tom.
> So you listen to me. Get that freedom for your
> baby, in writin' — while you still got what Masta
> Tom wants.

Sally nods. Mother and daughter hug. A deeper understanding having transpired.

EXT. MONTICELLO - PORCH AREA - DAY

The party continues. James, dressed in his French clothing and drinking far too much, joins the group listening to Randolph toast Jefferson's return.

>   RANDOLPH
>   Mr. 'Secretary', notwithstanding the important and
>   even turbulent scenes you have passed through,
>   you have not only the approbation of your own
>   stout heart, and that of your grateful countrymen,
>   but also the silence and, of course the constrained
>   approbation of your enemies.

Frowns and silence—as everyone attempts to understand what he means. But Martha is impressed with Randolph. Smittened.

>   MARTHA
>   How very true, Mr. Randolph.

>   JAMES
>   (sarcastic)
>   Oh yes. So well spoken, Master Randolph.

On Jefferson's signal fiddle music and dancing begins again. Jefferson dances in the crowd as Sally watches. James watches as well. His heart filled with contempt.

INT. MASTER SUITE - NIGHT

Jefferson and Sally in bed, facing away from each other.

>   SALLY
>   Everything is so different. I don't know how you
>   feel—what you feel.

His hand touches her belly.

>   DISSOLVE TO:

EXT. MULBERRY ROW - CLOSE ON NANCE - AFTERNOON

RINGING the BELL.

INT. MONTICELLO - CLOSE ON CRITTA - DAY

as Critta runs through and out of the house towards the Row.

>   CRITTA
>   It's come! Sally's baby is here.

PICK UP Martha coming down the hall toward the front porch followed by Randolph. Other house slaves follow to the porch.

EXT. KITCHEN AREA - ROW - CONTINUOUS ACTION - DAY

Betty rushes across from her cabin and yells into the kitchen.

> BETTY
> James, Robert, Peter. It's a boy!

> JAMES
> What color is he?

> BETTY
> White as snow.

INT./EXT. MONTICELLO - CONTINUOUS ACTION - DAY

Jefferson, hearing the commotion, comes out of his study and heads to the porch to join Martha and Randolph. Critta is out in the yard at the great tree.

EXT. BETTY'S CABIN - CONTINUOUS ACTION - DAY

Betty joins a crowd of slaves as Sukey comes out with a pale, red-haired infant in her arms. She raises him above her head.

> SUKEY
> Thomas Jefferson Hemings.

EXT. MONTICELLO PORCH - CONTINUOUS ACTION - DAY

Thomas Randolph turns to Martha.

> RANDOLPH
> Good God...

Jefferson's face registers a combination of embarrassment and pride.

INT. BETTY'S CABIN - NIGHT

Sally is in bed holding baby Tom. Betty and Sukey leave as Jefferson comes in. Sally smiles. Jefferson comes over and takes his child in his arms. He gives the baby back and Sally rocks him. Jefferson kisses her head as he sits with them.

EXT. MONTICELLO - DAY

> SALLY (V.O.)
> ... Three months later, Monticello celebrated in
> the marriage of Martha Jefferson and Thomas
> Mann Randolph. And even though Randolph
> wasn't mentally 'perfect,' we were all relieved
> that Martha had married. Thomas gave her a farm

SALLY (V.O.) (Cont'd)
and 25 slaves...
    (a beat)
...one of whom was Henry Jackson...

Martha and Randolph are leaving after their wedding. Their carriage is loaded behind them as well as three buckboards filled with slaves, including Henry Jackson. Polly steals glances at Jack Eppes as Sally stands to the side holding baby Tom. Critta and Betty are with her.

JEFFERSON
My joy is in seeing you happy, my dear son-in-law.

RANDOLPH
Sir... I am grateful...

JEFFERSON
...Martha, be kind to your new husband.

MARTHA
I shall, Papa. And I will come to Washington to visit once we are settled at Edgehill. Thank you for your generosity, Papa.

During this —

BETTY
I'm surprised there ain't more slaves on them wagons with them thousand acres they gotta clear.

CRITTA
Poor Henry. His heart is jus' broken.

Betty nods as Sally looks at Henry in the buckboard. Martha and Randolph depart.

SALLY (V.O.)
Thomas left to become the first Secretary of State. He took James as his cook and Robert drove him. I stayed behind to raise his son.

As the carriage and buckboards move off over the hill, Jefferson looks at Sally. She kisses their son and carries him back toward the Row.

END ACT FOUR

ACT FIVE

EXT. TOBACCO FIELDS - DAY (1791)

Sally and Critta are walking through the fields. Tom, one, and Critta's son, JAMY, four, are with them. Slaves are in the b.g., picking tobacco. Sally has a book in one hand, and reads a letter to her sister.

> SALLY
>
> Thomas and Alexander Hamilton, the treasury
> secretary hate each other.
> (reads further)
> He says: '... Mr. Hamilton has little regard for
> human rights.'
> (reads silently)
> '...and the Earth belongs to the living, not the
> dead.'

> CRITTA
>
> I don't know what he's sayin', but I likes how you
> talk, Sally. You talk good as white folks.

> SALLY
>
> I'll teach you. How to read, too.

> CRITTA
>
> What, an' get myself killed? No. Long as it's
> against the law, ain't nothin' 'round here worth
> readin' I wanna die for.

They walk awhile further.

> CRITTA
>
> You know, Sally.
> (a beat)
> I done fixed myself. I look at all those black folks
> out there pickin' corn an' tobacco, don' none of
> 'em know they daddies. An' white women on
> every plantation lookin' the other way when they
> men goes wit' us. An' us got to take it, an' be
> quiet, an' live with the shame, an' pain, an' the
> knowin' if we don' we gets sold or beat up.
> (shakes her head)
> I didn't want another child to grow up in this. So,
> I took a branch to myself one day after Peter done
> me...
> (cries; can't finish)
> ...anyway, I bled so bad, Sukey tol' me I can't
> never have no more children.

Sally hugs her sister as Critta weeps gently. Just then a wagon load of carpenters heading for Monticello passes by. Henry Jackson jumps off and approaches.

HENRY

Sally!!

CRITTA

Oh, Lord Henry Jackson. Don't you pay him no attention sister.

She jumps aboard the wagon with her child, calling out:

CRITTA

You mind yourself now, Henry.

SALLY

How've you been keeping?

HENRY

Been good, Sally. Real good. Been workin' over at Edgehill for Martha an' that mad man she married.

SALLY

Thomas Randolph is mad, isn't he?

HENRY

As a loon. An' Miss Martha be actin' like he fine, but the boy be mutterin' to hisself an' forgettin' to put his clothes on.

They laugh. Henry looks at Sally's book. Tries to read it.

HENRY

Mi... sum... sum...

SALLY

A Midsummer Night's Dream. It's a play by William Shakespeare.

HENRY

Real smart, ain't you? Read an' write, speak that French.
(re: Tom)
So. That's your boy, huh?

SALLY

Yes. Tom.
(then)
Henry...

HENRY

(serious)
...I didn't wanna see you, Sally. That's why I ask Masta Jefferson if I could go wit them others to Miss Martha's place. I couldn't be 'round you 'til the pain wus outta me.

Sally tries to change the subject.

> SALLY
>
> You still a carpenter?

> HENRY
>
> Yeah. Could be a furniture maker if I could
> measure and knew numbers an' readin'.

Sally picks up A Midsummer Night's Dream and indicates the first letter to
Henry.

> SALLY
>
> A. This is the letter A... A Midsummer Night's
> Dream... and this is B...
> (finding drawing inside) ...See? B is for Bottom, a
> character in this play. B...come on, say it...

> HENRY
>
> A...

INT. BARN - CLOSE ON BURNING CANDLE - NIGHT

> HENRY
>
> ... B-B, Bottom.

> SALLY
>
> C... Candle. Now D... Dark. It's dark outside
> tonight.

> HENRY
>
> D. Dark.

As they continue, CAMERA PULLS BACK and we:

CROSS FADE TO:

INT. CAPITOL (NEW YORK) - JEFFERSON'S OFFICE - NIGHT

Another candle. Jefferson reads a letter and we hear Sally's V.O. All the while
she teaches the alphabet to Henry—in the b.g. Jefferson walks to his window,
stares out during this.

> SALLY (V.O.)
>
> Dear Thomas. Your absence has made the days
> seem longer than ever. Yet I fill my time wisely
> with many activities in the big house and along
> Mulberry Row to distract me from my longings
> for you. You should see your spring garden. It has
> grown to over-flowing at summer's end. Our little
> son has discovered not only his own toes but mine
> as well. He has also learned to say the word
> 'Papa.'

INT. BARN - CLOSE ON HENRY'S HANDS - DAY

carving a wooden block. Just finishing the letter P.

> SALLY
> ... Papa. P is for Papa. Q. Queen. The Queen of
> France, and R... Reine. La Reine. The French
> word for Queen. You see, it all makes sense
> somehow.

CROSS FADE TO:

INT. JEFFERSON'S OFFICE - ON JEFFERSON'S HANDS - NIGHT

as he writes to Sally. His VOICE FADES IN over:

> JEFFERSON (V.O.)
> ... Where else has nature spread so rich a mantle
> under the eye but at Monticello, Sally? I often
> think of you as I wonder what majesty rides above
> the storms? How sublime to look down into the
> workhouse of nature, to see her clouds...

INT. BARN - NIGHT

Jefferson's voice continues over as Sally sits reading to Henry as he tries writing
his name in a book on the hay. He shows it to Sally who's pleased. Henry feels
proud.

> JEFFERSON (V.O.)
> ... hail, snow, rain, thunder, all fabricated at our
> feet! And the glorious sun, rising as if out of a
> distant water, just gliding the tops of mountains,
> and giving life to all nature...

CROSS FADE TO:

INT. BARN - DAY

Jefferson's VOICE FADES INTO Sally's as she reads his letter while Henry
carves letters.

> JEFFERSON/SALLY
> ... Oh, Sally, I long to be on our little mountain
> where all my wishes end, where I hope my days
> will...

During the last of the speech, Henry quietly leaves the barn.

> SALLY
> He's writing about Monticello, Henry.

She turns to find him gone.

SALLY

Henry...?

She moves to where he was carving. There are seven blocks laid out in a row.
They spell S-A-L H-E-N. Between the two blocks is a block with a heart carved
into the center.

EXT. FIELD - DAY (LATER)

Sally and Polly, now 15, sit on the grass, while Tom plays around them.

POLLY

Sally, do you think I'll ever be pretty enough for
Jack?

SALLY

Of course. Why do you ask?

POLLY

I don't think Jack thinks I'm pretty. Or smart.He
doesn't look at me as if I'm special. Not like Papa
looks at you. That's special.

SALLY

(cautious)
Y...you think your father favors me?

POLLY

Of course. I've known since France.

SALLY

What else do you know?

POLLY

That little Tom...is my brother.

SALLY

Polly, you know we must never...

POLLY

...I know, but you make him so happy, Sally. I
only hope I'll find that.

SALLY

Maybe I can help. Tonight when Jack arrives with
Martha and Randolph I'll make sure you're the
prettiest girl he's ever seen.

INT. ENTRANCE HALL - NIGHT

Martha, clearly pregnant, and husband Randolph come through the door. Jack
and Jupiter help with the baggage. Martha holds her stomach in slight pain.

MARTHA
God help me, those bad Virginia roads have made
me ill.

Sally brings Polly in. Polly is quite the beauty. She has on makeup, her hair
is up and her dress is cinched in tight at the waist. Jack's interest is piqued.

JACK
Polly? Why, you look ravishing.

POLLY
(with sophistication)
Call me Maria. 'Polly' is so childish.

MARTHA
Sister, that dress is far too bold for you.

MARTHA
Where is everybody... Sally, were you not
informed of my arrival? I will await the birth of
my child here and then travel to Washington to be
at Papa's side. He is in need of a link with his
family as he and Hamilton seem to be pitted in the
cabinet like two cocks. As for Adams, he is
growing absurdly mad with his delusions of
succeeding the President.
(then)
Sally, where is Betty? I wish to have a bath for
both myself and the child. My God. My insides
are burning.

She exits with Randolph in tow. As Sally watches hopefully, Jack holds out his
hand to Polly and the two go in the parlor.

DISSOLVE TO:

INT. HALLWAY - NIGHT

Sally moves through the front hallway by candlelight with a basin of fresh water.
Randolph is wandering outside Martha's room. Crying, confused. Sally runs
toward him.

RANDOLPH
Help us... help us, somebody...

INT. MARTHA'S BEDROOM - NIGHT

Polly stands near the bed as Martha lays on her side, clutching her stomach,
moaning in pain. The sheets are bloody.

MARTHA
Sally, please... help me.

EXT. JEFFERSON FAMILY CEMETERY - LATE AFTERNOON

The family Martha, Randolph, Polly, Jack, Samuel, and Peter, along with a minister gathers at the Jefferson family cemetery near the bottom of the plantation, Martha's stillborn baby is buried in a tiny casket.

At some distance outside the gates, Sally, Betty, Critta and other house slaves gather under the trees and watch quietly. Two field slaves stand ready to cover the coffin with dirt.

SLOW DISSOLVE TO:

EXT. FIELDS - NEAR CREEK - NIGHT

We hear the BAYING of small HOUNDS in the tall grass. CLOSE ON the face of a female RUNAWAY and CLOSE ON her feet, running for her life. Over this we hear Henry struggling to read.

> HENRY (V.O.)
> Oh t-that this too solid flesh w- would melt,thaw,
> and re re—sss...

> SALLY (V.O.)
> ... Resolve...

INT. BARN - NIGHT

Henry is reading to Sally by candlelight.

> HENRY
> ...resolve itself into a dew.

EXT. BARN - NIGHT

The runaway comes closer... breathing hard, gasping for air, crashing against the barn door.

INT. BARN - NIGHT

Hearing the crash, Henry and Sally jump to their feet, frightened. Sally hides the books as the runaway collapses into the barn. Through her dress we see blood.

> RUNAWAY
> Jesus, help me... the dogs is loose on me. I stole, I
> did... an' he beat me... now he want me dead...
> Jesus, help me. Help me get to...

> SALLY
> (to Henry)
> The river. Help me.

SMASH CUT TO:

EXT. BARN - NIGHT

Sally and the runaway ride away.

EXT. RIVER ROAD - CLOSE ON HORSES' HOOFS - NIGHT

PAN UP TO the team pulling the small buggy. CLOSE ON Sally, Henry and runaway.

EXT. BARN - NIGHT

The SLAVERS arrive at the barn with the horses and dogs. The DOGS BAY and run toward the road.

                    SLAVER #1
          The river!

EXT. CREEK BANK CLEARING - NIGHT

Sally, Henry, and the Runaway arrive, get out and rush to the banks.

                    SALLY
          This creek leads to the river. Don't be afraid. Just
          follow it. Hide by day, travel by night. God be
          with you.

The woman runs into the river. Out of the woods come the DOGS SNAPPING and GROWLING. Surrounding Sally and Henry. The Slavers call the dogs off, then come out of the darkness.

                    SLAVER #1
          There be two of 'em. One buck here...

He comes closer to Sally with his torch lit.

                    SLAVER #1
          ...God a'mighty, look at this. Just as white as my
          mama.

                    HENRY
          We belongs here, Massa.

                    SLAVER #1
          Well you mus', boy, 'cause you ain't one o' my
          niggas. I jus' lost my nigga cus you done helped
          her go...
                    (to Sally; intentions clear)
          Now I gotta get a new one.

He places his hands on Sally's hair. Whispers gently.

                    SLAVER #1
          C'mere, gal.

Henry cannot bear what he is seeing. He moves forward.

> SLAVER #1
>
> Hold that buck, Martin.

> SALLY
>
> I warn you, sir. I am the property of Thomas
> Jefferson.

CUT TO:

EXT. MONTICELLO HOUSE - NIGHT

The Slaver drives the buggy with Henry being pulled along behind, both hands tied by rope. Sally sits beside the driver. Jefferson's carriage is being unloaded outside by James and Robert. James rushes toward the buggy.

> JAMES
>
> Sister, what has happened?

> SLAVER #1
>
> (to James)
> You just step back there, friend, till we clear this up.

Jefferson appears.

> SLAVER #1
>
> Mr. Jefferson, sir, we are very sorry to wake you,
> but these two were down to the river helpin' one
> of mine escape and claim you as their owner.

Jefferson speaks softly... but is clearly angry.

> JEFFERSON
>
> Untie my servants at once.

> SLAVER #1
>
> No harm meant, sir... but I'm going to have to get
> $800.00, sir... or maybe we could settle...

He looks at Sally. His interest clear.

> SLAVER #1
>
> I admire your taste, sir.

> JEFFERSON
>
> (close to him)
> How dare you! Now leave my property or I'll kill
> you with my bare hands.

The men leave.

JEFFERSON

James, see to Henry. Sally, did they harm you?

She cannot meet his eyes. Shakes her head.

CUT TO:

INT. MASTER SUITE - LATER

Jefferson is livid.

JEFFERSON

How dare you!!

SALLY

They would have killed her.

JEFFERSON

This plantation is not a haven for escapees! Is that clear to you!?

SALLY

Is it clear to you that I cannot stand by and watch another slave hunted like an animal?

JEFFERSON

Yes, yes, damn you!
        (a beat)
I cannot reconcile what happened to you with those men. Your humiliation is mine in my inability to keep you safe.

INT. SALLY'S ROOM - NIGHT

Jefferson and Sally lie in bed.

JEFFERSON

I handed Washington my letter of resignation. I was going to tell you last night before...
        (a beat)
I'm going to retire here to Monticello for good. Sanctum, sanctorum, Sally. And safety.

SLOW DISSOLVE TO:

EXT. MULBERRY ROW - DAY (1796)

Spring day. Jefferson leads a curious parade, of two French architects, a group of slave carpenters, including Henry Jackson and several children, among them grandson, JEFF RANDOLPH, four, Jamy Hemings, nine, and TOM HEMINGS, six, down the road to Mulberry Row. He rambles happily.

JEFFERSON
As it is we are now living in a brick kiln! This is
not acceptable. There fore we shall remodel and
redefine our environment.
(to the children)
The environment is therein where you live. So
onward!

He carries plans rolled under his arm as he rambles on. Tom Hemings and
Jeff Randolph play and joke around with each other. They're friends.
He enters the row and moves on to a long table outside the nailery. A scale
model of the "new" Monticello sits in the center. Some slaves back away,
unsureof how to react.

JEFFERSON
Now, now. Let us not stand in the path of
progress! Come, Jeff, Tom, Jamy. Try my latest
invention. Swivel chairs!

The children gather around as Tom, Jeff and Jamy try the chairs. Jeff falls
from his. Jefferson happily continues spreading his drawings to show the
architects and others.

JEFFERSON
This represents what shall be the new Monticello.
We shall tear down the front facade and part of the
second story. We'll expand the front into an
impressive foyer even though those whom we
might wish to impress will never come here
according to my daughter.
(a beat)
Now, the new dome, through which we might see
the heavens at play, will be built on the same
principle as the great Roman temple of Vesta as
interpreted by the French at the Halle aux Bleds...

Henry motions to another slave re the model of Monticello.

HENRY
(sotto voce)
We's looking at least 20 years of our lives, boy.

During Jefferson's speech, Sally comes over carrying her new baby, Edy,
who has a cough.

JEFFERSON
Virtue, beauty and progress...

There is great applause at this impromptu speech.Jefferson, pleased, walks
over to Betty and Critta who are working on a large quilt. Sally trails
behind him with the baby.

                        JEFFERSON
        Betty, pray what is this ornate creation?

She shows him the quilt.

                         BETTY
        This is the Hemings' family quilt. See, this is my
        mama from Africa. An' this is my daddy, Cap'n
        Hemings, an' here's Sally an' Critta's daddy,
        Masta Wayles, and his daughter Martha, your late
        wife and Sally's half-sister...

Jefferson becomes uneasy. The crowd is quiet. Betty goes on.

                         BETTY
        ... An' now here's James an' Critta, an' Critta's
        boy, Jamy, an' this is Sally, Peter, Robert an'...
        your little Tom an' Edy.

Jefferson nods, then walks away uncomfortably. The slave women chuckle.

INT./EXT. KITCHEN PATIO AREA - DAY

Sally is breast feeding Edy while Critta washes dishes. James is drinking
heavily while showing Peter Hemings how to cook tonight's French
culinary delight.

                         JAMES
        12 cueillerres de sucre en poudre. Put them in
        little by little. See?

Peter nods just as Martha suddenly appears with her baby.

                        MARTHA
        Sally, I had to walk all the way down here to find
        you. Ellen needs to be changed and dressed.

But EDY STARTS COUGHING. Martha stops and looks.

                        MARTHA
        What is wrong with little Edy?

                         SALLY
        Edy won't take my milk. She's sick.

                        MARTHA
        Oh my, I shall inform Papa.

She carries her own baby back down the road.

                         JAMES
            (mimicks)
        'Oh my. I shall inform Papa.' As if he can do

JAMES (Cont'd)

anything about your sick baby. She acts as if he can walk on water!

SALLY

James, stop it.

Peter Carr has come up the road on horseback.

PETER

How is everyone this fine evening?

CRITTA

(nervous, looks down)

Jes' fine, suh.

JAMES

No, suh... no, suh.

SALLY

James...

JAMES

No, suh, we are not fine this evening and we would request that you remain on your side of the plantation...

PETER

Why, James, you are inebriated.

JAMES

I want you to stop raping my sister everytime you come to this plantation!

Critta runs off, ashamed. James keeps up his assault on Peter.

JAMES

How dare you think all Negro women are for the taking, just because you got that high and mighty white skin.

PETER

If you are not careful in your drunken insolence, you uppity Sambo, I am likely to turn you out to the fields.

James glares at him.

PETER

Turn your eyes away from me.

James rushes him. Peter draws his whip. Betty intervenes.

BETTY

Master Carr, you put up that whip and git back to

BETTY (Cont'd)
the house!
> (to James)

An' you get back to the kitchen and clean up. I ain't havin' you serve dinner like some drunken fool.

James walks off.

INT. DINING ROOM - NIGHT   (LATER)

MARTHA
President Alexander Hamilton?
Madness.

RANDOLPH
Good God.

Dinner is over, the family shares after dinner conversation. Sally and Betty clear up. Young Tom is helping. INCLUDE Samuel, Peter, Jack with Polly, Martha and Randolph. Jefferson reads a newspaper and watches Sally and Tom as she teaches him.

MARTHA
He would make a worse President than Adams.
Papa, you must run.

JEFFERSON
Nonsense.

SAMUEL
Martha's right. It does America no good having your brilliant mind retired here designing swivel chairs and domes and allowing Hamilton or worse John Adams to become dictator.

JEFFERSON
We have had a dictator, sir... George Washington.

MARTHA
Please, Papa, be serious.

PETER
And God help us should Hamilton win, the dismantling of the South won't be far behind. He's a Northerner.

Young Tom drops a handful of silverware on the floor. Sally bends to help him pick it up. Jefferson smiles.

RANDOLPH
The nationalization of cotton and tobacco. Indeed.

SAMUEL

Uncle, tell the Republicans you'll run.

RANDOLPH

Oh, Republicans are we now?

JEFFERSON

Well there are some issues I feel require a man of
some vision. The idea of States' rights, the
economy. Slavery.

Sally throws Jefferson a look.

JACK

There's an issue teeming with debate.

RANDOLPH

Debate?

MARTHA

Be silent, Mr. Randolph. Father...

PETER

There's nothing to debate. The South cannot
continue to provide three quarters of the country's
cotton, and tobacco without a slave work force.
It's the Southern way of life.

MARTHA

That doesn't make it right, Peter.

Everyone looks at Martha.

MARTHA

We really don't have to hold human flesh in
bondage just for commerce. Papa, you've said
yourself in the genuine scheme of things, all any
of us truly wants is a piece of earth to live on,
loved ones around us and food on our tables. I
think slaves would work the same as now if they
knew at the end of the day their labors were for
their families and their own bit of land.

For a moment we see Martha in a new light.

MARTHA

Well...

The door opens and James Hemings steps in.

JAMES

Master Jefferson...

JEFFERSON

Yes, James, come in.

                                JAMES
        I'll be leaving Monticello. Our agreement in Paris, sir.
            (a beat)
        I cannot turn down freedom twice.

Sally is dismayed. Looks to Jefferson.

EXT. MONTICELLO SIDE PORCH - DAY   (NEXT DAY)

Sally and James come out.

                                JAMES
        By returning here I kept my promise to you. But if
        I stay I fear I'll kill one of these white folks, or
        we'll all be hurt in my trying.

EXT. MULBERRY ROW - STABLES - DAWN

Morning cooking fires burn as we FIND Sally, carrying little Edy, walking
through the row. Slaves watch silently as she goes to Betty's cabin and looks in.
There, in the cold dawn light, Betty weeps, held by Sukey and Critta. Betty looks
out to Sally. The two women cannot speak through their pain.

EXT. MONTICELLO MAIN ROAD - CLOSE ON JAMES - DAWN

James Hemings is riding away from Monticello. Young Tom Hemings and a
group of slave children run after him, waving and calling their good-byes. Sally
cries near her tree, her baby weak in her arms. Henry stands beside her,
comforting.

                            SALLY (V.O.)
        ...A cloud passed over Monticello. James leaving
        was a kind of death...

EXT. SLAVE CEMETERY BY RIVER - DAY

The Hemings family, other slaves, Sukey, Henry and Polly are gathered as
Edy is buried. Sally is in tears as a group sings a capella. Martha places a
rose on the little mound of dirt covering the grave. She looks at Sally with an
understanding only another mother can have.

                            SALLY (V.O.)
        ...My daughter's was another. When Martha's
        baby died, she was buried in the elegant family
        cemetery down the hill. But when my Edy died of
        whooping cough, she, Jefferson's blood daughter,
        was buried in the slave cemetery...

Jefferson is at a distance, unable to outwardly reveal his grief.

END ACT FIVE

ACT SIX

INT. MONTICELLO - DAY (1800)

A string quartet plays as Polly is brought in by Jefferson and married by a minister to Jack Eppes.

> SALLY (V.O.)
> ...Thomas lost his bid for President to John Adams
> and thus became Vice- President. Then he and
> Adams clashed on every issue and Thomas could
> do nothing of consequence about anything.
> Especially slavery...

Samuel and Peter Carr, Martha, Randolph and the children, Betty, Critta and the rest of the house servants also attend. Other guests include friends from nearby plantations.

EXT. MONTICELLO PORCH - DAY

Jefferson toasts.

> JEFFERSON
> To my dear sweet Polly and husband, Jack, I pray
> you long, happy, fruitful lives in loving company.
> With the deepest love I bestow upon you our
> beautiful Pantops plantation, 819 acres and 26
> slaves in service to your happiness.

Music begins again as she looks toward Mulberry Row. The field slaves are under the trees watching the festivities. She spots Henry near her old swing. She goes over.

EXT. MONTICELLO TREES - CONTINUOUS ACTION - DAY

Sally approaches Henry.

> SALLY
> Henry, why don't you come closer?

But Henry just stares at the house. He's in a strange mood.

> HENRY
> No. I soon as bring a musket up here an' put a
> bullet in one o' dem peckerwood's heads.

> SALLY
> Henry!

He has a newspaper. Shows Sally a story.

HENRY

See this?
>(reads crudely)

The r-revolts led by freed slave Gabriel Prosser,
have now caused i-injury to over two dozen
plantation owners. What he's doin' is how you
gotta handle things sometimes.

SALLY

No, Henry. Gabriel Prosser means to kill people.
You know killing isn't right.

HENRY

'Course it ain't to you—or any of you Hemings
'house negroes.' All yall do is cook an' serve an'
go to weddings.

Henry's passion takes over. He attempts to kiss her.

HENRY

Don't you feel nothin' for me?

SALLY

I do, just...

HENRY

Jus' not what you feel for him, huh?

She says nothing. Henry slams his fist into a tree.

HENRY

An' he up there in the Capitol wit' another
woman... a white woman.

Sally is in shock.

HENRY

Her name is Margaret Bayard Smith, an' he been
seein' her ever since he been vice-president. Yo'
brother, Robert, tol' me he drive 'em 'round.
>(anger building)

Then he come back here to you, an' you jus' lie on
your back goin'...
>(demonstrates)

...Oooh, Massa, thank you, Massa, here be a baby.
Ohh, Massa, here be another.

Sally slaps him hard across the face. But he grabs her wrists.

HENRY

Don't you remember how it felt when that white
bastard touched you? Grabbed you? Jus' knowin'
he could take you if he wanted? That's how it is
for most of us in the fields.

Sally weeps.

> HENRY
>
> But now you in danger, Sally. The rising gonna
> come and them loyal to the big house gon burn up
> in it. Come with me, Sally. Bring the children.

> SALLY
>
> Henry, please. Stop this! No.

He looks at her, realizing she'll never be his, then pulls a small carved wooden
heart from his pocket. Recites Shakespeare from memory.

> HENRY
>
> 'Being your slave, what should I do but tend upon
> the hours and times of your desire? I have no
> precious time to spend. Nor service to do, till you
> require...'

He hands her the heart.

> HENRY
>
> Take it. It's my heart. I love you.

And after touching her face sadly, he runs into the woods. Sally tearfully stares
down at the heart. In the b.g., guests wave good-bye to the bride and groom as
their carriage moves down the long road.

EXT. MONTICELLO - HILL OVER RIVER - DAY

Jefferson stands on the bluff overlooking the Rivanna River still in his wedding
clothes. He has set up a telescope and is looking across the river to a distant hill.
Sally walks angrily towards him. He is unaware of her mood.

> JEFFERSON
>
> Sally, you left the party...never mind, look through
> here. This is the ideal site to build the university.
>> (senses her mood)
> What is the matter...?

> SALLY
>
> 'Twenty-six slaves in service to your happiness.'

> JEFFERSON
>
> Let me explain...

> SALLY
>
> You just gave them away.

> JEFFERSON
>
> No, no. It is merely a transfer from this location to
> Polly's.

> SALLY
>
> Martha was right. It's wrong to own human beings for commerce.

> JEFFERSON
>
> No one has worked harder than I...

> SALLY
>
> ...Who is Margaret Bayard Smith?

This stops him. Jefferson is careful.

> JEFFERSON
>
> Mrs. Smith is a friend... a social companion. I only spend time with Margaret when...

> SALLY
>
> 'Margaret?'

> JEFFERSON
>
> ... when her husband is away from...

> SALLY
>
> ... 'Husband'...?

> JEFFERSON
>
> ... away from Washington. We keep similar company. And that is all!

> SALLY
>
> I too keep similar company!

> JEFFERSON
>
> With whom?

> SALLY
>
> My own!

> JEFFERSON
>
> Who is he?

Sally turns and runs toward the house.

> SALLY
>
> What do you care?

SMASH CUT TO:

INT. SALLY'S BEDROOM - DAY

Jefferson POUNDS on the door.

> JEFFERSON (O.S.)
>
> Open this door.

INT. FRONT HALLWAY/PORCH -DAY

Martha, Critta and Betty — all cleaning up from the wedding — react to the NOISE from above.

INT. SALLY'S BEDROOM - DAY

Jefferson bursts through the door.

> JEFFERSON
> Have you lost your mind?

> SALLY
> Why? Because I keep company with a slave?

> JEFFERSON
> I forbid this! I will not have another man touch you!

> SALLY
> I shall do as I wish!

Jefferson advances on her, pushing her roughly down to a submissive position on the edge of the bed. Sally struggles.

> JEFFERSON
> Do you understand! You belong to me!

Sally suddenly goes limp beneath his strength. Stares at him a moment.

> SALLY
> You don't have to hurt me, Mr. Jefferson. You own me.
> (pointedly)
> Remember?

Jefferson is confounded by his actions. He melts, holding her tightly.

> JEFFERSON
> My God, Sally. I...I'm. Oh God.

> SALLY (V.O.)
> ...In April 1798 I gave birth to another son. I named him Beverly Jefferson Hemings. Six months later, when Thomas Jefferson finally decided he would run for President again, I became pregnant with our daughter, Harriet...

FADE OUT:

END OF ACT SIX

ACT SEVEN

INT. DINING ROOM - NIGHT (1800)

Dolley Madison — ever the hostess — seats the guests. They include her husband James, Jefferson, Martha and Randolph, Polly and Jack, Peter andSamuel and...

...JAMES THOMPSON CALLENDER, a 52-year-old Englishman and journalist.

> DOLLEY
> ...and Mr. Callender shall be opposite Martha and me.

Sally, pregnant, young Tom (now 12), and Peter Hemings are serving.

> MARTHA
> Thank you, Mrs. Madison. Commence service,
> Sally.

> MADISON
> A toast to our guest. Mr. James Thompson
> Callender, distinguished scribe for the Richmond
> Recorder...

> DOLLEY
> ...who we hope shall aid us in Mr. Jefferson's bid
> for the Presidency.

They toast.

> CALLENDER
> Mrs. Madison, do you recall the Elias Theater in
> New York City where we last met? What was the
> play that evening? You were in the company of
> Mr. Aaron Burr were you not?

> DOLLEY
> (somewhat flustered)
> Sir, I do not discuss my previous social circles.
> Now if we may...

> CALLENDER
> ... Mrs. Madison, I speak of a decade ago. Surely
> you are not a creature plagued with
> embarrassment over prior indiscretions?

> RANDOLPH
> Indiscretions...?

> SAMUEL
> Reporters feed upon such things sir.

CALLENDER

Feed, sir? Indeed we kneel at the trough. Truth
Society's demand. Ragged, rubbed and scribbles
by this humble pen. Truth is knowledge, or
whatever.

MARTHA

But we are all protectors of the first amendment in
this household are we not?

CALLENDER

And I give thanks for that, madame, as I have
printed more items against the Federalists for your
father than any journalist might deem wise.

Callender motions to Sally to serve his soup. His tone is now softer as he sips.
He looks at Sally and says pointedly.

CALLENDER

Delicious.
          (indicates Tom)
Is that your boy?

SALLY

Yes, sir. He is.

CALLENDER

And I see you're plump with another. Is the boy's
father also a servant?

Sally glances at Jefferson nervously. Callender looks to Jefferson as well.

CALLENDER

And so they speak of Monticello's fair-skinned
slaves—auburn, blond, and red-hair abounding.
Such mixed beauty no doubt created by...

JEFFERSON

They are members of the same family.

CALLENDER

And which family might that be, sir?

JEFFERSON

The Hemings family, sir.

CALLENDER

Then I must commend you on acquiring such a
rare family and allowing this dusky beauty here to
function as...

He stands and lifts his glass.

CALLENDER
Mistress of Monticello.

Sally leaves, pulling Tom with her. Randolph mumbles. The rest of the room is
dead silent.

EXT. MONTICELLO PORCH - NIGHT

Jefferson accompanies Callender down the steps. He silently represses his anger.

CALLENDER
Let us be candid with each other, Mr. Jefferson. I
would favor withholding any embarrassment with
regard to your family or friends for consideration
of a bit of pocket change.
(a beat)
Or, should you ascend to the Presidency, perhaps
the consideration of Postmaster in Virginia?

JEFFERSON
Mr. Callender, you cannot be so bold as to attempt
to blackmail me in my own home.

CALLENDER
(pointedly)
You are a candidate for President of the United
States, sir. A delicate business with regard to
reputation.

EXT. TOBACCO FIELD - DAY

SHERIFF CLENON and four deputies all ride up on horseback. Jefferson is on
horseback, Sally and Critta walk next to a buggy along the road.

SHERIFF
Mr. Vice-President. I'm Sheriff Clenon and these
are my deputies. Governor Monroe has dispatched
us to protect you, sir. There was some trouble
outside of Richmond with regard to several
armed, escaped slaves intent on killing plantation
owners and white citizens. We would ask those on
your plantation to remain inside until we've
quelled this insurrection.

JEFFERSON
How did this come to be, sir?

SHERIFF
A runaway by the name of Gabriel Prosser
gathered a ruthless group of young bucks
including one we believe was under your
ownership.

JEFFERSON

Who?

SHERIFF

Henry Jackson. But we caught him and he'll be
hanged at first light.

OFF Sally we:

CUT TO:

EXT. CLEARING - DAY

Sally arrives in a buckboard with Tom. Dozens have gathered under the trees to
witness the hangings. Two have already been hanged, the bodies swing.

When Henry sees Sally, he stops and a moment of contrition reflects on his face,but
the guards force the noose to his neck. He fights them. His fierce determination is
primal, animal-like as the deputies try to control him.

Finally, one of the deputies pulls out his GUN and SHOOTS Henry in the head...
Sally is shocked and horrified as she tearfully watches Henry's proud body fall.

SLOW DISSOLVE TO:

INT. BETTY'S CABIN - NIGHT

Jefferson stands in the doorway as Sally huddles with Tom and Beverly.
Her face is swollen from crying.

JEFFERSON
He took part in the murder of a family, Sally, there
was nothing I could do.

SALLY
...I feel like killing people too. Does that surprise
you? That people can be strained so tight at the
yoke of slavery it makes them want to murder?
(pause)
I taught Henry to read and write.

JEFFERSON
... and you could be hanged for that.

SALLY
And then what is your solution? Where do you
stand on slavery because that's what killed Henry.

JEFFERSON
I have fought against this...

SALLY
Not enough.

                    JEFFERSON
I believe so strongly in the cessation of slavery
that I wrote to that issue specifically in my first
draft of The Declaration of Independence.
Southern delegates—men I respected—tore and
plundered those passages to shreds, obliterating
every reference to slavery. Not one idea survived
the final draft, not one.

                    SALLY
Then you must fight again. In Paris you told me
that this abomination must end—be true to your
words, Thomas, for if you become President you
can not come to my bed, then go to your white
congress and do nothing about this plague on my
people.

                    SALLY (V.O.)
...But James Thompson Callender made good on
his threats, and all our lives changed forever...

INT. PARLOR - DAY

Jefferson, Martha, Polly (who is pregnant) Randolph, Peter, and Samuel are
joined by James Madison. The discussion is heated. Young Tom Hemings and
Betty are serving.

Martha reads from the Richmond Recorder.

                    MARTHA
'It is well known that the man, whom it delighteth
the people to honor, keeps and for many years has
kept, as his concubine, one of his slaves...'

                    PETER
...'by this wench Sally, our President has had
several children...'

                    RANDOLPH
        Absurd.

                    PETER
Betty, Tom, please excuse yourselves.

They leave, but eavesdrop outside the door.

                    SAMUEL
All this because you would not appoint their man
as Postmaster?

MADISON

Callender has spread these allegations of your
personal life for all the world to see.

JEFFERSON

Then I damn the eternal medicant!

MADISON

I have come to tell you that members of congress
ridicule you and speculate on how soon you shall
resign.

JEFFERSON

The charges of this clot-hearted bastard will be
ignored.

MADISON

Ignored? Thomas? Though our Southern
colleagues might forgive in the face of their own
slave dalliances, the rest will pile high their scorn
upon your office. You must respond!

JEFFERSON

To respond is to engage.

MARTHA

(still reading)
'Her name is Sally. The name of her eldest son is Tom.'

SAMUEL

My God, he calls him 'the little president.'

Young Tom is reacting to this.

MARTHA

'... His features bear a striking resemblance to the
President himself.' Oh, Lord. Sell them both,
Papa.

POLLY

No, Papa, Sally's my friend.

Tom bolts from the hallway. Betty Hemings follows. Peter catches the boy.

PETER

You better run, you little bastard, because the
country won't stand for it.

Madison pulls Jefferson aside.

MADISON

(out of earshot)
You are the President, man! Your conduct must be
above reproach! Now take immediate action...

MARTHA
(continues reading)
'The woman has a room to herself at
Monticello...' Who told him that?
(then)
And this from the Gazette— 'Jefferson's
daughters have the mortification to see illegitimate
mulatto siblings sharing the same parental
affections as themselves...'

MADISON
... Unless...
(sudden realization)
... do you love her?

JEFFERSON
For God's sake, Martha, be silent!
(to Madison)
Do you love your wife, sir?

MADISON
Yes, but she is...

JEFFERSON
...White? Perhaps you are right, James. Perhaps I
should answer these claims and say, yes, I am an
unattached widower who has a black mistress and
children with her, and, as President, I intend to
take the position of my youth and end slavery.

MADISON
Then good God, man. You will no longer be
President!

EXT. MONTICELLO ROAD TO ROW - DAY

Tom is running towards the row, Betty in pursuit calling.

BETTY
Tom... Thomas... please, boy...

EXT. MULBERRY ROW - DAY

Several slaves gather at the commotion. Sally comes out of the kitchen with Critta.
Runs to Tom, following him to his cabin.

SALLY
Tom, Tom? What is it, boy?

Betty stops her as Tom enters his cabin.

                              BETTY
            You and Massa Jefferson. It's all in the papers
            now. They be namin' Tom. Mockin' him. Call him
            names.

Sally stares at Betty, unsure.

                              BETTY
            He can't take it. Talk to him.

INT. SLAVE CABIN - DAY

The cabin sleeps six or more on a row of rough mattresses spread on the floor.
Tom kneels facing away from the door. Holding back tears. Sally enters.

                              TOM
            I'm runnin', Mama, as soon as I can pack my
            clothes. This is all my fault.

                              SALLY
            No, Tom... it's not your fault.

                              TOM
            By God, Mama, they mean to sell us all. I ain't
            livin' here.

Sally looks down at him. Her face reflects her pain. She turns and bolts out the
door, passing Betty, Critta and the others who are gathered outside.

INT. MONTICELLO PARLOR - DAY

ON Sally as she enters and addresses Jefferson.

                              SALLY
            I wish to speak to you, sir!

                            JEFFERSON
            This is not an appropriate time, Sally.

                              SALLY
            I wish to speak to the President now!

                             MARTHA
                    (upset: to Jefferson)
            Papa!
                    (then to Sally)
            If you must know, we are discussing what must be
            done in the light of the growing scandal you have
            brought on our household...

                            JEFFERSON
            Silence, Martha. Sally, I cannot speak with
            you now.

SALLY

...And what must be done? Am I to be sold? Is our
son to be sold?

MARTHA

Be silent, Sally! Papa do you not have authority in
your own home!

JEFFERSON

I cannot speak with you now, Sally...

SALLY

Answer me, sir!

JEFFERSON

Kindly leave the room, Martha.

Martha grunts, leaves. Jefferson snatches Sally by the arm, takes her aside.

JEFFERSON

What is wrong with you? Did you not hear me? I
cannot speak with you now!

SALLY

All I hear from you are words. 'We hold these
truths to be self-evident.' What truths, to whom?
'Endowed by their creator with life and liberty.'
You are plotting to sell my life and liberty now!
You hypocrite! Our son...

JEFFERSON

... Sally.

SALLY

...Our son, Thomas, he's leaving us. He is leaving
this place, and you and me...and I am allowing
this and you will not stop him.

Jefferson has turned away. Tortured, he does not respond.

EXT. MULBERRY ROW - DAY

Young Tom finishes loading his saddlebags. Little Harriet and Beverly watch
silently as Sally comes up close to her son and produces Jefferson's gold pocket
watch (the one we saw in Paris) and hands it to Tom.

SALLY

I want you to have this. You remember who you
are. Mr. Jefferson has a cousin in Greenbriar
county—Drury Woodson. Stop there for food.

TOM

He's gonna sell you, Mama.

SALLY
Be strong, son. I love you, Tom.

Sally kisses him, he mounts his horse and rides off. Little Harriet and Beverly weep and run with their mother to the old tree to see their brother galloping away from Monticello.

INT. MONTICELLO ENTRANCEWAY - DAY

Jefferson looks out the large window at the scene outside. He sees his son riding away and Sally and the children under the great tree. Behind him we see Martha in the shadows.

MARTHA
Sell her, Papa...

EXT. MONTICELLO GREAT TREE - DAY

Sally is clutching her two remaining children. Will he sell her?

MARTHA (O.S.)
...Sell Sally now!

FADE OUT:

END NIGHT ONE

SALLY HEMINGS: AN AMERICAN SCANDAL

[NIGHT TWO]

ACT EIGHT

FADE IN:

MAIN TITLE AND CREDITS IN OVER:

INT./EXT. MONTICELLO - DAY

ESTABLISH Monticello OVER CREDIT SEQUENCE.

EXT. MONTICELLO - DAY

SALLY HEMINGS walks across the yard toward the house.She stops at the
window and sees Jefferson at his desk.

> SALLY (V.O.)
> By January 1803, the scandal had plagued Thomas
> and me for months. Newspapers from New York
> to the Mississippi were filled with every manner
> of cruel speculation on our relationship and even
> Monticello was no longer safe for me...

EXT./INT. JEFFERSON'S STUDY - REVERSE ANGLE - DAY

Sally is at the window as THOMAS JEFFERSON sits alone at his desk,
anguished over the newspaper articles in front of him — all dealing with his
relationship with Sally. In the b.g. we hear Martha's muffled voice from
elsewhere in the house.

> MARTHA (O.S.)
> ...If you, for one moment wish to doubt the danger
> of this attack upon us read this— 'the Aristocracy
> of this neighborhood is one of the vilest in
> America...' James Callender.

INT. PARLOR - DAY

MARTHA stands in front of the gathered family — PETER and SAMUEL
CARR, and THOMAS MANN RANDOLPH, JR.

> RANDOLPH
> James Callender be damned!

> MARTHA
> Since Papa has chosen not to address this issue,
> we, as a family, must be mindful of his legacy. All
> of us.

MARTHA

Samuel, Peter, you're his nephews, Randolph,
you're his son-in-law. We must all agree. Papa is
the President. And it shall be the position of this
family that these accusations regarding Sally are
false and the events never occurred.

EXT. CROSSROADS (OUTSIDE RICHMOND) - DAY

A sketch artist is finishing a scathing sexual caricature of Jefferson and "Black
Sal." Sally is depicted with exaggerated lips, eyes and corkscrew hair. PULL
BACK and we see JAMES THOMPSON CALLENDER sitting at a long table
with the reporters drinking, laughing at the sketch.

CALLENDER

Yes! Ha, ha. We'll print it! Let me titillate you
with the accompanying text.

A crowd from the outdoor market begins to gather in curiosity. A white man
having his shoes shined by a black man with his BACK TO CAMERA reading
the Richmond Recorder. The headline reads: "Jefferson and Negro Paramour?
Truth? Or Federalist Propaganda?"

CALLENDER

'President Jefferson has been for years living in a
habitual, loathsome relationship with his slave,
Sally Hemings, and through that unholy union he
has bred several mixed offspring.' Well I ask you
now, how do we present such an alliance to our
wives? What do we say to our children...?

Some people in the crowd respond.

CALLENDER

... Is this slave fornicator really the man we want
to reelect for another four years? An atheist from
whom we must hide our Bibles, whose character
and personal behavior is so beneath reproach it's
contemptible...?

Great applause and laughter through the crowd. Callender is now in the middle
of the gathering. His hands quiet them. As the crowd yells, we notice a shocking
sight. The man shining shoes is none other than...

JAMES HEMINGS...

...disheveled and drunk! He stands and begins staggering through the crowd. His
clothes are the now worn and filthy French garments we first saw him wear in
Paris. Callender continues.

CALLENDER

... Well the ruin of Mr. Jefferson and his party and
indeed this very nation, lies in the hands of a slut
as common as the pavement!

The crowd cheers. But suddenly James cries out in a drunken rage of French and English.

> JAMES
> Blasphemy! Lies! I am James Hemings. You will not defame my sister.

The crowd is shocked by the outburst. Callender laughs.

> CALLENDER
> Your sister, indeed. Witness the result of such repulsive liaisons before us. A savage — blaring in the language of romance. Silence me, sir? I think not. Or do you even comprehend my words?

> JAMES
> Then you, sir, will comprehend my words. The words of a free man. Liberty is a gift of God and not to be violated but with his wrath. Indeed I tremble for my country when I reflect that God is just and that his justice will not sleep forever. Thomas Jefferson.

The crowd is silent, uneasy, unsure. Then Callender begins to sing to the tune of "Yankee Doodle Dandy."

> CALLENDER
> (sings)
> 'Of all the damsels on the green, On the mountain or in the valley, A lass so luscious ne'er was seen as Monticello Sally...'

Others who know the now famous lampoon, join, singing:

> CALLENDER & CROWD
> '... Yankee Doodle, who's the noodle? What wife were half so handy? To breed a flock of slaves for stock . A blackmoor's the dandy...'

Callender motions for someone to remove James, and the crowd pushes James aside who in his drunken state can hardly stand. A fiddle and banjo take up the tune.

> CALLENDER & CROWD
> '... She's black you tell me grant she be Must color always tally? lack's love's proper hue for you, And white's the hue for Sally.'

OVER the verses we CUT the FOLLOWING IMAGES —

EXT. CROSSROADS - DAY

CLOSE ON the humiliated James Hemings as he stumbles down the road from the Crossroads.

CLOSE ON newspaper headlines—Washington, New York, Philadelphia,
Richmond— Drawings and stories by all manner of reportage. Pro and con.

INT. HALLWAY - DAY

Sally approaches the door to Jefferson's study when the sound of MARTHA'S
AGITATED VOICE stops her. She listens as we...

INT. JEFFERSON STUDY - DAY

> MARTHA
> Papa, you must extricate yourself from this
> madness. Deny these claims. Sally must be sold.

> JEFFERSON
> Martha, was it not you who said selling human
> flesh for commerce was wrong? Do you revile all
> our servants—or just Sally? Why must you make
> me choose between you?

> MARTHA
> Because the devil is at our very door, now.

Jefferson sighs, feeling the weight of the moment. He rubs his temples.

> JEFFERSON
> Martha, I must leave for Washington in the
> morning. I want you to arrange to have Sally and
> the children transferred...

> MARTHA
> ...Sold, Papa.

> JEFFERSON
> Transferred, Martha. Am I clear? Arrange for Mr.
> Lilly to transport Sally and her children to
> Pantops. She can care for Polly in her illness.
> Now leave me, Martha, my head is throbbing and
> I wish to be alone.

Martha attempts to hug him, but Jefferson is stiff and aloof.

EXT. MONTICELLO - DAWN

In front of the house the Presidential caravan is loaded and ready for departure.

EXT. MULBERRY ROW - DAWN

Word of Sally's "transfer" has reached the row. The slaves watch silently as
Jefferson dressed in formal traveling clothes, walks alone through the area. He
knocks on the door of Betty's cabin—there is no answer. He turns to see Sukey
behind him.

JEFFERSON
(uncomfortable)
Sukey, I am looking for... I am looking for Sally
Hemings.

Sukey stares at him, tears in her eyes. The door to the cabin opens. It is Betty.

BETTY
Yes?

JEFFERSON
Betty, where are Sally and the children?

BETTY
Ain't here, sir.

JEFFERSON
Betty, please... I am leaving for Washington and I
wish to see Sally and the children.

Betty is silent.

JEFFERSON
Betty... why has it come to this?

BETTY
They, can't none o'them, leave us be 'round here.
Now, go'on. They's waitin'. We'll all be here.
Sally'll see you when she's up to it..

JEFFERSON
But I need to get a message to Sally, Betty.

BETTY
Your silence been message enough, massa.

Betty closes the door. Jefferson stands there a moment before turning and leaving.

EXT. MONTICELLO - DAY

Jefferson's coach moves down the road and away from the house with Jefferson
leading on horseback. CAMERA FOLLOWS it to reveal Sally CLOSE as she
watches it go.

INT. SALLY'S ROOM - CLOSE ON MARTHA - DAY

ransacking Sally's room. Going through every piece of furniture, opening
drawers. Looks under the bed. Then she sees the pigskin trunk and
rummages through it. Pulls out the lilac dress, books, perfume bottles, etc.

Finally, she finds Sally's love letters from Jefferson bound in ribbon. She
opens them and starts reading —becoming more and more furious with
each passage. She then finds Sally's diary. But just as she is closing the
trunk, she turns to find... Sally standing.

SALLY

What are you doing in my room?

MARTHA

Your room? This is no longer your room. Nothing
here is yours. It all belongs to Papa and therefore
to me. And upon my orders, you — are barred
from this house and most especially from this
room. Now pack your things and get out!

Martha hurls the letters and diary into the fireplace. Sally fights to retrieve them,
but Martha holds her back.

MARTHA

Oh no. I will not have these shameful letters make
their way into history as the humiliation of you
has already! My father will be remembered as the
righteous and honorable man he is. And, you, you
will be grateful for his generosity to you and your
family and you will be silent. Silent! Do you hear
me? He will return to Washington and he will look
his colleagues in the eye and assure them that
their faith in his character is beyond reproach. And
lastly, with God's help he will find a woman of his
standing and color to share his Presidency and in
his greatness. Go back to the row where you
belong, Sally, and prepare for your departure.

Martha leaves. Sally looks at the fire. Tearfully watches her letters go up in
flames.

DISSOLVE TO:

EXT. PRESIDENT'S HOUSE - EVENING (MATTE SHOT)

Pennsylvania Avenue is a swamp in front of the first White House. A dirt path
is near the unfinished West Wing where 2x4's stand exposed to the elements.

INT. PRESIDENT'S HOUSE - RECEPTION AREA - EVENING

In an old waistcoat and worn pants, Jefferson is entertaining six guests. Peter
Hemings serves drinks in the sparsely furnished, chilly room. Among the guests
are Thomas Paine, now 65; Dolley Madison, who is introducing him around...

...And MARGARET BAYARD SMITH, 40, a beautiful dark-haired socialite who
hangs on Jefferson's arm and his every word as he and James Madison talk.

MARGARET

Pray, Mr. President, what intrigues have you
brought from home this time.

Dolley, overhearing, quickly comes over with Paine.

                              DOLLEY
Such thoughtless attire for so elegant a dinner,
Thomas.
                 (to Margaret)
Margaret, do use your influence and introduce the
President to brocade. Preferably Italian.

                              MARGARET
More difficult than you can imagine, Mrs.
Madison. He so loves the French.

                              JEFFERSON
I'll have no trappings of monarchy in this
administration. I'm a man of the people.

                              PAINE
Then perhaps 'the people' should buy you a new
suit. Preferably Italian.

The others chuckle. So does Jefferson as Paine sips his wine.

                              JEFFERSON
Pay Mr. Paine no attention. He's an old friend.

                              PAINE
Yes. As old as this very expensive wine in this
equally expensive crystal. 'Man of the people,'
indeed.

                              JEFFERSON
Well, I did splurge a bit for our meal. My famous
Virginia hams, aged and cured on my plantation,
were brought here just this morning and prepared
by my chef. And we're going to have ice cream.

They enter the dining room beautifully outfitted with a long lace-covered
dining table. Margaret looks over the table.

                              MARGARET
Are there no place cards?

                              JEFFERSON
No need. We dine pell-mell here.

                              DOLLEY
                 (eyes to heaven)
Pell-mell?

They all find seats where they may. Then Jefferson rings his small serving bell...
which signals for Peter who, followed by two servants, brings out several platters
of food. The guests marvel at the array of corn, beans, sweet potatoes, macaroni
and rolls culminating with the piece de resistance—a Virginia baked ham—brought
out by none other than...

Sally Hemings.

Jefferson, sitting next to Margaret Bayard Smith, almost chokes on his wine. Paine, realizing who she is, looks at Jefferson. James and Dolley are mortified. Margaret is completely unaware.

                    PAINE
          Mr. President, there's a rumor...

Everyone stops — praying he isn't referring to the scandal.

                    PAINE
          ...that you're also in negotiations with the French
          government with regard to the Louisiana
          Territories. Is it true?

A sigh of relief from all except Sally who meets Tom Paine's gaze with a slight smile.

                    MADISON
          We're in luck, you know. Monroe wrote from
          Paris to say the little Corsican is willing to sell
          Louisiana and the Floridas.

                    PAINE
          Then your good fortune is due to those Haitians
          refusing slavery.

                    MARGARET
              (referring to Sally)
          She is lovely, is she not? One could well
          understand how a man might favor a creature of
          such complexion.

Paine to the rescue — stands.

                    PAINE
          A toast, shall we... To the Louisiana Purchase!

Jefferson raises. His eyes lock with Sally's.

                    DOLLEY
              (knowing)
          Raise your glass, Mr. President.

INT. WHITE HOUSE - BACK STAIRS - NIGHT

Dolley stands across from Sally and speaks frankly.

                    DOLLEY
          This was very bold of you, Sally.

SALLY
I know I should not have come but...

DOLLEY
Ultimately we are women, aren't we? Given to the
same second class concerns no matter our color.
Do you think it's easy being a political wife? The
way you're thrust aside and forced to be a
charming, albeit silent, accouterment? No. And
before we were married, I had to fight several
earnest widows showing their ankles for Mr.
Madison. But I had to learn to adapt to situations.
(a beat)
And you must do the same. Perhaps in another
time your presence would be acceptable here. But
Thomas is fighting for his political life.
(softly)
Learn to adapt, Sally. Steel yourself to this horrid
situation. Times will change. You realize, do you
not, this Bayard woman is but a beard to throw the
press off the scent. If that is why you have come
rest assured you still have Thomas's heart.

Sally nods.

DOLLEY
Now come with me. It is late and the President is
no doubt waiting.

INT. JEFFERSON'S QUARTERS - CONTINUOUS ACTION - NIGHT

Jefferson, readying for bed, looks up as Sally enters. He comes to her, then stops.

JEFFERSON
I cannot believe it. How in God's name did you
make your way here?

SALLY
Robert brought me—along with the hams and
your mockingbird.

JEFFERSON
But why? Was your plan to give the two
Federalists at dinner ammunition for my
impeachment? What on earth were you thinking?

SALLY
What was I thinking? What does it matter? What
have I to lose? My diary and private letters have
been burned, I have been locked out of the house.

JEFFERSON
By whose authority were you locked out?

SALLY

Martha's, the one who wants me sold. The one
whose authority comes from you when you're
away from Monticello.

JEFFERSON

I'm sure she means you no harm. She has reacted
to these troubles with fear and misguided emotions.

SALLY

Misguided emotions, which will result in my sale
and that of our children.

JEFFERSON

She is completely out of order in this regard.
Monticello is also your home. I will see to Martha.

He finally holds her desperately. She lingers in his embrace.

JEFFERSON

(softly)
Sally, I've missed you. Do you have any idea how
I've ached to hold you? I was bereft when you
would not see me. A thousand times reason told
me to carve you from my heart. But my affections
grow ever deeper and stronger each time I see you...

SALLY

I've given you four children. And yet I am not the
one sitting next to you at dinner. I want to be at
your side.

DISSOLVE TO:

INT. WHITE HOUSE RESIDENCE - DAY

Sally wakes up to find Jefferson writing a letter. He hands it to her.

JEFFERSON

Return to Monticello. Give this to Martha.

There is a KNOCK on the door. They freeze.

MALE SECRETARY (O.S.)

Mr. President, sir? The Spanish Ambassador is
already here.

JEFFERSON

Tell Ambassador Ysidro I shall be on my way shortly.

They relax and almost giggle.

JEFFERSON
Go home, Sally. And know you take my heart with you.

DISSOLVE TO:

EXT. ROAD OUTSIDE WASHINGTON - DAY

ROBERT is driving Sally in Jefferson's carriage back to Monticello. A group of men on horseback ride up to them, stop their carriage in the process. James Thompson Callender dismounts and approaches.

CALLENDER
Good day.
(stops, as if confused)
I am James Thompson Callender, a scribe for the Richmond Recorder I mistook this carriage for the President's and was alarmed to find it unguarded. This is the President's carriage, is it not?

Callender looks inside. He draws closer to Sally.

CALLENDER
Why you are the negress Sally Hemings. The subject of much negative speculation recently.
(sees she's nervous)
It's alright, you have nothing to fear from me as I seek only the truth. Indeed this chance meeting on the road might give you the opportunity to share your story with the hungry public through my personal reportage.

SALLY
I have nothing to say to you.

CALLENDER
You are much maligned, lady. Seize this chance to set things a'right.
(hands her his card)
This is my card. Please contact me if you experience a change of heart.

Sally looks at Callender. Scorn and hatred fill her eyes.

SALLY
You are an abomination of mankind, sir.

CALLENDER
No. It is your lover who has that dubious distinction. And you can tell the man whom it 'delighteth the people to honor,' there may be those who question the integrity of my words, but they're dwarfed compared to the arrogance of his conduct. Jefferson may fool his colleagues with

CALLENDER (Cont'd)
his self-righteous, man-of-the-people horse
manure, but not me. He talks white, but he sleeps
black!

Robert cracks his whip and the horses ride off leaving Callender laughing on
the road.

INT. JEFFERSON'S CARRIAGE - CLOSE ON SALLY

looking at Callender's card as we:

FADE OUT:

END OF ACT EIGHT

ACT NINE

FADE IN:

INT. MONTICELLO - PARLOR - DAY

Martha registers concern as she reacts to...

EXT. MONTICELLO - LONG SHOT - CARRIAGE - DAY

...The carriage containing Sally arrives at the front of the house. Betty and Critta are running from the row as Martha comes out of the house.

> MARTHA
> Peter! Samuel! Come quickly!
> (to Sally)
> What are you doing here?

Sally stands calmly at the bottom of the stairs...

> SALLY
> Forgive me, Martha, I believe there has been some misunderstanding.

> MARTHA
> The circumstances have not changed.

Sally walks to her, hands her the letter from Jefferson which Martha opens and gasps in reaction to...

> SALLY
> Now, if you will excuse me.

> MARTHA
> You will not defy me.

> SALLY
> Oh, yes, I almost forgot. Upon my journey from Washington, I was met on the road by a Mr. Callender who appeared quite solicitous of my opinion with regard to our troubles here. See, here is his card.

> MARTHA
> You would not dare...

Martha glares and slowly steps aside as Sally heads into the house, a deadly look between Martha and Peter Carr.

> MARTHA
> (to the watching staff)
> Get back to work!

INT. SALLY'S ROOM - AFTERNOON

Sally is fishing through her armoire. But something on the floor catches her eye.
It's Tom's baby breeches. She pulls them out. Holds them a moment. Smells
them. Caresses them. She begins to weep when, at the door, Betty appears,
comes to her and rocks her in her arms.

SLOW CROSSFADE TO:

EXT. FIELD - WIDE SHOT - DAY (SLOW MOTION)

A PISTOL and a puff of smoke drives James Hemings backwards and slowly
down onto the grass. His wound is self-inflicted.

FADE TO:

EXT. ROAD - SLAVE CEMETERY NEAR RIVER - DAY

In a SERIES OF CROSSFADING IMAGES, we see—a wooden coffin is being
hauled by buckboard to the cemetery by the river's edge, followed by the
Hemings family and a hundred slaves.

GRAVESITE

Martha reads a letter from Jefferson. The rest of the Jefferson family is in
attendance.

                    MARTHA
          'I know well and feel what you have lost, what
          you have suffered, and what you have to endure
          and I pray our dear James Hemings will find
          himself in a heaven which shall be an ecstatic
          meeting with the friends and family he has loved
          and lost, and whom he shall never lose again.'
                    (closes the letter)
          All of us join President Jefferson in his sentiments
          upon your loss.

The slaves are silent as Sally steps forward to address the crowd.

                    SALLY
          I remember in Paris a man tipped his hat to me and
          my brother turned to me and said, 'You like that,
          don't you?' The way people look you in the eye
          and acknowledge you like a human being.' James
          spent his life hoping to be looked in the eye with
          respect.
                    (a beat)
          But all of his skills, education, and manners—
          even his freedom—could not gain him this simple

SALLY (Cont'd)

wish ...and so he died in despair. A man who
encouraged me to want better, to improve, to
learn. I honor my brother here today because he
did not live in vain. He showed us what we can,
should— and will be.

INT. SUKEY'S CABIN - EVENING

SUKEY opens the door. Sally is there with money...and Callender's card.

SUKEY

Who you want gone?

SALLY

An enemy.

SUKEY

Who you want back?

SALLY

My son...Tom.

She gives Sukey the card and the money. Sukey goes to a table inside and pulls
down a jar of green liquid and another jar of dried bones. Sukey puts Callender's
card into the liquid, along with a few of the bones.

EXT. TOBACCO FIELDS - DAY

As Sally walks along, she is approached by Samuel Carr on horseback.

SAMUEL

Sally... I'm so sorry about James.

SALLY

Are you, Samuel?

Slaves carry heavy bales to various wagons, among them Jamy Hemings who,
unused to the hard field work, stumbles under a bundle. Lilly, the overseer, rides
up and calls out.

LILLY

Get it up there, boy. Now!

Jamy tries to pick up the bale and the leaves scatter under the horse's foot. Lilly
rides up hard. His whip out.

LILLY

That's money you scatterin', fool!

Jamy looks over as crack — the whip comes down across Jamy's face, and he
falls to the ground in agony. Lilly's whip comes up and cracks on the boy again.
Sally, at the water wagon, sees this and runs over.

                              SALLY

        Oh my God! Jamy!!

Sally runs over in a rage. Grabs Lilly's arm.

                              SALLY

        Mr. Lilly! Stop it! What are you doing! Mr.
        Jefferson doesn't allow beatings on this
        plantation! Stop!

                              LILLY

        Back up, girl, get away now...

                              SALLY

                    (screaming)
        Damn you, Mr. Lilly.

Lilly slaps Sally's face, knocking her to the ground.

                              LILLY

        Don't ever put your hands on me! I don't take
        back talk from any of you uppity niggers. I'm in
        charge.

Samuel rides up hard and draws a pistol on Lilly.

                              SAMUEL

        Put up that whip, Mr. Lilly or I shall drop you...
        back away, Mr. Lilly... your work here is finished!

                              LILLY

        I was hired by Mr. Peter Carr.

                              SAMUEL

        My brother did not hire you to abuse our
        slaves...and Mr. Jefferson has strict orders on that
        fact, sir. Now your work here is finished, Lilly.
        Collect your wages and get off the property.

Lilly wheels and gallops away. Samuel dismounts and comes to Sally.

                              SAMUEL

        Are you alright?

                              SALLY

        Yes. But I must see to Jamy.

                              SAMUEL

        Sally, let me help you. I can make things better for
        you here...

But Sally ignores Samuel. Tends to her beaten nephew, Jamy.

                                                    CUT TO:

INT. MONTICELLO PARLOR - CLOSE ON LILLY - DAY

He stands before Peter Carr as he counts out his pay.

> LILLY
>
> It ain't right, sir. These niggers runnin' the place.
> It ain't right.

WIDEN. Martha stands in the doorway.

> MARTHA
>
> I fear we must stand by the Plantation rules
> established by the President, Mr. Lilly.

> PETER
>
> I'm sorry about this, Lilly. As you have sadly
> discovered, we are faced with a serious problem.

> LILLY
>
> We'll have to deal with this problem at another
> time, Mr. Carr.

> PETER
>
> Sooner or later, Mr. Lilly.

A knowing look between them. Peter then glances at Martha as we hear
SOUNDS of RAIN beginning.

DISSOLVE TO:

INT. BARN - NIGHT

Reading lessons in progress. Critta reads from a book. Betty, Peter, Harriet,
Beverly and Jamy, bandaged and bruised, listen as Sally coaches.

> CRITTA
> (reads)
> ... and the woods were so thick with trees she
> could not see. She heard the sound of a horse win,
> winny...

> SALLY
>
> Whinnying...

> CRITTA
>
> What kinda word is that...

Sally makes a whinnying sound.

> SALLY
>
> It's that word, Critta...

The slave outside gives singsong warning. Books are thrust under a quilt as a
young slave, RUFUS, enters. He appears to be a runaway.

> RUFUS
>
> I's lookin' for Miss Sally.

> SALLY
>
> I'm Sally.

> RUFUS
>
> (quietly)
> I hear you helps folks git north?

SMASH CUT TO:

EXT. ROAD - NIGHT

Still raining. A small buggy winds its way through the darkness. CLOSE ON
Sally reacting as: A group of men ride out into the middle of the road, blocking
their progress. Muskets drawn. Hats obscuring their faces.

> LILLY
>
> Get down from the buggy.

But when Sally doesn't move fast enough, a man rides up close and pulls Sally
from the buggy by her hair. She struggles as a large burlap bag is pulled over her
head. Lilly approac hes Rufus.

> LILLY
>
> You done good, boy! Not a word, understand?
> Now git!

He flips a silver piece to Rufus who disappears into the woods.

CUT TO:

INT. OUTBUILDING - NIGHT

Darkness. A voice. Familiar. The bag is taken off Sally's head. She focuses.
It is Lilly.

> LILLY
>
> You think you're so damned superior, don't you?
> So much better than anybody with your hifalutin'
> ways an' your influence on the President.
> (comes closer)
> Race mixing is an aberration and you with your
> indecent randiness which disgraces Southern
> honor will be sold into Georgia like a field hand.
> Some folks would soon as see you dead...

Lilly unravels his bullwhip from his belt and cracks it.

> LILLY
>
> ...and I'm happy to oblige 'em.

Sally trembles. Lilly nods to the two others who grab Sally, turn her around, and tear the back of her dress to her waist. CLOSE ON her bare back as...

CUT TO:

EXT. BUILDING - NIGHT

...we hear the CRACK of the WHIP and the SCREAMS of Sally Hemings tearing into the rainy night.

EXT. MONTICELLO - VERANDA - NIGHT

The rain still falls as Peter and Samuel Carr, Martha, and Randolph sit on the veranda. The men smoke. Peter reads yet another newspaper article.

> PETER
> '... We feel for the honor of our country. We do most honestly and sincerely wish to see the stain upon the nation removed by the appearance of some...'

> SAMUEL
> '...Evidence of his innocence.' I read it, Peter.

> PETER
> Nigger lovers, half-breeds, infidels. Aren't you sick of it? The way people are making fun of us?

> SAMUEL
> How many of these 'half breeds' around here are yours, brother?

> PETER
> I am breeding free labor.

> MARTHA
> Stop it. We are dealing with only one subject here, that of Sally Hemings.

> PETER
> You see, she's the perfect example of white people's fears. She's smart, beautiful — and yellow. A negress who looks white, capable of seducing white men. And if every man followed uncle's example and educated negroes, freed them, mixed and married them, by the end of the century there will be no more white people.

> RANDOLPH
> Sally is dangerous.

> PETER
> Fear not. I am under the impression the situation is being dealt with.

SAMUEL

How so, brother?

PETER

I shudder to imagine how Mr. Lilly might right his
current humiliation.

SAMUEL

What in God's name are you talking about?

CUT TO:

EXT. BUILDING - NEAR DAWN

The rain has stopped. CLOSE ON Sally's naked back as a bucket of water is
thrown on her. She reaches for her locket, dislodged during the whipping. Her
back is bloody, raw.

LILLY

Clean her up. She won't fetch a dollar like that.

The men grab Sally and towel off her back. It's killing her, but she won't give
them the satisfaction she's in pain.

EXT. BUILDING - CONTINUOUS ACTION - DAWN

As Sally is brought out of the door and dragged across the muddy yard, there is
a MUSKET CLICK and Samuel steps from the tree-lined perimeter with his
weapon pointed.

SAMUEL

Put your weapons on the ground, Lilly, or I'll kill
you where you stand.

LILLY

Mr. Carr, now why would a white man defend this
wicked creature?

SAMUEL

I said—leave your weapons on the ground and
walk down the road, Lilly. Sally, don't you move.
Go on, Lilly!

Lilly and his men begin to walk down the road. Sally's body is quivering in the
morning light as we:

FADE OUT:

END ACT NINE

ACT TEN

INT. WHITE HOUSE - DAY

White gloves carry a stack of official papers, laying them carefully for signature before a distinguished group of politicians seated about a long table. In the center is Jefferson, quill in hand, signing document after document.

We hear Jefferson's voice OVER the IMAGES that follow.

> JEFFERSON (V.O.)
> ... Dear Sally, first and foremost I miss you
> terribly and send my warmest love to all at
> Monticello. I am witness to a glorious day for our
> new country. The 820,000 square miles of the
> Louisiana Territories are today part of the United
> States —from the Mississippi to the Great Plains
> and mountains beyond...

INT. BETTY'S CABIN - DAY

CLOSE as Betty weeps to see: CLOSE ON Sally's face. WIDEN to see she is in a tub. Sukey dabs oils and herbs on her back, mumbling in patois. CLOSE ON Sally's hand gripping her locket.

> SUKEY
> More mullet weed an' syrup, or she burn. I don'
> want she scar bad...

INTERCUT WITH:

INT. WHITE HOUSE - CLOSE ON HANDS - DAY

signing, quills scratching. Men in government at work.

> JEFFERSON (V.O.)
> ... sixty million francs — four cents an acre to
> double our national geography, and open the door
> to a vast new world of unlimited resources...

INT. CABIN - CLOSE ON BLACK HANDS - DAY

stitching up Sally's torn back.

> JEFFERSON (V.O.)
> ...It's a new beginning for America...

CLOSE ON Sally, bearing the pain. Betty weeps in a corner. Women slaves watch silently in the doorway.

JEFFERSON (V.O.)
...Tomorrow, I'll open the doors to the President's
House to the citizenry in celebration, and draw the
nation around the strength of our central
government to show that together, as one, we are
strong and resourceful...

INT. PRESIDENT'S HOUSE - DAY

Jefferson stands to applause and congratulations by his peers.

INT. BETTY'S CABIN - ON FACES OF SLAVES - DAY

It is Sally's voice we hear, OVERLAPPING Jefferson's.

SALLY
'...Sally, no foe will ever disturb our peace of
mind again or the pursuit of our happiness. It is
over, my love and our trials are now behind us.
The country is now focused on the glorious
achieve ment and not the intricacies of my
personal affairs. And when my duties here are
complete I shall return to my little mountain and
the warmth of your arms. Thomas.'

Sally, letter in hand, looks up, at the slaves, at her mother, a forced smile.
Betty simply nods. The cruel irony of their existence is not lost on her.
Betty holds her daughter realizing she's come through a terrible ordeal.

EXT. SWAMP - DAY

Two slaves silently look on from the bank as a group of white men with a
rope hitched to a team of horses drag a bloated body from the murky water.
When the body is turned over we recognize it as the body of James Thompson
Callender.

SALLY (V.O.)
... Four days later, James Thompson Callender
was found drowned in three feet of water. Some
blamed Callender's drinking and womanizing,
others blamed Jefferson sympathizers.
(a beat)
Either way, the Bible says, 'So as you sow, ye
shall reap...' Yes. It was over...

DISSOLVE TO:

INT. MONTICELLO - PARLOR - SERIES OF SHOTS - NIGHT (1805)

Accompanied by Beverly Hemings on harpsichord and Old Jupiter on fiddle,
favorite songs are sung at a harvest party in celebration of Jefferson's return
from Washington. Jefferson stands in the center of the hall, playing his violin,

surrounded by his family and grandchildren. Sickly Polly is brought into the music room by slaves and placed next to Jack in a sitting chair. She appears deathly ill, but holds one-year-old Francis' hand. Sally stands next to her, holding her hand.

Food has been lavishly prepared and is served by Critta, Sukey, Isabel and Nance. All the Jeffersons Polly, Jack, Peter Carr, Martha, Randolph, and a host of grandchildren, including JEFF, now fourteen are singing.

Three generations of Hemings women Betty, Sally and four- year-old HARRIET, very white with bright red hair, already somewhat spoiled, are having a good time. Betty pours a small glass of punch and calls out to Harriet playing with Martha's four-year-old daughter, VIRGINIA RANDOLPH.

BETTY

Harriet? Take this punch to Virginia.

Harriet gives her grandmother a look. Shakes her head. Betty's hands go to her hips.

CRITTA

(to Sally)

Your little girl! It's you all over again.

SALLY

Harriet, you come get this glass right now and
don't talk back to your grandmother like that!

Harriet slowly comes over and gets the glass. Gives it to Virginia. Still resentful.

SAMUEL

Miss Hemings, may I have a word with you,
outside?

Something in his voice causes her to set her tray aside and follow him out. Jefferson sees Sally and Samuel talking through the window. He keeps playing.

EXT. VERANDA - NIGHT

SAMUEL

Do you know you could be arrested for harboring
and helping runaways?

SALLY

What are you talking about, Samuel?

SAMUEL

I know of several incidences, Sally.

He touches Sally's arms, shoulders in a familiar way. Sally reacts with nervous suspicion.

SAMUEL
If you thought what Lilly did to you was bad,
imagine what the sheriffs would do. Brand you,
maim you. Cut off a hand..

... which he grabs to pull her to him. Sally gasps.

SAMUEL
... But I'm always here, aren't I? To take your
side. And why? Because I keep dreaming one day
you'll realize I'm the one, Sally. Me.

He kisses her. Sally pushes him away. He grabs her again.

INT. PARLOR - NIGHT

Jefferson sees Sally is agitated. He stops playing and moves through the crowd
to the front door.

EXT. VERANDA - NIGHT

SALLY
I thought you were different.

SAMUEL
From whom? My uncle?

He reaches into his jacket pocket, pulls out a book.

SAMUEL
Read the folded pages. Then you'll realize my
uncle is no different from any other slave holder.
But I am different...

He grabs her hand and puts the book into it. It's Jefferson's "Notes on the State
of Virginia."

SAMUEL
...It's time you knew just exactly what my uncle
thinks about you Godforsaken Negroes, Sally.

And he kisses her again. But before she can push him away, they both hear:

JEFFERSON (O.S.)
What's going on here?

Samuel is caught off-guard. Sally runs off with the book, upset.

JEFFERSON
I believe you owe me an explanation.

SAMUEL
What do you mean?

JEFFERSON
I have eyes! I just saw you kiss Sally. Am I to be
made a fool of?

SAMUEL
This is ridiculous. I'm her friend. I've tried to
make her feel at ease when you're gone. To take
away some of the pain of the scandal.

JEFFERSON
Which requires you to touch her? To kiss her!

Samuel says nothing. Jefferson comes closer.

JEFFERSON
Have you been intimate with her?

Again, Samuel says nothing. Jefferson becomes irate.

JEFFERSON
Speak up, damn you! Have you done something
shameful?

In a sudden flurry of anger, Samuel turns on Jefferson.

SAMUEL
Haven't you? Haven't you to the detriment of us
all? Did you ask yourself if she might be attracted
to me? I'm younger, stronger, here when she
needs someone, when she's in danger instead of
you, who's up in Washington disavowing and
denying all claims to her—or your children!

Jefferson is outraged. Grabs Samuel, hurls him to the floor.

JEFFERSON
How dare you! I have treated you like a son. Now,
I suggest you return to your own farm and your
own wife, or I will not take responsibility for my
actions should I look at you another second! Now
leave my sight!

Samuel leaves without apology. We can still hear the SINGING as Jefferson's
anger almost over- takes him. He takes a moment to compose himself, then
heads toward the row, looking for Sally.

INT. MONTICELLO - NIGHT

With the celebration on-going, Jefferson is still looking for Sally. Can't find
her. He sees Betty arranging her cookies on the food table. Goes over to her.

JEFFERSON
Betty, where is Sally?

BETTY

I don't know.

But Jefferson senses she does know. Takes her arm and walks her around into a hallway where they are alone.

JEFFERSON

I need to speak to her.

BETTY

(firm)
Well she don't wanna speak to you.

JEFFERSON

What is this tone you've taken?

BETTY

It's a mother's tone! Long before I was your slave,
I was her mother!

Betty just looks at him. He walks off.

INT. BETTY'S CABIN - NIGHT

Jefferson enters to find Sally sitting alone with the book.

JEFFERSON

What are you doing here?

Sally says nothing. Jefferson approaches her.

JEFFERSON

Sally...why after all these years, after all there has
been between us. He says you want a younger
man. Is that true?
She stares at him in disbelief.

JEFFERSON

Samuel's feelings could not have progressed
without some prompting on your part.

SALLY

How dare you insinuate I've been intimate with
him. You're the only man I've ever known that
way.
(a beat)
Oh, but I forget. Naturally you'd believe your
white nephew and not your black concubine...
because you wrote this.

She waves his book. Jefferson goes blanch as she reads.

SALLY

'... Whites are superior to blacks in reason and in
beauty. Yet in music, blacks are more gifted than
whites with accurate ears for tune, time and
rhythm.' 'In imagination they are tasteless and
dull. They secrete less by the kidneys and more by
the glands which gives them a strong
disagreeable odor.'
    (a beat)
Did it occur to you your slaves don't have brass
bathing tubs or perfumed oils? And this? 'Among
blacks is no poetry. I have never yet heard a black
utter a thought above the level of plain narration.'
    (flings the book)
You disgust me.

JEFFERSON

You've taken my observations out of context.

SALLY

Then here's one in context.
    (quotes from memory)
'An amalgamation between blacks and whites
produces a degradation to which no one can
innocently consent.'

JEFFERSON

Sally, please.

SALLY

    (almost tearful)
Are our children a degradation? Is my mother?
Am I?

JEFFERSON

I was wrong.

SALLY

And I was a fool. Every time you said, "No, Sally,
I can't do anything about slavery now. Wait 'til
I'm elected. Wait 'til I'm reelected." Wait. Wait. It
was all lies! Even your own law against
miscegenation prevents us from marrying.

JEFFERSON

I was ignorant. I wrote that book 25 years ago!

SALLY

You bought the Louisiana Territory 25 days ago.
Are you going to admit it as a slave state? And
keep perpetuating the horror? Or will you sit on
your hands like you always do—and blame your
'Southern constituents.

She tears the back of her dress down from her shoulders to reveal her scarred back. He's shocked.

SALLY

Because this is what they think of slavery.

JEFFERSON

(in shock)
My God. What has happened to you?

SALLY

You! You and your ambiguities, and your nonchalance. So, here's an utterance above plain narration: I am finished with you. I'm leaving you.

JEFFERSON

Sally, no. No. Stop, please...

SALLY

... I hate you. I hate what I've allowed you to turn me into.

JEFFERSON

No, you love me. I know you do...

But Sally ignores him. Jefferson is desperate. Knows he's about to lose the woman he loves and he must prove himself.

JEFFERSON

You love me, Sally. The same way...
(finally)
...that I love you.

There. He finally said it. This stops Sally.

JEFFERSON

I love you. God help me, I do. I never thought I would ever feel it —let alone say it again.

He falls to his knees. Holding her. Clutching her almost in desperation as we:

FADE OUT:

END OF ACT TEN

ACT ELEVEN

EXT. MONTICELLO - CLOSE ON DOME - DAY (SUMMER, 1815)

The structure of the main house is finally finished, but scaffolding still remains on at least half the facade.

EXT. ROW - DAY

We hear a CONCERTO played on HARPSICHORD in the b.g., as we FOLLOW Sally Hemings leaving Betty's cabin along with two red-headed white boys ages 10 and seven. She's carrying flowers.

CONCERTO CONTINUES as Thomas Jefferson, age 72, his once red hair now graying and sparse, rides atop Eagle, his white stallion. He calls to Sally and the boys.

> JEFFERSON
> Have you spied the garden today, boys? Those
> who labor the earth are the chosen people of God!

He rides off into the fields.

> SALLY (V.O.)
> ... By 1815, Thomas had retired to Monticello and,
> although to some becoming more and more
> eccentric, was more active than ever...

As they walk through the row, slaves load wagons with lumber and barrels of nails.

> SALLY (V.O.)
> ...A lot happened in the intervening years. He got
> a bill approved by Congress prohibiting slave
> trade to America...

Sally and the boys pass Critta, 44, outside the fabric mill. Critta waves as she carries dyed cloth to be dried.

> SALLY (V.O.)
> ...We went to war with the British in 1812, and
> both Louisiana and Ohio were admitted into the
> union.
> (a beat)
> But with these successes came tragedy.

EXT. JEFFERSON CEMETERY - DAY

The three walk past the Jefferson graveyard. CAMERA PASSES OVER Polly's gravestone, which reads: "Maria Jefferson Eppes, 1778-1804. Beloved daughter, wife and mother."

SALLY (V.O.)
Polly died the same year Thomas was reelected,
and I kept my promise to see after her son,
Francis...

EXT. SLAVE CEMETERY - DAY

They enter the slave cemetery by the river and walk to Betty Heming's grave site.
The crude wooden grave marker says: "Elizabeth Hemings, 1734-1807. Beloved
mother."

A bouquet of flowers is placed on the grave. The CAMERA PULLS BACK ON
Sally, who stands and turns TO CAMERA. She is now 42, and matriarch of
Monticello.

SALLY (V.O.)
...and Mama died in 1807. After 40 years of
faithful service to Thomas Jefferson, she, too, was
buried in the slave cemetery with James, Henry,
and my baby Edy...

With Sally are her two new sons, MADISON, age 10, and ESTON HEMINGS,
age seven. Both boys have red hair and look white.

SALLY (V.O.)
...My brother Robert was given his freedom and I
was blessed with two more sons Madison and
Eston...

EXT. MONTICELLO - CONTINUOUS ACTION - DAY

CONCERTO CONTINUES as they all slowly walk back toward the mansion
holding hands. As they go, we see how parched the tobacco fields are now. A
shadow of its former glory.

SALLY (V.O.)
... Monticello hadn't been prosperous in years.
Cotton and tobacco crops had failed all over the
state. And for us, it was four years in a row...

The tobacco yield is small and the leaves are yellow and dry. Sally shakes her
head. To her left are only three buckboards filled with droopy leaves. To her
right she sees:

ANGLE

Thomas Mann Randolph walking around naked and muttering. Martha, now 43,
rushes out of the house, covers him with a blanket and brings him back inside.

SALLY (V.O.)
...And as crazy as Thomas Mann Randolph was,
somehow he got elected Governor of the state, and
fathered a total of 12 children with Martha...

Sally and the boys go into the house, passing several slaves hammering on the side porch, and/or carrying lumber and nails to buckboards parked along the side of the house.

INT. RECEPTION ROOM - CONTINUOUS ACTION - DAY

Sally comes in and listens to her son, Beverly Hemings, now 18, and Harriet Hemings, red-haired and lovely, now 16, finishing the harpsichord and violin concerto.

Beverly is handsome, brooding, talented. When they finish, they look over at Sally, who applauds.

                    SALLY
          That was beautiful, my children.

                    SALLY (V.O.)
          ... But Thomas had his dream project. He was
          building the University of Virginia and he spent
          every dime he earned or didn't on it.

EXT. MONTICELLO - DAY

Jefferson rides up and calls to his lead foreman, MR. BATISTE.

                    JEFFERSON
          Mr. Batiste... I had an epiphany last night and I
          feel we should employ the same stepped dome
          roof design for the university rotunda we
          employed here at Monticello.

                    BAPTISTE
          But, Mr. President, sir, it requires yards more
          lumber and personnel. Since I have split my
          workers between here and the university grounds,
          and the draftsmen have not been paid for their
          plans...
               (follows Jefferson up the stairs)
          ...and these men have not been compensated since
          May, I am afraid, sir... I am afraid...

                    JEFFERSON
          Don't worry, don't worry. They'll receive their
          funds shortly. The Lord will provide. You'll see.

EDMUND BACON, the overseer, is instructing the slaves loading up the supplies.

                    JEFFERSON
          Mr. Bacon, you and Mr. Batiste coordinate it so
          this shipment arrives on the university site by
          tomorrow.

Sally is on her way around the building, catches up.

SALLY

If you insist on taking these men to the university,
how shall we manage the tallowing? Guests are
coming.

JEFFERSON

Guests?

SALLY

The Du Ponts.

JEFFERSON

Du Pont, Mr. Batiste, tell the boys in the nailery.
Three inch will not do for the facings... six inch,
six inch...

BAPTISTE

Yes, sir.

JEFFERSON

And tell them we need more nails!

Jefferson spies Harriet and VIRGINIA RANDOLPH, 15, plain and unassuming,
running out the front door onto the porch.

HARRIET

But he was not looking at you. He was looking at
me.

VIRGINIA

Harriet, why on earth would Daniel Johnson be
looking at you?
          (spotting Jefferson, curtseys)
Grandfather.

JEFFERSON

Virginia, my little lamb, how's my favorite
grandchild?

HARRIET

          (also curtseys)
Sir...

Jefferson striding into the front door, the girls, and Martha following him through
the hall and into his study.

INT. HALLWAY - CONTINUOUS ACTION - DAY

JEFFERSON

Come with me, young ladies, I have something
quite amazing to show you.

INT. LIBRARY/STUDY - DAY

The study is cluttered. Maps, elk antlers, correspondence, sketches and
Jefferson's model design for the university, are on his desk. Crates of books and
other oddities are piled on the floor near his telescope.

He walks over to a huge bone on one of the tables.

JEFFERSON

> A skull fragment of the great mastodon, found at
> Big Bone Lake.

Harriet has put an Indian headdress on her head. Jefferson comments.

JEFFERSON

> ...The ceremonial headdress of the great Chief...
> > (pronunces)
>
> Po-o-wat-a-tan of the Manotin Nation, brought to
> me by Meriwether Lewis. A a gift to the Great
> White Father. Now get me some tea, Harriet.

HARRIET

> But...

JEFFERSON

> ...Go, go. Get me some tea.
> > (to Virginia)
>
> And you run to your brother Jeff and tell him the
> damnable bankers are descending upon us this
> afternoon.

As Harriet and Virginia leave, in comes Sally, following six slaves carrying
boxes of books.

SALLY

> More books?

JEFFERSON

> Very rare. I cannot live without them.

SALLY

> I thought they were for...

JEFFERSON

> ...The University library. They are. But they are on
> loan to me until its completion.

He looks out the window. A group of children are chasing sheep across the
grounds.

JEFFERSON

> Good Lord. Who are all those people?

                    SALLY
Thomas, they're your grandchildren. See? Thomas
Jefferson Randolph, Benjamin Franklin Randolph,
George Wythe Randolph, James Madison
Randolph, Meriwether Lewis Randolph and their
four sisters.

                  JEFFERSON
          (shakes his head)
All by that idiot? All living here?
          (then sighs)
Well, as you say, Du Pont is coming. Hopefully
he's still rich, and hopefully I can interest him in
investing in the university.

Sally falls silent. Jefferson notices it. Becomes irritated.

                  JEFFERSON
What? What? Say it.

                    SALLY
This constant entertainment is costing you a
fortune. Hordes of visitors, all wanting something
from you, eating like vultures, staying forever.

                  JEFFERSON
Du Pont... for a week...

                    SALLY
He'll bring others, they'll stay five. Care to
wager?

Jefferson sighs.

                                        CUT TO:

EXT. GARDEN ROAD - DAY (ONE MONTH LATER)

An elegant carriage turns onto the property. Inside are three people.
PIERRE DU PONT, now 76, his son, E.I., 49, and his handsome grandnephew,
WILLIAM ALEXANDER, 17. They spot the dome in the distance.

                  DU PONT
My God, he has recreated the Halle aux Bleds in a field!

                  WILLIAM
Granduncle, who is that?

They look towards the gardens to see Jefferson, in a broad- brimmed straw hat
and white breeches covered by a dirty apron-like covering, walking toward
them, carrying an assortment of wildflowers and herbs. Sally follows him as does
Harriet. He spies Du Pont. Harriet eyes the handsome William.

JEFFERSON
(excited, in French)
Pierre, Pierre, is that you, sir?

DU PONT
(also in French)
Thomas, you wonderful, dear man. And who is
this?
(English now)
No. It cannot be. Mademoiselle Sally? How lovely
to see you again. How long has it been, my dear
girl?

SALLY
Not since Paris, 1789, sir.

DU PONT
27 years and still a beauty. This is my son,
Eleuthere call him E.I., and William Alexander,
who is, one half of him, my American nephew...

William cannot take his eyes off Harriet Hemings.

JEFFERSON
Welcome, gentlemen, to Monticello! Please do me
the favor of dropping these ox- tongue and bee
balm leaves to the kitchen so that we might enjoy
them as our teas this afternoon.

He tosses the cuttings onto the back of their carriage.

JEFFERSON
Centaurea maculosa, spotted knap weed and
carduus nutans, sweet nodding thistle. Go on now,
Martha is waiting.

ON the Du Ponts as the carriage heads to the house.

WILLIAM
He's quite the eccentric, isn't he, Granduncle?

DU PONT
But hopefully, still a wealthy one.

CUT TO:

INT. KITCHEN - DAY

The kitchen is abuzz with activity and preparation for the dinner to welcome the
Du Ponts. Sally is in charge and reminds us of Betty in her manner. INCLUDE
Peter cooking.

                              SALLY

We shall all do the best we can with what we
have. Peter, this must appear to be beef
bourguigonne, despite our lack of chervil and the
proper amount of meat...

Harriet enters with a pile of napkins.

                             HARRIET

You mean no meat, Mother. Do you realize that
almost every sheet in this house has a hole in it?

                              SALLY

Make dumplings, Peter. Add some more flour and
water, we are serving at least a dozen.

                             HARRIET

...I have been upstairs for two hours mending
sheets left over from Grandma's era...

                              SALLY

This stew's still missing something.

                             HARRIET

Yes. Meat, mother.
        (then)
Have any of you seen that boy with the Du Ponts?
He's quite pleasing.

Sally hands one of the help a tray filled with the ox-tongue and bee balm teas.

                              SALLY

Israel, take Mr. Jefferson's dreadful tea up, please.
        (after he goes)
Harriet, aren't there any Negro boys you like
around here, like Israel? He's sweet.

                             HARRIET

A sweet slave.

                              SALLY

And you're not? Harriet, I didn't raise you to
discriminate against other slaves.

                             HARRIET

Well, what would you have me aspire to? Not
anyone around here. You certainly haven't.

Sally reacts. Hands Harriet a tray.

                              SALLY

Take this up for me.

Harriet is not pleased with this. Ties a dishrag around her head, mocks slave dialect.

> HARRIET
> Yes'm. Needs me to do anythin' else for Massa?
> Wash his feets or sumthin'?

The rest of the servants look on. Sally swings Harriet around. Snatches off the dishrag. Pulls her out of earshot.

> SALLY
> Harriet, we've been through this before. We
> serve. That's what we do.

> HARRIET
> No. It's what you do! You and slaves like Israel.

> SALLY
> Harriet, all slaves here or anywhere else in
> America are the same. The light ones and the dark
> ones. You're no different from Sukey or Jupiter,
> do you understand?

> HARRIET
> No different? Last year when that Negro boy so
> much as talked to me in Richmond? The store
> owner slapped him and told him not to ever flirt
> with a white girl again.
> (holds out her arm)
> Look at my skin. It makes me too white to be
> black, and too black to be white.
> (a beat)
> I don't know where to belong.

Sally thinks. Takes Harriet's hand.

> SALLY
> Honey. I think it's time we talked. Come with me.

INT. PARLOR - EVENING

Informal dinner. A buffet of food on the long table. Critta circulates hors d'oeuvres. Guests include Martha, Randolph, several of their grandchildren including Virginia, who stands flirting with William Alexander Du Pont, E.I. and Jefferson. Beverly plays the harpsicord.

> E.I.
> When should we ask Mr. Jefferson about an
> investment in our company?

> DU PONT
> Not on the first night. It wouldn't be proper. We
> wouldn't be good guests.

Just before they approach Jefferson and Thomas Mann Randolph...

RANDOLPH
When will you ask Du Pont about the investment?

JEFFERSON
Not on the first night. It wouldn't be proper. We wouldn't be good hosts.

INT. SALLY'S ROOM - EVENING

They come in. Harriet has never been in Sally's private bedroom. She's in awe and looks around. Though the room needs new paint it's still elegant.

HARRIET
So this is it...?

SALLY
My room. Thomas built it for me.

HARRIET
You call him 'Thomas'?

Sally opens the weathering pigskin trunk and pulls out the Richmond Recorder and other newspapers now yellowing and aged. Hands them to Harriet, who reads them and reacts.

HARRIET
So, all my life...the rumors, the whispers, they're true?

SALLY
(nods reflectively)
I was about your age when I went to Paris. It was so wonderful. Thomas and I could go anywhere and people would tip their hats to us and smile. No one judged us...

CLOSE ON the yellowing Richmond Recorder as Harriet reads:

SALLY
...Then the French Revolution began. I was pregnant with your brother, Tom—the 'Tom' in that newspaper article—and I wanted to be with your father. So I made an arrangement with him...and I came back.

Harriet folds the paper. Sally pulls out Tom's baby clothes from the trunk.

SALLY
You were born out of love, too, Harriet. You and your brothers.

> HARRIET
>
> What happened to my brother Tom?

Sally caresses Tom's baby clothes longingly.

> SALLY
>
> He ran away. Because of the scandal. And I
> haven't seen him since. I miss him. He was so
> beautiful. Such a beautiful boy.
> (tries to compose herself)
> Oh, Harriet. I want so much for all of you. I just
> want you to understand.

She becomes emotional. Harriet wipes her mother's eyes, then puts the newspaper back in the trunk. She then finds the lilac chiffon gown and pulls it out.

> HARRIET
>
> Oh, Mama. Look at this.

Harriet marvels at the dress. Holds it up to herself in a nearby mirror. Sally smiles, transported back in time.

> SALLY
>
> Thomas had it made for me in Paris. I wore it to
> the palace at Versailles.

Harriet turns back to the mirror, admiring how she might look in the dress.

INT. RECEPTION ROOM - NIGHT

The Du Ponts, Jefferson, Martha and Randolph in conversation with Nicholas. Suddenly Harriet floats into the room wearing the lilac dress. She's stunning. Jefferson looks over and for a flash, she becomes Sally in Paris at Versailles. He excuses himself and goes to Harriet who trembles knowing for sure he's her father.

> JEFFERSON
>
> You look lovely, child. As lovely as I've seen your
> mother.

> HARRIET
>
> I... thank you, Mr. Jefferson.

Jefferson furtively glances at Sally and winks before going back to his guests. Sally smiles, then goes to Harriet. The two squeeze hands. But Martha, recognizing the dress, goes over to the food table and picks up a tray. Brings it to Harriet. Hands it to her.

> MARTHA
>
> Harriet, dear, we've run out of the little fish rolls...

Harriet takes the tray mortified. As Martha returns to her group, she turns away almost bumping into William Alexander. She quickly puts the tray on the table.

Both speak at once.

> ### WILLIAM
> Excuse me.

> ### HARRIET
> Excuse me, sir.

Just a flash of question at the word "sir."

> ### WILLIAM
> No, no... I... I've been admiring you. Might I
> inquire your name?

> ### HARRIET
> It's Harriet...

> ### WILLIAM
> ...Ah, Harriet Randolph.

Harriet looks around slightly. Doesn't correct him. Smiles demurely.

> ### WILLIAM
> Well, Harriet Randolph, I'm William DuPont
> Alexander, at your service.

He extends his hand, they shake, but William holds hers a moment longer..

> ### WILLIAM
> They said looks did not run in the Randolph
> family, but dear Lord, you give lie to that. You're
> breathtaking.

Harriet blushes. Across the room, Sally sees Jefferson and the Du Ponts talking, knowing how important an investment is to Jefferson. She eases over closer so she can hear.

> ### JEFFERSON
> The boys of this rising generation are to be the
> men of the next. I shall bring the Scot, Samuel
> Knox, and his staff to lay the intellectual
> cornerstones of the University of Virginia and
> "numinibus secundis" the holy fire shall burn
> forth from these hills throughout the world.

> ### DU PONT
> Er...Thomas, we also have several projects. One of
> which involves the many uses of the rubber tree
> found in the Carib. Another, is gunpowder.

Beverly starts playing. Jefferson is pleasantly distracted by the music as are the Du Ponts as they see William take Harriet's hand.

                    WILLIAM
        Will you dance with me?

Before Harriet can respond, she sees Virginia and Martha glaring. She smiles at
William.
                    HARRIET
        I...I'd be delighted.

He takes her hand and they dance. Harriet loves the attention. Virginia turns
to her mother then hurries away. Martha goes to Jefferson. Gives him a look.
Jefferson bends in to her.

                    JEFFERSON
        Martha, let it go.

Sally watches them dance and is transported back to Paris. She smiles, then
leaves the room.

INT. LIBRARY/STUDY - NIGHT

Sally comes into the study. Sits on Jefferson's desk. She glances down and
sees a few letters and correspondence. One strikes her and she picks it up.
It's a bill of sale for Shadwell plantation signed by Thos. Jefferson. She
frowns, real concern reflecting on her face.

END OF ACT ELEVEN

ACT TWELVE

EXT. RIVANNA RIVER - AFTERNOON

Harriet and William are lazily rowing up the river in a small boat.

> WILLIAM
> What about you? What are your dreams?

> HARRIET
> (thinks)
> I dream about going to Paris. Mother talks about
> it. Seeing the Louvre. Maybe be a painter—there
> are lots of women painters in France, you know.
> Then I'd like to drift down the Seine with the man
> of my dreams under a parasol. Perhaps live in an
> apartment on the Champs Elysees...
> (caught up, forgets)
> ...and have servants wait on me for a change so
> my hands wouldn't be red from scrubbing and
> dusting and...

> WILLIAM
> ...But you have servants now—Sally, Critta,
> Sukey...

William referring to her family snaps Harriet out of her reverie. William takes
her hand.

> WILLIAM
> Maybe I could be that man with you on the Seine,
> Harriet.

INT. BETTY'S CABIN - EVENING

A fire burns in the fireplace of Betty's cabin (which is Sally and Harriet's
cabin now). Sally is awake when Harriet comes in all giddy from being
with William.

> HARRIET
> Oh, Mama! I'm so happy. He's so wonderful, so
> sweet. He's already mentioned he wants to take
> me to Philadelphia with him.

> SALLY
> And what did you say?

> HARRIET
> I said, I'd love to go.

> SALLY
> Does he know and accept you for what you are?
> Harriet?

Harriet says nothing. Sally frowns.

                    SALLY
          Harriet...

                    HARRIET
          ...Mama, he doesn't need to know.

Sally reacts.

                    HARRIET
          Mama, this is my chance to leave here. To live the
          life I want. To be truly free.

                    SALLY
          And that's what you want? To pass? To deny that
          part of me in you?

                    HARRIET
          I'm the daughter of an ex-President. But was I
          given my privileges as a presidential daughter?
          No! He denied me...as he's done you!
                    (a beat)
          Mama, the world is run by white people, and I
          have white skin just like William. I can be with
          him.

                    SALLY
          What about children? How will you explain it?

                    HARRIET
          I won't have children.

                    SALLY
          You'd reject motherhood by rejecting your
          ancestry? Harriet, you can't lie forever.

                    HARRIET
          Yes I can. I'd rather tell a white lie, than live a
          black life.

INT. LIBRARY/STUDY - LATE AFTERNOON

Sally has the household account books spread before her. She is reading
several bills of sale as Jefferson comes in and, seeing her, stops.

                    JEFFERSON
                    (irritated)
          Yes, I've had to sell Shadwell... and Pantops, and
          perhaps even...

                    SALLY
          ...Where will your servants be quartered? Or will
          they be next?

JEFFERSON

Stop it, Sally! They will go to Poplar Forest and
Tufton. While exploring my ledgers, woman, did
you come across the forty-five hundred pounds
owed to the English creditors in Bristol? The two
thousand to Glasgow unpaid?!

SALLY

I was merely...

JEFFERSON

(loud)
To Madison, to Meriweather Lewis?! I am in the
thralldom of debt and must rescue my lands from
the ravages of overseers...

A KNOCK on the door—Critta appears.

CRITTA

Mr. Du Pont is here for your meeting.

JEFFERSON

...and now an afternoon devoted to explosives.
Send them in.

Sally leaves, crossing Du Pont and E.I. entering.

EXT. VERANDA - DAY

She takes us out onto the veranda where Randolph sits playing chess at a
table. STAY ON Randolph as William Alexander approaches.

RANDOLPH

Would you like to play?

WILLIAM

Love to. I'll take green.

RANDOLPH

(as they play)
Sorry I have not spent very much time here
during your visit. Martha and I are having crop
failures at Edgehill.

WILLIAM

Quite alright. I've been spreading my time quite
nicely, thanks to your daughter. She's wonderful.

RANDOLPH

Which one? Virginia?

WILLIAM

No. Harriet. I'm crazy about her.

RANDOLPH
(has to think)
Harriet...I don't have a daughter named 'Harriet.'

WILLIAM
Of course you do, sir. The beautiful one with the
long red curls. The one I danced with at our
arrival party.

RANDOLPH
(thinks back, suddenly)
Not the one wearing the lilac dress?

WILLIAM
Yes, sir, I'm afraid I'm falling in love with her.
She knows French, poetry, music. She's divine...

Randolph bursts out laughing—in William's face.

RANDOLPH
That's Harriet Hemings! She's one of our slaves,
you imbecile!

WILLIAM
But she looks...

RANDOLPH
(indicates Beverly)
...Surely you've noticed Monticello is crawling
with 'white' looking slaves!

William is beyond humiliated. He storms out.

INT./EXT. KITCHEN - AFTERNOON

Harriet is preparing food along with Critta when a red-faced William walks
up, grabs her and shoves her to the ground.

WILLIAM
How dare you pass yourself off as a Randolph!
How dare you pass yourself off as white! You
mongrel!

Beverly comes to the rescue and jumps on William wrestling him to the ground.
Sally tries gto break them up. But William lashes out at her.

WILLIAM
You get your hands off of me, nigger!

SALLY
You will never use that word to me— or my
children do you understand me?
Mr. Bacon, escort this boy off the row and back to
his family. Mr. Jefferson will deal with him.

Bacon does so. Meantime, Harriet is overcome. In tears. Resigned. Sally's arms go around her daughter.

INT. PARLOR - AFTERNOON

Things are not going well.

> JEFFERSON
> An investment from me — in gunpowder? No, no,
> no. Education is designed to propel mankind forward.
> Gunpowder is designed to blow us all to hell.

> DU PONT
> But, sir, when building new roads and cities to
> open up the western frontier, people will need
> gunpowder.

> JEFFERSON
> And surveyors and scientists and artisans to build
> each new hamlet, doctors and educators, not
> weapons, explosives...

Du Pont and E.I. begin laughing.

> DU PONT
> Don't you see what's happening? Mr. Jefferson
> invited us to invest in his University — and we
> came for him to invest in our gunpowder
> company. This is priceless. No more, Thomas.
> Our old friendship is worth far more than this!

The men rise realizing there's no deal to be had.

> DU PONT
> Forgive us, dear man.
> (extends his hand)
> Still friends of the Republic?

Jefferson shakes his old friend's hand, embraces him. But from Jefferson's side of the hug, this is a disappointment.

EXT. MONTICELLO - MORNING (NEXT MORNING)

The Du Ponts are preparing to leave. Valises and boxes are being loaded by slaves. E.I. and Du Pont say good-bye to Jefferson, Martha, and Randolph. William is already seated in the carriage. Everyone is aware of what has happened.

> JEFFERSON
> Perhaps this will teach the boy some manners.

> DU PONT
> Thomas, I am mortified at my nephew's behavior.
> Please forgive us.

Jefferson and Du Pont hug. Du Pont then gets into the carriage along with E.I. After waving their goodbye's, the carriage pulls off. Jefferson stands with Sally. Martha and Randolph go into the house. As he turns, Jefferson sees Harriet walking out.

> JEFFERSON

Harriet?

> HARRIET

Sir?

> JEFFERSON

Sometimes we get hurt because of what we do not say. Truths we do not speak.

> HARRIET
> (pointedly)
> What truth are you talking about...
> (a beat)
> ...Father?

She walks away. Jefferson and Sally exchange a look of parental understanding. Then suddenly, Jefferson's right hand shakes in uncontrollable quivers. Sally gently grabs his hand to stop the shaking.

> JEFFERSON

I know you're worried. You're afraid I'm going to die and leave you alone and overwhelmed.

She says nothing. Her silence answering him.

> JEFFERSON

I beg you to remember you're the spirited woman who showed up in Washington to remind me she was still in my heart. The same woman who survived scandal and a son running, when I know how much you miss him.
> (a beat)
You're strong, Sally, and I've come to depend on your strength. Don't underestimate yourself.
> (lifts her head)
I prefer the dreams of the future to the errors of the past, my darling. We'll be fine. And no matter what.
> (avoiding emotion)
Now I must be off to the stable. My Eagle awaits his afternoon ride.

Jefferson walks down the road as Sally watches.

FADE OUT:

END OF ACT TWELVE

ACT THIRTEEN

EXT. MONTICELLO BARN AREA - DAY (1816)

A large auction in progress. Jefferson's farm equipment is spread out and piled outside the barn. Horses, and other livestock are on the block as well as manufacturing equipment, plows, wagons, and harvesting equipment.

> SALLY (V.O.)
> ...But debt was consumming Thomas and by 1816,
> little by little he began selling off all he held dear
> just to survive...

An AUCTIONEER calls out the bidding.

> AUCTIONEER
> Whatamibid... etc.

Mr. Batiste follows Jefferson who, now with a cane, walks through the small crowd Martha approaches.

> MARTHA
> The campeachy chairs John Hemings made, the
> speedpress, the revolving bookholders, all made in
> our joinery have gone for a mere $50.00. I cannot
> bear to see the Fauteuils en Cabriolet and the a La
> Reines go!

The fine French pieces we recognize from Paris are being loaded onto a wagon, along with linens.

> SALLY
> From Paris, Thomas, I remember...

The very bed Jefferson slept in in Paris is loaded into the wagon. Sally reacts as her dresser and bed are loaded into another wagon. Jefferson notes this.

> BATISTE
> The accessors from Philadelphia are in the foyer.
> They will settle a sum for the European paintings
> and the maps.

> JEFFERSON
> The European maps!...not my maps of this country.
> Those shall be given to the university...along with
> my drawings, my designs, the architect's
> instruments, those shall be.
> > (He stops, almost confused).
> Sally? The clocks? They're not taking the clocks,
> are they?... it is warm today...humid. My
> barometer...

Sally's arm goes over his shoulders, he leans against her. Will he weep? Then...Beverly and his brothers, Madison and Eston, run up the road from the row. They excitedly point out to the main road.

MADISON HEMINGS
Sir, sir! Mama, look. Look!

Down the road, led by at least six military guards on horseback, comes the Presidential caravan. President James and Dolley Madison inside. It is an impressive sight. Martha takes off running for the house.

SALLY
...It's the President...

JEFFERSON
(emotional)
James...and Dolley...

CUT TO:

EXT. MONTICELLO - DAY

The Presidential carriage pulls up to the house. Madison and Dolley, get out as Critta, Harriet, and Sukey come out onto the porch, tying aprons, curtseying, trying to make up for the disarray of the entrance way where all manner of furnishings, including paintings etc. are set out for appraisal.

MADISON
Dear me.

Martha comes out of the house, out of breath and somewhat embarrassed.

MARTHA
Mr. President...Dolley... I fear you have caught us
in the middle of, er, Spring cleaning...all of
this...we had no warning...

DOLLEY
Stop it, Martha. James and I were enroute. Dare
we enter the state of Virginia without a stop here?

Sally is out the door, white apron on.

MADISON
Sally Hemings.

But Jefferson, arms outstretched, comes out. He has left his cane inside and embraces Madison with great bravado.

MADISON
Mr. President.

JEFFERSON
No, no. Mr. President to you! James, look at you,
man. Look at where all of this has led us. Dolley,
beautiful Dolley. Come in.

Everyone follows as the party moves inside. Sally looks at Critta... What now?

INT. LIBRARY/STUDY - DAY

Jefferson pours wine for Madison, Dolley, Martha and Randolph.

JEFFERSON
A salute to the man who triumphantly led our
country through war.

They drink. Madison then strolls past all the books filling up shelf after shelf.

MADISON
Damned fine collection, my friend. Extraordinary.

JEFFERSON
And you shall have them.

MADISON
Thomas...

JEFFERSON
No, I soon shall go, James...to meet God, if indeed
he exists. So I will divest myself of these material
things whilst I still live to see who might deserve
them. The British, damn them, burned our
National Library but somehow spared my humble
collection. So my luck shall be this nation's.

MADISON
And 'this nation' would be honored to pay you
handsomely for them, sir.

Martha reacts. This will help them.

EXT. MONTICELLO GROUNDS - DAY

as Sally and Dolley walk the grounds.

SALLY
He grows old, Mrs. Madison, and I'm afraid for
him. He's dispossessing himself of all things he
once held dear, and I'm afraid losing everything
important to him will kill him.

DOLLEY
Well, I could not help but notice Monticello is
threadbare. But those of us who love Thomas,

> DOLLEY (Cont'd)
> know that not to pursue that which he has made a
> mission, would kill him as well. He needs his
> dream,and we need his vision. We'll help all we
> can.

Dolley pats Sally's hand—and they stroll on.

INT. LIBRARY - DAY

The shelves are now empty.

EXT. MONTICELLO - DAY

The last of the books are being loaded onto a buckboard outside where three
other buckboards are filled with books bound in twine. One book falls from
a pile and Sally retrieves it. It's A Midsummer Night's Dream. She opens it.
Inside is the legible scrawl of "Henry Jackson." The first time he was able to
write his name. She puts the book back.

> SALLY (V.O.)
> ... 8,000 books. Some from around the world he'd
> owned for decades. Books Thomas had taught me
> to read from. Books I'd taught my children and
> other slaves with...

Sally and Jefferson watch the 8,000 volumes leave Monticello in the
buckboards. The sight affects Sally and a tear rolls down her cheek. Jefferson
is pained. Martha comes out of the front door with Batiste. The assessors
are in the b.g., still looking over the valuable paintings.

> MARTHA
> And how much for the books, Papa?

> JEFFERSON
> That is my private affair, Martha.

> MARTHA
> If it is not over $50,000.00 then we shall be forced
> off this planation.

Jefferson, agitated, begins to walk onto the road to the row. Sally and Martha
follow.

> JEFFERSON
> I still own all the equipment, machinery, livestock
> here.

> MARTHA
> ...which is being sold.

> JEFFERSON
> ...and Varina and Poplar Forest...

MARTHA
...which are mortgaged! One hundred and fifty-two slaves, Papa.

Sally reacts, coming to Jefferson.

JEFFERSON
No. I will not sell my servants.

MARTHA
Selling 60 of them will hold off the bank for six months! Forgive me, Papa, though it's noble in the face of demise to be uncompromising, we need money. Our slaves provide it.

JEFFERSON
My slaves. And I will not sell them!

Martha sinks down, sits on one of the benches beneath the great tree. She weeps.

MARTHA
I will tell you then, Papa, it has already happened. We thought if perhaps we sold everything we might...

She stops. Jefferson's face fills with fear. Sally is concerned.

SALLY
What has happened, Martha?

MARTHA
We are bankrupt.

Jefferson reacts. Martha can hardly go on.

MARTHA
The bank... cannot bring themselves to face you, Papa. They will refinance the loan only if they receive the money owed them. We are over $100,000 in debt!

Silence between them. Jefferson speaks, almost formally.

JEFFERSON
Forgive me, I must take a ride.

CUT TO:

EXT. ROW - ON SALLY - DAY

as she watches. Jefferson slowly rides his horse Eagle through what is left of the once-lively area. The familiar slaves, all older now watch as the old man silently rides through. OVER this we hear the sound of WAILING as we...

INT. BARN - DAY

Sally is helping Eston and Madison with writing. Other slave children are practicing their writing as well. Soon, Beverly comes inside the barn.

                    BEVERLY
        Mama, something's going on.

EXT. BARN - DAY

Sally comes outside. Beverly points and she sees...

                    SALLY
        Oh no.

EXT. BARN - DAY

SOUNDS of CRYING and SOBBING continue as five buckboards are out front with white owners in them purchasing slaves.

                    SALLY (V.O.)
        ...Buyers came and picked any slave they wanted
        for any chore they wanted. But none of the
        Hemings were sold. Thomas would not allow it.
        Still...

Sally, Harriet, Critta, Madison, Eston and Beverly run up and hug various slaves we've seen throughout the piece— including Sukey—who sits at the back of a wagon weeping and holding Sally.

                    SALLY (V.O.)
        ...Sukey. Even Sukey, who birthed my children
        and Thomas' grandchildren, was sold because a
        buyer needed a midwife...

                    SUKEY
        Why? Why, Sally?
            (screams at Jefferson)
        Why, Massa? I ain't don' nothin' but love yo'
        family all my life...!

But the wagon holding her begins to pull away as Sukey is pulled from Sally's arms. Sally cries. Madison is scared. Harriet grabs Beverly's hand. Sally cries tearfully.

                    SALLY
        Sukey, Sukey, I'm sorry. I'm sorry...

Sally crumbles to the ground in despair.

INT. LIBRARY/STUDY - DAY

As the buckboards with his servants pull off, Jefferson's head falls into his hands as he hears Sukey CRYING, O.S.

FADE OUT:

END OF ACT THIRTEEN

ACT FOURTEEN

EXT. MULBERRY ROW - LATE AFTERNOON (1822)

All the slaves are gathered in the row including all the Hemings'. Jefferson stands in the center with Sally at his side. He looks at them all with pain in his heart.

                    JEFFERSON
          It was never my plan to sell any one of you. It is
          why I sold everything else— equipment, land,
          livestock and stripped Monticello. Some of you
          have been with me before I built Monticello and
          many of you were born here.
                    (becoming emotional)
          I've tried to insist you not be treated poorly. You
          have been a hard working part of my family for
          generations and I care for you...

As he continues, we see the faces of his slave workforce. He becomes emotional.

                    JEFFERSON
          ...My dream has failed.. because the foundation
          upon which I built that dream.. has been slavery.
          And any dream built on slavery is doomed. This
          abominable institution is like holding an angry
          wolf by its ears. Sooner or later, reason and sheer
          exhaustion will force us to let go—and we will be
          devoured by it. But like so many, I've been
          complacent and afraid, and that inexcusable fear
          and complacency has brought us to this painful
          moment. Our plantation no longer supports us and
          my creditors now own Monticello--and I'm
          afraid.. I'm afraid you will all be sold...

Groans and reactions from all. Jefferson wipes away a tear.

                    JEFFERSON
          I am sorry. I am so sorry.

INT. LIBRARY/STUDY - DAY

Jefferson is sitting up in a chair reading, Sally beside him. The room is sparse, lonely. Jefferson looks up as Harriet enters with Beverly.

                    HARRIET
          Mr. Jefferson, mama says if we want to leave
          Monticello, we can anytime we choose to. Is that
          true?

JEFFERSON
(somewhat confused)
Sally? What is this...

SALLY
I told them that you would allow them to
walk off the plantation and would not try
to find them.

JEFFERSON
I see... But what shall you do?

SALLY
They'll use their skills, their minds, their talents.
(then to her children)
But you need to know that even up North there's a
kind of slavery. Not in shackles or chains... but in
attitudes and opportunities denied you. Don't let
that stop you from being who you are.

Jefferson slowly rises, opens a drawer and pulls out the lock box containing
the plantation expense fund. He opens it and counts out $50. Hands it to Harriet.

JEFFERSON
You are a smart, prideful girl, Harriet, not unlike
your mother...

He cannot go on. Harriet kisses his forehead and moves toward the door with
Beverly.

JEFFERSON
Tell Mr. Bacon to escort them to the stage in
Charlottesville. I want them seen after properly.

He looks to Beverly.

JEFFERSON
Beverly...perhaps you might play for me, one last
time.

Sally and Harriet watch as Beverly goes to the harpsichord and plays,
beautifully, the tune we first heard him play as a child. OVER this we...

FADE TO:

EXT. MONTICELLO - DAY

HARPSICHORD continues to PLAY. Several slaves gathered, including
Critta. A carriage is waiting outside. Sally walks with Beverly and Harriet
dressed in traveling clothes. Madison and Eston carry the trunks and valises
and place them on board the carriage. Sally gives her daughter a brand new
leather-bound book with clean, blank pages.

                              HARRIET
        I love you, Mama.

                               SALLY
        I love you too. Be strong.

She kisses both children as they climb into the carriage driven by Mr. Batiste.
And as the slaves wave good-bye to the departing carriage, Sally stands determined
to be strong.

                            SALLY (V.O.
        ...Harriet went to Philadelphia and stayed with
        Thomas's friends until she could join Beverly in
        Washington. I knew they would both pass for
        white and I'd never hear from them again.
                (a beat)
        Three children gone—all masquerading as white.
        And I wondered if the Hemings name would
        survive...

                                                      DISSOLVE TO:

EXT. MONTICELLO - DAY

Laundry is flapping in the breeze. Sally, now 51, and Critta, 53, put clothes
on the line.

                            SALLY (V.O.)
        ...But then a passionate wish I made long ago was
        unexpectedly fulfilled...

Then Sally notices something in the distance..

HER POV

A LONE RIDER coming toward the crest of the hill. Sally stands there
transfixed. Critta notices the change on her face..

                              CRITTA
        Sally? Sally what is it?

But Sally doesn't hear her. She has recognized the rider and tears up. She runs
toward him, arms outstretched. Her face stretched in a huge grin. The rider
dismounts. He is a tall man with red hair. In the wide field, he and Sally run to
each other's arms, crying.

                               TOM
        Hello, mother...

                               SALLY
        TOM!!!!

Critta turns to the other slave women.

CRITTA

It's Tom. Tom Hemings come home.

INT. JEFFERSON STUDY - DAY

Jefferson, at his desk, hears Critta calling out. He looks.

EXT. FIELD - DAY

Madison, Eston and others come up to see. Tom has his arm around Sally.
Mother and son walk toward the house.

TOM

...Oh yes, mama everything is fine. We have a
large house in the "Roads" and Jemima and I even
help runaways get to Canada. I learned a lot from
you mama.

SALLY

Jemima...?

TOM

My wife. I'm married 20 years. You have 10
grandchildren, mama.

SALLY

Good lord. 20 years? 10 children!

TOM

I want you to come back with me, mama. When I
heard of Mr. Jefferson's financial troubles, I could
not bear the thought of you being sold or
dispossessed. I've come to ask Mr...

But Sally shakes her head. She is about to answer when she sees Madison
and Eston.

SALLY

Madison, Eston, this is your...

But before she can finish, Jefferson appears.

JEFFERSON

Welcome to Monticello, sir.

SALLY

Thomas... this is...

TOM

(cuts in)
...Tom Woodson...of Ohio, Mr. President.

                         JEFFERSON
          "Woodson" did you say? I have some Woodson
          cousins in Greenbriar county Virginia.

There is a strange silence as everyone just stands there.

                         JEFFERSON
          Do you have the time, Mr. Woodson?

Tom takes a moment, then reaches into his pocket. Pulls out the same gold
watch given to him by Sally decades ago. Sally reacts as Tom hands it to
Jefferson— who, seconds later, surprisingly produces the gold chain
belonging to it.

                         JEFFERSON
          A handsome watch, sir. I just happen to have a fob
          belonging to a watch I misplaced some years ago.
          Perhaps you can use it.

He hands the watch and fob back to Tom. There is a long eerie look between
father and son as both know who the other really is...but chooses to say nothing.

                           TOM
          Thank you, sir.

Jefferson nods, then goes back to the house. Sally turns to Tom.

                          SALLY
          I can't go with you, Tom. My life is here. This is
          my home, Tom. We Hemings are as much a part
          of Monticello as the Jeffersons.
                    (a beat)
          But I am so very proud of you. You've carved out
          a good life for yourself...and you've done it
          without denying your roots.
                    (a beat)
          I love you.

                           TOM
          I love you too, mama. I always have.

Mother and son embrace as we :

                                                    DISSOLVE TO:

EXT. GARDENS - DAY (1826)

Jefferson and Sally are naming the flowers in the garden.

                          SALLY
          ... honeysuckles, strawberries, French marigold...

SALLY (V.O.)

...Though I knew the Hemings name would survive, it was now the Jefferson legacy in question...

In the distance we SEE Martha hurrying across the field from the house, a paper in her hand. When she finally reaches them, she hands a letter to Jefferson highly distressed. Jefferson begins to read. His body quivers, then struggles under his own weight.

MARTHA

They have foreclosed. The auction is set for January. Monticello is no longer ours.

JEFFERSON

But they...they cannot...they... No!

Jefferson is reeling. He stumbles through the garden towards the field as the CAMERA RISES ABOVE HIM. He falls to the ground as Sally rushes to his side, and we:

DISSOLVE TO:

INT. BEDROOM/STUDY- DAY

The CAMERA DROPS DOWN ABOVE the dying Jefferson attended by Sally and Martha.

JEFFERSON

No more laudanum. It's finished.

Dr. May looks at Martha, shakes his head, leaves. Martha kisses her father on his cheek. Her tears spill onto his dressing gown. He struggles to wipe her eyes. His voice weak.

JEFFERSON

I want the stone as we discussed.

Martha nods. She kisses him again and he smiles. As she moves off, he finally motions for Sally to come close. Sally does. We can hear the TICK TOCK of the grandfather's CLOCK in the b.g. as Jefferson takes her hand and manages a smile.

JEFFERSON

I never told you enough, but I've loved you.

SALLY

I have always known.

The grandfather's CLOCK CHIMES twelve. He smiles faintly.

JEFFERSON

Is it the Fourth...?

Sally nods. Then a strange calm comes over Thomas Jefferson's face and he breathes his last. Sally goes to the window. She can hear the CRYING in the room, and closes her eyes.

                    SALLY (V.O.)
          ...The man I spent 38 years loving and challenging
          died July 4, 1826 on the 50th anniversary of the
          Declaration of Independence...

                                                    DISSOLVE TO:

INT. LIBRARY/STUDY - MATCH SHOT - DAY

When Sally opens her eyes, she is standing in Jefferson's now half-empty study. Martha stands in the window looking out, eyes swollen from crying. When she turns around, she and Sally share a look. She waves a paper.

                    MARTHA
          This is Papa's will. He's left me in charge—of
          what, pray, I will never know. But he's been most
          generous as he could for a man in such debt our
          lives are a complete pretense.

Sally just stares at Martha, who tries not to cry again.

                    MARTHA
          He's left nothing. No inheritances, no bequeaths
          only instructions for five slaves he could afford to
          free. Madison and Eston are among them.

Sally remains silent. Martha shoves the will in her face.

                    MARTHA
          Read it, Sally. Because it says nothing about
          freeing you!

Sally finally takes the will from Martha. She reads it, then hands the document back. Martha, with grief welling up inside her, lashes out at the only person she can.

                    MARTHA
          But your name does appear on the slave inventory
          list here. I told you one day I'd have my
          recompense. And here we are. Now, my job is to
          send you to the auction block where an old
          strumpet like you will hardly fetch us fifty dollars.

Sally turns away. But Martha forces Sally's face toward hers.

                    MARTHA
          Oh my. Have I rumpled the feathers of Papa's
          Galitea? Did he provide for you? Because God
          knows he didn't provide for me or his
          grandchildren. So you look at me.

Sally yanks her head away and turns.

> MARTHA
>
> Look at me if you want your freedom!

Sally turns to Martha her look suggesting rage.

> SALLY
>
> No. You look at me! What do you see? Family! I
> am your aunt, Martha! Your mother's sister! We
> have the same blood and you can't deny me...
> > (pointedly)
> Or sell me. Because decades before Thomas died
> he gave me this...

She pulls an aged, yellowing paper from her bosom. Throws it at Martha, who reads it.

> SALLY
>
> ... I've been free since Paris.

> MARTHA
>
> He freed you? Yet you stayed?

Sally takes back the manumission papers. Puts it in her bosom.

> SALLY
>
> Thomas promised to free any children we had on
> their18th birthday. But slaves cannot live in
> Virginia without a dispensation from the
> legislature. Using those papers to take my
> freedom meant leaving Virginia, Monticello,
> Thomas and my children before that age. And it
> meant my name would be tied to your father's in
> public papers for all eternity to comment on. No,
> Martha. I couldn't do that.
> > (a beat)
> Even you wouldn't want me to do that.

Martha realizes the depth of Sally's sacrifice for her father. Sally's voice softens.

> SALLY
>
> Martha, you and I have been at war all this time
> over a man whose deepest affections were for
> Monticello.
> > (beat)
> I've never forgotten something you said years ago.
> That slavery was wrong. That human beings had
> the right to be where they wanted. Well, I always
> wanted to be here. Was it too much to ask that I
> live and toil and sacrifice on this little bit of
> earth...just like you?

Martha tearfully remembers saying that. Sally looks around the room. Sighs.

> SALLY
> Well, it doesn't matter now. We're both displaced,
> aren't we?
> > (then)
> Where will you go?

> MARTHA
> I'm forced to live with my eldest, Ellen and her
> family. You?

> SALLY
> According to you, I'm on that list.

Martha looks at the list, then back at Sally. It takes her a moment, then:

> MARTHA
> No, Sally. It stops here. Go and be with your sons.

Sally acknowledges this. Leaves. Martha looks after her knowing both women are victims of their relationship to Jefferson. Martha crosses Sally's name from the list as we:

SLOW DISSOLVE TO:

EXT. FAMILY CEMETERY - DAY

Sally is looking at Jefferson's fine headstone proclaiming:

HEADSTONE

"Here was buried Thomas Jefferson, Author of the Declaration of American Independence, of the Statute of Virginia for Religious Freedom, and Father of the University of Virginia."

RESUME SCENE

Madison and Eston are with Sally as she places a rose there. In the b.g., we HEAR a slave auction taking place. The AUCTIONEER'S fast rant announcing:

> AUCTIONEER (V.O.)
> ...WhatamIbid, whatamIbid, for prime stock
> Negro, Martin. Hardworking field hand, good
> teeth—sold $200 to Mr. Warrell from Alabama...

As the slave auction continues O.S., Sally keeps staring at Jefferson's headstone until Madison and Eston take her hand.

> ESTON
> Come on, mama. Time to go.

SALLY (V.O.)
...Who knows how history will treat the legacy of
Thomas Jefferson. So, I must entrust my story to
my children, so that perhaps they will pass down
an oral history of who they are, and how they
came to be...

Sally, Madison and Eston slowly walk away from Monticello.

SALLY (V.O.) (Cont'd)
...For our roots—the Hemingses and Jeffersons —
a black family and a white one— not only
represents the intricate tapestry of Monticello, but
the complex, diverse and interwoven history ...of
America itself

ON SALLY

As she, Madison and Eston make their way back toward Monticello,
Sally's face slowly transforms into Harriet's, then another descendant, and
another one, and another one with increasing speed into blacks, whites,
light-skinned, dark-skinned...to the present Hemings descendants...

...while a CRAWL COMES UP OVER:

"On March 13, 1873, Madison Hemings told the story of his parents, Sally
Hemings and Thomas Jefferson to the Pike County Republican Newspaper.
The story was dismissed as conjecture and remained an unproven rumor in
history despite the oral histories of numerous Jefferson/Hemings descendants.

Not until 1998, when DNA tests were conducted through the male descendants
of Sally's youngest son, Eston Hemings Jefferson, was a link in the relationship
finally established."

FADE OUT:

THE END

HERE WAS BURIED
THOMAS JEFFERSON
AUTHOR OF THE
DECLARATION
OF
AMERICAN INDEPENDENCE
OF THE
STATUTE OF VIRGINIA
FOR
RELIGIOUS FREEDOM
AND FATHER OF THE
UNIVERSITY OF VIRGINIA

BORN APRIL 2, 1743. O.S.
DIED JULY 4. 1826.

PHOTO GALLERY

Carmen Ejogo and Sam Neill as Sally and Tom

From

"Sally Hemings: An American Scandal"

Top left
Amelia Heinle as
"Harriet Hemings"

Top:
Željko Ivanek as
"Thomas Mann
Randolph"

Left:
Kevin Conway as
"Thomas Paine"

Far left:
Mare Winningham
as "Martha
Jefferson" and
Jessica Townsend
as "Maria 'Polly'
Jefferson"

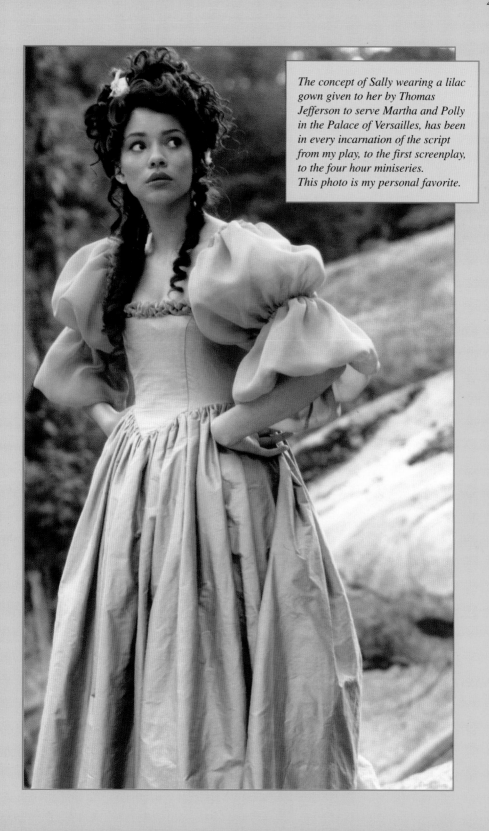

The concept of Sally wearing a lilac gown given to her by Thomas Jefferson to serve Martha and Polly in the Palace of Versailles, has been in every incarnation of the script from my play, to the first screenplay, to the four hour miniseries.
This photo is my personal favorite.

Klea Scott as "Critta Hemings" and Larry Gilliard, Jr. as "Henry Jackson" talk to Sally about her pregnancy with Jefferson's child.

Sam Neill as "Thomas Jefferson" apologizes to the slaves for not freeing them. At this point in the film, Jefferson is 80 years old.

Rene Auberjonois as "James Thompson Callender"

Callender has been referred to as the most "vile and unscrupulous scandalmonger of his day." He was the first to reveal Jefferson's affair with Sally Hemings in the Richmond Recorder in 1802. The scandal almost cost Jefferson his presidency. Rene played Callender with a delicious wickedness.

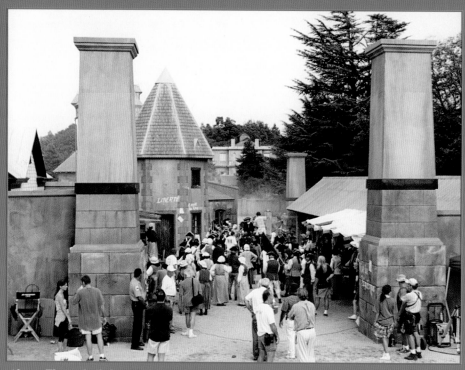

Above: The set built for an 18th century Parisian market street. Later we used it for the start of the French Revolution.

Below: In foreground, Peter Bradbury as "Samuel Carr" at right , Chris Stafford as his brother "Peter Carr."

Right:
Paul Kandel as "Pierre
Samuel Du Pont" with Sam
Neill as "Thomas Jefferson."

Below:
Carmen Ejogo with Diahann
Carroll as "Betty Hemings"

Below Right:
Kelly Rutherford as "Lady
Maria Cosway. "

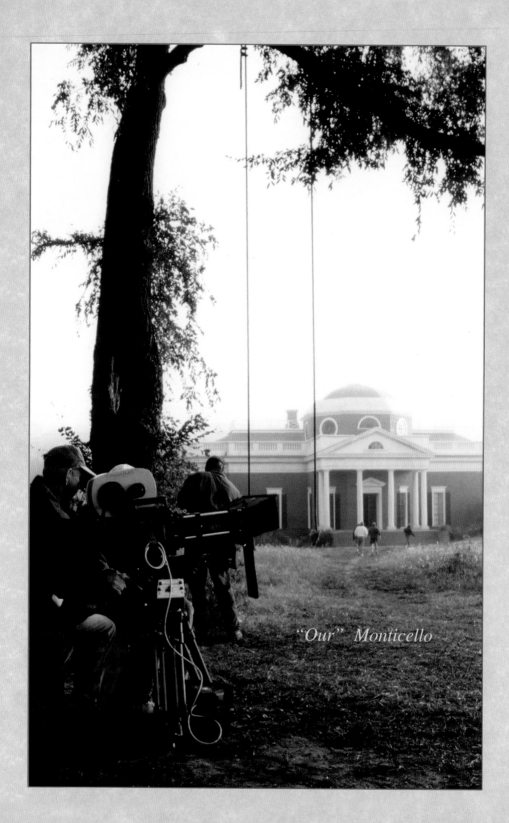

"Our" Monticello

Production Credits for:
"SALLY HEMINGS: AN AMERICAN SCANDAL"

STARRING:	Sam Neill......................... Thomas Jefferson
	Carmen Ejogo.................... Sally Hemings
	Diahann Carroll................ Betty Hemings
	Mare Winningham .... Martha Jefferson
	Mario Van Peebles .... James Hemings
ALSO STARRING:	Rene Auberjonois.............. James Callender
	Zeljko Ivanek................... Thomas Mann Randolph
	Klea Scott.......................Critta Hemings
	Jessica Townsend..............Maria "Polly" Jefferson
	Larry Gilliard Jr................ Henry Jackson
	Kevin Conway.................. Thomas Paine
	Amelia Heinle.................. Harriet Hemings
	Peter Bradbury..................Samuel Carr
	Kelly Rutherford.............. Lady Maria Cosway
	Jesse Tyler Ferguson........... Young Tom Hemings
	Paul Kandel.....................Pierre Du Pont
	Kathryn Meisle................. Dolly Madison
	Reno Roop...................... James Madison
	June Gable..................... Madame Dupre
	Jefrey Alan Chandler......... Adrien Petit
FEATURING:	Kweli Leapart................. Sukey
	Zachary Knighton.............. William Alexander
	Sean Pratt.......................Tom Hemings Woodson
	Alex Draper.................... Jean Michel Salveaux
	Chris Stafford................. Peter Carr
	Duke Lafoon....................Jack Eppes
	Elisabeth Harmon Haid....... Margaret Baynard Smith
	Mark Joy........................Gabriel Lilly
	David Bridgewater.............E.I. Du Pont
	Brian Franklin................. Beverly Hemings

EXECUTIVE PRODUCER:	Craig Anderson
CO-EXECUTIVE PRODUCERS:	Tina Andrews, Wendy Kram
PRODUCER:	Gerrit van der Meer
SUPERVISING PRODUCER:	Marty Eli Schwartz
LINE PRODUCER:	Ric Rondell
DIRECTED BY:	Charles Haid
WRITTEN BY:	Tina Andrews
EDITED BY:	Andrew Doerfer
DIRECTOR OF PHOTOGRAPHY:	Donald M. Morgan, ASC
PRODUCTION DESIGNER:	David Crank

COSTUME DESIGNER:	Michael T. Boyd
CASTING BY:	Reuben Cannon & Associates
	Kim Williams
HAIR DESIGNER:	Linda De Andrea
MAKE-UP:	David Atherton
KEY MAKE-UP:	Gil Mosko
MUSIC BY:	Joel McNeely
PRODUCTION SOUND MIXER:	Jay Patterson, C.A.S.
HISTORIAN:	Leni Ashmore Sorenson
DIALECT COACH:	Lilene Mansell
CHOREOGRAPHER:	Gwendolyn Glenn

Bibliography used for "Sally Hemings An American Scandal" and Sally Hemings An American Scandal: The Struggle to Tell the Controversial True Story

1. Thomas Jefferson An Intimate History, Fawn M. Brodie, W.W. Norton & Company, New York, 1974
2) The Great Jefferson Taboo, Fawn Brodie, American Heritage Magazine, June, 1972
3) Thomas Jefferson's Unknown Grandchildren, Fawn Brodie, American Heritage Magazine, October, 1976
4) The Slave Children Of Thomas Jefferson, Samuel H. Sloan, Orsden Press, Berkeley, California, 1992
5) Down From The Mountain: The Oral History of the Hemings Family, Judith P. Justus, Herald Printing Co, New Washington, Ohio, 1990
6) Memoirs of Madison Hemings, Life Among the Lowly - Pike County Republican, (Ohio) newspaper March 13, 1873
7) The President Again? - by James Thompson Callender, The Richmond Recorder, September 1, 1802
8) Thomas Jefferson and Sally Hemings An American Controversy - by Annette Gordon-Reed, University Press of Virginia, 1997
9) American Sphinx: The Character of Thomas Jefferson, Joseph J. Ellis, Alfred A. Knopf, New York, 1997
10) The Thomas Jefferson Papers, Frank Donovan, Dodd, Mead & Company, New York, 1963
11) The Hemings Family of Monticello, James A. Bear, Jr., Virginia Cavalcade, Vol XXIX, No 2 (Autumn, 1979)
12) Notes on the State of Virginia, Thomas Jefferson, (1787), edited by William Peden, W.W. Norton & Company, Inc. New York, New York, 1954
13) Monticello, A Family Story, Elizabeth Langhorne, Algonquin Books of Chapel Hill, Chapel Hill, North Carolina, 1987
14) The Jefferson Scandals, a Rebuttal; Virginius Dabney, Dodd, Mead & Company, New York, 1981

For additional information on the Hemings family, read: **"Jefferson's Children"** by Shannon Lanier and Jane Feldman, and **"President In The Family"** by Byron Woodson.

APPENDIX

The Memoirs of Madison Hemings

Originally printed in The Pike County (Ohio) Republican newspaper on March 13, 1873, under the heading:

"Life Among The Lowly, No. 1"

I never knew of but one white man who bore the name of Hemings. He was an Englishman and my great grandfather. He was captain of an English whaling vessel which sailed between England and Williamsburg, Va., then quite a port. My [great-] grandmother was a fullblooded African, possibly a native of that country. She was the property of John Wales, a Welchman. Capt. Hemings happened to be in the port of Williamsburg at the time my grandmother was born, and acknowledging her fatherhood he tried to purchase her of Mr. Wales who would not part with the child, though he was offered an extraordinarily large price for her. She was named Elizabeth Hemings. Being thwarted in the purchase, and determined to own his own flesh and blood he resolved to take the child by force or stealth, but the knowledge of his intention coming to John Wales' ears, through leaky fellow servants of the mother, she and the child were taken into the "great house" under their master's immediate care. I have been informed that it was not the extra value of that child over the other slave children that induced Mr. Wales to refuse to sell it, for slave masters then, as in later days, had no compunctions of conscience which restrained them from parting mother and child of however tender age, but he was restrained by the fact that just about that time amalgamation began, and the child was so great a curiosity that its owner desired to raise it himself that he might see its outcome. Capt. Hemings soon afterwards sailed from Williamsburg, never to return. Such is the story that comes to me.

Elizabeth Hemings grew to womanhood in the family of John Wales, whose wife dying she (Elizabeth) was taken by the widower Wales as his concubine, by whom she had six children – three sons and three daughters, viz: Robert, James, Peter, Critty, Sally and Thena. These children went by the name of Hemings.

Williamsburg was the capital of Virginia, and of course it was an aristocratic place, where the "bloods" of the Colony and the new State most did congregate. Thomas Jefferson, the author of the Declaration of Independence, was educated at William and Mary College, which had its seat at Williamsburg. He afterwards studied law with Geo. Wythe, and practiced law at the bar of the general court of the Colony. He was afterwards elected a member of the provincial legislature from Albemarle county. Thos. Jefferson was a visitor at the "great house" of John Wales, who had children about his own age. He formed the acquaintance of his daughter Martha (I believe that was her name, though I am not positively sure,) and an intimacy sprang up between them which ripened into love, and they were married. They afterwards went to live at his country seat in Monticello, and course of time had born to them a daughter whom they named Martha. About the same time she was born my mother, the second daughter of John Wales and Elizabeth Hemings. On the death of John Wales, my grandmother, his concubine, and her children by him fell to Martha, Thomas Jefferson's wife, and consequently became property of Thomas Jefferson, who in the course of time became famous, and was appointed minister to France during our revolutionary troubles, or soon after independence was gained. About the time of the appointment and before he was ready to leave the country his wife died, and as soon after her interment as could attend to and arrange his domestic affairs in accordance with the changed circumstances of his family in consequence of this misfortune (I think not more than three weeks thereafter) he left for France, taking his eldest daughter with him. He had had sons born to him, but they died in early infancy, so he then had but two children – Martha and Maria. The latter was left home, but was afterwards ordered to follow him to France. She was three years or so younger than Martha. My mother accompanied her as a body servant. When Mr. Jefferson went to France Martha was a young woman grown, my mother was about her age, and Maria was just budding into womanhood. Their stay (my mother and Maria's) was about eighteen months. But during that time my mother became Mr. Jefferson's concubine, and when he was called back home she was enciente by him. He desired to bring my mother back to Virginia with him but she demurred. She was just beginning to understand the French language well, and in France she was free, while if she returned to Virginia she would be re-enslaved. So she refused to return with him. To induce her to do so he promised her extraordinary privileges, and made a solemn pledge that her children should be freed at the age of twenty-one years. In consequence of his promises, on which she implicitly replied, she returned with him to Virginia. Soon after their arrival, she gave birth to a child, of whom Thomas Jefferson was the father. It lived but a short time. She gave birth to four others, and Jefferson was the father of all of them. Their names were Beverly, Harriet, Madison (myself), and Eston – three sons and one daughter. We all became free agreeably to the treaty entered into by our parents before we were born. We all married and have raised families.

Beverly left Monticello and went to Washington as a white man. He married a white woman in Maryland, and their only child, a daughter, was not known by white folks to have any colored blood coursing in her veins. Beverly's wife's family were people in good circumstances.

Harriet married a white man in good standing in Washington City, whose name I could give, but will not, for prudential reasons. She raised a family of children, and so far as I know they were never suspected of being tainted with African blood in the community where she lives. I have not heard from her for ten years, and do not know whether she is dead or alive. She thought it in her interest, on going to Washington, to assume the role of white woman, and by her dress and conduct as such I am not aware that her identity as Harriet Hemings of Monticello has ever been discovered.

Eston married a colored woman in Virginia, and moved from there to Ohio, and lived in Chillicothe several years. In the fall of 1852 he removed to Wisconsin, where he died a year or two afterwards. He left three children.

As to myself, I was named Madison by the wife of James Madison, who was afterwards President of the United States. Mrs. Madison happened to be at Monticello at the time of my birth, and begged the privilege of naming me, promising my mother a fine present for the honor. She consented, and Mrs. Madison dubbed me by the name I now acknowledge, but like many promises of white folks to the slaves she never gave my *mother anything. I was born at my father's seat of Monticello in Albemarle county Va., near Charlottesville, on the 19th day of January, 1805. My very earliest recollections are of my grandmother Elizabeth Hemings. That was when I was about three years old. She was sick and upon her death bed. I was eating a piece of bread and asked if she would have some. She replied: "No; granny don't want bread any more." She shortly afterwards breathed her last. I have only a faint recollection of her.*

Of my father, Thomas Jefferson, I knew more of his domestic than his public life during his life time. It is only since his death that I have learned much of the latter, except that he was considered as a foremost man in the land, and held many important trusts, including that of President. I learned to read by inducing the white children to teach me the letters and something more; what else I know of books I have picked up here and there till I now can read and write. I was almost 21 years of age when my father died on the 4th of July, 1826.

About his own home, he was the quietest of men. He was hardly ever known to angry, though sometimes he was irritated when matters went wrong, but even then he hardly ever allowed himself to be made unhappy any great length of time. Unlike Washington he had but little taste or care for agricultural pursuits. He left matters pertaining to his plantations mostly with his stewards and overseers. He always had mechanics at work for him, such as carpenters, blacksmiths, shoemakers, coopers, etc. It was his mechanics he seemed mostly to direct, and in their operations he took great interest. Almost every day of his later years he might have been seen among them. He occupied much of the time in his office engaged in correspondence and reading and writing. His general temperament was smooth and even; he was very undemonstrative. He was uniformly kind to all about him. He was not in the habit of showing partiality or fatherly affection to us children. We were the only children of his by a slave woman. He was affectionate towards his white grandchildren of whom he had fourteen, twelve of whom lived to manhood and womanhood. His daughter Martha married Thomas Mann Randolph by whom she had thirteen children. Two died in infancy. The names of the living were Ann, Thomas Jefferson, Ellen, Cornelia, Virginia, Mary, James, Benj. Franklin, Lewis Madison, Septemia, and Geo. Wythe. Thos. Jefferson Randolph was Chairman of the Democratic National Convention in Baltimore last spring which nominated Horace Greeley for the Presidency, and Geo. Wythe Randolph was Jeff. Davis' first Secretary of War in the late "unpleasantness."

Maria married John Eppes, and raised one son – Francis.

My father generally enjoyed excellent health. I never knew him to have but one spell of sickness, and that was caused by a visit to the Warm Springs in 1818. Till within three weeks of his death he was hale and hearty, and at the age of 83 years he walked erect and with stately tread. I am now 68, and I well remember that he was a much smarter man physically, even at that age, than I am.

When I was fourteen years old I was put to the carpenter trade under the charge of John Hemings, the youngest son of my grandmother. His father's name was Nelson, who was an Englishman. She had seven children by white men and seven by colored men – fourteen in all. My brothers, sister Harriet and myself, were used alike. They were put to some mechanical trade at the age of fourteen. Till then we were permitted to stay about the "great house," and only required to do such light work as going to on errands. Harriet learned to spin and to weave in a little factory on the home plantation.

We were free from the dread of having to be slaves all our lives long, and were measurably happy. We were always permitted to be with our mother, who was well used. It was her duty, all her life which I can remember, up to the time of our father's death, to take care of his chamber and wardrobe, look after us children and do such light work as sewing, etc. Provision was made in the will of our father that we should be free when we arrived at the age of 21 years. We had all passed that period when he died but Eston, and he was given the remainder of his time shortly after. He and I rented a house and took mother to live with us, till her death, which event occurred in 1835.

In 1834 I married Mary McCoy. Her grandmother was a slave, and lived with her master, Stephen Hughes, near Charlottesville, as his wife. She was manumitted by him, which made their children free born. Mary McCoy's mother was his daughter. I was about 28 and she 22 years of age when we married. We lived and labored together in Virginia till 1836, when we voluntarily left and came to Ohio. We settled in Pebble township, Pike county. We lived there four or five years and during my stay in that county I worked at my trade on and off for about four years. Joseph Sewell was my first employer. I built for him what is now known as Bizzleport No. 2 in Waverly. I afterwards worked for George Wolf Senior and I did the carpenter work of the brick building now owned by John J. Kellison in which the Pike County Republican is printed. I worked for and with Micajah Hinson. I found him to be a very clever man. I also reconstructed the building on the corner of Market and Water from a store to a hotel for the late Judge Jacob Row.

When we came from Virginia we brought one daughter (Sarah) with us, leaving the dust of a son in the soil near Monticello. We have born to us in this State nine children. Two are dead. The names of the living, besides Sarah, are Harriet, Mary Ann, Catharine, Jane, William Beverly, James Madison, and Ellen Wales. Thomas Eston died in the Andersonville prison pen, and Julia died at home. William, James and Ellen are unmarried and live at home, in Huntington township, Ross county. All the others area married and raising families. My post-office address is Pee Pee, Pike county Ohio.

Reprinted by permission from, "Thomas Jefferson An Intimate History" by Fawn Brodie, W.W. Norton and Company, New York, 1974

Photos and Archival Images Credits

All photos © CBS Worldwide, Inc./Cliff Lipson except as indicated below:

Page VI, photo of wall at Jefferson memorial, Tina Andrews. Page X, photo of Thomas Jefferson's spectacles, courtesy of Mary Cassels Kearney. Page 7, Sally Hemings Bell, courtesy Monticello/Thomas Jefferson Memorial Foundation/Howard University. Page 8, Sam Neill, Carmen Ejogo, Shannon Lanier, © Jane Feldman. Page 10, Excerpt from The Los Angeles Times, copyright, 1977, reprinted by permission. Page 11, photo of Tina Andrews and Richard Guthrie, courtesy author's archives. Page 19, author at Monticello,© Stephen Gaines. Page 20, Chart of Hemings/Jefferson descendants by Stephen Gaines. Page 24, James Hemings deed of manumission, courtesy University of Virginia Library. Page 32, Ad for Executor's Sale, courtesy, American Antiquarian Society. Page 34, Codicil of Jefferson's will, courtesy University of Virginia Library. Page 44, photo of Alex Haley Courtesy Bettmann/ Corbis Archives; Page 54, photo of Hemings quilt, © Tina Andrews. Page 61, Illustration of female slave beating, courtesy of Library of Congress. Page 62, photo of the author and Wendy Kram, courtesy Cliff Lipson. Page 64, photo of Leni Ashmore Sorensen © Tina Andrews. Page 67 & 68, photos of Woodson descendants, courtesy of Mary Cassels Kearney. Page 68, photo of Michelle Cooley-Quille, © Peggy Harrison. Page 69, photos of Harriet Hemings Butler and Francis Butler Spears, courtesy of Shay Banks-Young archives; photo of Madison Hemings descendants, courtesy of Patti Jo Harding. Page 70, photo of Shay Banks-Young, courtesy of Shay Banks-Young archives; photo of William F. Dalton, © Tina Andrews; photo of Shannon Lanier, © Peggy Harrison. Page 71, photo of John Wayles Jefferson, courtesy of State Historical Society of Wisconsin. photos of Eston Hemings Jefferson descendants, courtesy Julia Jefferson Westerinen archives; Page 72, photo of current Eston Hemings Jefferson descendants, © Jane Feldman. Page 86, Sam Neill, Mare Winningham, Julia and Dorothy Jefferson Westerinen, © Tina Andrews. Page 89, photo of Gerrit van der Meer and Craig Anderson, © Tina Andrews. Page 90, photo of Mare Winningham © Tina Andrews. Page 96 & 97, Hemings descendant's group photo, © Jane Feldman. Page 97, Thomas Jefferson painting by Rembrandt Peale, © Bettmann/CORBIS archives. Page 102, author with young extras, courtesy of William Dalton. Page 106, photo of descendants and author at Jefferson's grave © Jane Feldman. Page 112, photo of Hampton Inn, © Philip Beaurline; photo of William Beverly Hemings' grave, courtesy of Leavenworth National Cemetery. Page 205, photo of slave children, © Tina Andrews. Page 234, photo of slaves, © Tina Andrews. Page 258, photo of Jefferson's grave, courtesy Monticello/Thomas Jefferson Memorial Foundation. Page 264, photo of French market street, courtesy David Crank; photo of Peter Bradbury and Chris Stafford © Tina Andrews. Page 265, photo of Kelly Rutherford © Tina Andrews.

My sincere thanks to Francis Cavanaugh and CBS Entertainment for use of the many production photos in this book. Videocassette copies of "Sally Hemings: An American Scandal" are available on Artisan Entertainment at your local video store.

Visit our web site at: www.malibupress.com.
Visit the author's web site at www.tinaandrews.com.

Sally and Tom. The Controversy Continues